Anthony Boucher

To Kate Stine and Brian Skupin,
two wonderful friends who gave advice
for this book on everything
from locked rooms to the Runcible Spoon

Acknowledgments

No book is written in a vacuum, and many people help in its creation. As a result, thanks are in order for the people who have helped shepherd this book along through its years of preparation and writing. The book was first conceived during a conversation with Keith Kahla. His modest suggestion turned into this work.

Since Boucher touched so many lives and held so many interests, I had to contact a number of people to help me get all of my details correct. They've talked with me and answered questions. If there are errors in the book, they are mine and not the work of wonderful people such as Andi Shechter who helped answer my science fiction questions, and Barry Zeman and Margery Flax, who offered me details on Boucher through Mystery Writers of America. Bill Vande Water and Jon Lellenberg along with Leslie Klinger and Ted Schulz assisted me with information on the Baker Street Irregulars. Gordon Van Gelder was instrumental in not only kindly agreeing to write the foreword, but also to help introduce me to a host of science fiction writers from *The Magazine of Fantasy & Science Fiction* who knew Anthony Boucher.

So many people have helped with the history of mystery, including Allen Hubin, and the members of the Golden Age Detection group online with special thanks to Barry Ergang and Lynne Fraser. I certainly could not have completed this work without Doug Greene, who has answered a million and one questions for me about this work. He knows more than I can ever hope to learn.

The staff of the Indiana University Lilly Library deserves special thanks for all the boxes of material they hoisted from the back to my table. I've spent numerous hours at the library over the past three years and enjoyed its silence and comfortable chairs.

TABLE OF CONTENTS

As Editor   *192*
Translations   *193*
Articles About Boucher   *197*
Appendix: Boucher Choices for Best Books, 1951–1967   *199*

Bibliography   *205*
Index   *209*

Foreword

by Gordon Van Gelder

You know the old saying about how the way to know someone is to walk a mile in their shoes, right? Well, I'm here right now because I've sat a few years in someone else's saddle — that is, I've spent the last decade filling the role that Anthony Boucher created nearly sixty years ago, the position of editor of *The Magazine of Fantasy & Science Fiction.*

In that role, I've gotten to know Tony well (well enough that I feel like I'm on a first-name basis with him, even though we never met — and in fact, I wasn't even two years old when he passed away). I've heard from writers whose work he fostered, like Robert Silverberg, Arthur Porges, and Ron Goulart, who had a friendly competition with another student of Boucher's, Philip K. Dick, to be the first to appear in *F&SF* (Goulart won). I remember Judith Merril saying that most writers unconsciously work with an ideal editor in mind, and for her — like so many other writers — that ideal was Boucher. I've spoken with Sidney Offitt about what fun it was working in the East Coast office of Mercury Press while Boucher worked from California. I've even heard Phil Klass describe what it was like after Boucher stepped down as editor and his successors inherited a slew of stories that were bought but, as Phil said, "had a long way to go before they were ready for publication."

And my respect for the man is tremendous. What he and Mick McComas did advanced the SF/fantasy fields immeasurably, and I am proud to stand on the shoulders of these giants.

What I like most about Jeffrey Marks' thorough and much-needed biography is that it makes clear how *small* a part of Tony Boucher's overall career frequently heard attendees pronounce the event as "Boo-cher-con" instead of the proper "Bow-cher-con."

Some ties to the past remained. In recent years, the Bouchercon committee has come up with a memorial booklet to Boucher, so that new members might know who he was and learn his place in the genre. Phyllis White, Boucher's widow, was still given membership number one. She faithfully attended the event until her death, but as time progressed, fewer people could pick her out of the crowd.

Even as direct memories of Boucher fade with the passage of years, his reputation lives on. Bouchercon continues to thrive in its fourth decade. Boucher is still widely regarded as the *New York Times'* preeminent mystery reviewer. Mike Nevins recently collected three volumes of Boucher's reviews for Ramble House, a project that was long overdue. Boucher's periodical, *The Magazine of Fantasy and Science Fiction,* still publishes some of the best genre fiction available. A biography of Anthony Boucher is long overdue. Other than a few short articles and introductions, no attempt had been made to chronicle Boucher's short, but very full life.

After his death, Boucher's wife, Phyllis White, sold all of Boucher's professional papers to Indiana University in Bloomington, Indiana. I have visited frequently to review the forty-plus boxes of papers and correspondence. I was awarded the Helm Fellowship from IU to defray expenses in studying Boucher's papers. Additionally, I have researched Phyllis White's papers, which are still in the family's possession in Berkeley, California.

Part I

The Man

The point is that I might undertake to do a competent biographico-critical essay on just about any other writer, but I don't see how one approaches oneself.
— Anthony Boucher, "Author, Author," *The Fanscient*

William Parker White, better known to millions of mystery readers and science fiction fans as Anthony Boucher, possessed almost as many names as he did interests. To most people, he was known as Anthony or Tony Boucher. To those who had known him the longest, friends and family, he was A.P., or fondly "Apey." Boucher joked in his later years that he only reverted to the White name on tax day, a thought he could do without.

William Parker White was born in Oakland, California, on August 21, 1911. His given name was his maternal grandfather's. His middle name was his mother's maiden name.

Like his name, Boucher's upbringing relied heavily on his mother. Before Boucher's first birthday, James Taylor White passed away at age 46. His short life portended Boucher's own early demise.

Boucher's father had been born on December 13, 1866, in Port Townsend, Washington. When he was just a boy, White's family settled in a hill district of Oakland named Highland Park.

Boucher's father showed some of the same precociousness and diversity of interest as his son. He participated in the Highland Park Amateur Band where he played piccolo and clarinet. He served as secretary for the Highland Park Photographic Amateurs, the president of the Hillcrest Tennis Club, and still found time to collect nature specimens.

By age 40, James Taylor White still had not married, but he had nearly been around the world. After graduating from the Medical College of the University of California, White began traveling extensively. In 1890, he went on a six-month tour of the Arctic, providing medical assistance to a ship's crew and the natives. He came home and settled in Seattle, but not for long. By 1894, he had sailed with another ship to Alaska and Siberia. He returned to America briefly to study at the New York University Post-Graduate Medical School. However, he followed that education with trips to Yokohama, Hong Kong, Honolulu, Manila, and the Yukon.

White had to quit the naval life when a new policy was issued that required ships to use Marine Hospital officers on-board revenue cutters. The San Francisco–based hospital became the only one to provide medical men for the larger ships in what would become the Coast Guard.

White settled in Bridgeport, California, where he met Mary Ellen Parker, another doctor. They married in 1906. White encouraged her with his wayfaring ways, and the couple was soon on their way to Europe to study.

Boucher with his mother, Mary Parker White, and his grandfather, William Owen Parker (courtesy Lilly Library, Indiana University, Bloomington).

They returned home in 1911, expecting their first child. White died of typhoid just seven months after the birth of his son.

Although left a widow, Mary White was capable of handling her new family. Boucher's wife, Phyllis, remembered, "His mother was an unusual woman because in her time there weren't so many woman doctors. And what was also pretty unusual for her time, she smoked and drank, too. She was about average height with white hair and blue eyes. She was very intelligent and very opinionated."[1]

Boucher's mother was born Mary Ellen Parker, on July 6, 1874 in Stockton, California. Unlike her future husband, she lived in Bridgeport for most of her childhood, but moved to Ogden, Utah to earn a teaching certificate. She taught briefly, but by 1900, she had returned to California to begin study for a medical career. She moved to Eugene to complete her studies at the University of Oregon, graduating in 1903. She returned to San Francisco for her internship and later began an ear, nose, and throat practice in Portland. Mary White had a difficulty delivery with her only son and was still recovering when her husband passed away.

The paternal role fell to Boucher's maternal grandfather and namesake, William Owen Parker. The old man was a lawyer and Civil War veteran. He had been an ironworker in Scotland. In 1864, Parker had come to the United States with free passage for agreeing to fight during the Civil War. He'd left behind a wife and son in Glasgow. Parker never saw fighting in the war, stationed with the Union Army at Fort Vancouver, Washington. At the war's end, he settled in Northern California.

In 1871, Parker married again, this time to Annie Boucher Hine, a Catholic woman from Ireland. She is the relative from whom Boucher got his pseudonym and his faith. It wasn't until 1879 that Parker bothered to divorce his Scottish wife. Ten years later, he divorced Annie Parker and he married another woman, who Boucher referred to as "Bridgeport's fallen woman." Parker divorced again in 1897 for unknown reasons and remarried Annie Parker. This final marriage didn't seem to be a happy one, and the couple rarely spent time in the same city, much less the same household. When Annie Parker died in 1913, Parker renounced all claims to her estate. Parker passed away in 1930 before he'd had a chance to see his grandson prove his writing talent.

Boucher adopted his maternal grandmother's maiden name, of French-Irish extraction at a young age. He liked the sound of the name (which rhymes with voucher), and frequently used it as an alter ego in his active imagination. By the time he started writing, Boucher decided to use the

White name for his more "serious" plays and writings and Boucher for the more commercial, genre work. The move was practical as well as homage to his grandmother; many other "William White's wrote. As a name, Boucher stood out. He admitted that by the time of his death, he thought of himself mainly as Boucher and his wife as Mrs. Boucher. White became the name used solely for taxes and official records.

Not only did Boucher take on his grandmother's maiden name, he adopted her faith as well. Boucher was a lifelong Catholic, even though his father had been Episcopalian. His deep faith in the Catholic Church was a lifelong commitment, shown through every area of his life, including his writings. Boucher's faith was not that of a hard-lined Bible thumper, but he held that all men should help the less fortunate, do unto others, and care about a wide group of family and friends. It was an ideal faith for a man coming of age during the New Deal and the Great Depression.

Boucher's faith stemmed from his mother who urged the boy to participate more in the church and follow the Catholic law. Many of her letters to Boucher as he matured consisted of lectures regarding what she considered to be his frivolous ways and irreverent writings.

Boucher is one of a few mystery novelists who have had their faith appear in their works. Dorothy L. Sayers, who wrote the Lord Peter Wimsey series, later abandoned crime fiction to complete a translation of Dante's *Divine Comedy*, which she considered her best work. G.K. Chesterton, known for his priest-detective Father Brown, wrote Christian apologetics as well as mystery short stories.

Boucher's faith also had a light-hearted air, even though it was central to his life. Family members credit his grandfather with the sense of humor that allowed Boucher to laugh about religious-based matters. For example, Boucher was christened William Anthony Parker White at his confirmation in 1923. Boucher would later say that naming him after Anthony of Padua, the patron saint of lost objects, did not help him at all with his penchant for losing things and not being able to find them. This lighthearted, but in-depth Catholic upbringing would play a major part in his adult life.

Boucher was frequently bedridden as a child, struggling with a lifelong asthma condition. Asthma is a chronic disease of the lungs marked by constriction and inflammation of the airways. The condition leaves the patient with wheezing, coughing and shortness of breath. A patient with asthma feels like he cannot get a lungful of air. The disease has many triggers, and Boucher spent much of his life unable to take a decent breath. By his own admission, paint fumes were one of his worst triggers and he had to make special arrangements to avoid the fumes when possible.

For his condition, Boucher took inhalers using epinephrine. In the middle of the twentieth century, asthma treatment was quite primitive. Boucher used a "puffer," a glass nebulizer that had a rubber bulb and a tube that Boucher had to place his lips around. The medicine was atomized by repeating squeezes of the bulb.

During the 1940s, Boucher received bi-weekly shots for his condition in addition to the puffer. The shots of adrenal cortex were an early version of steroids that are currently used to relieve allergy and asthma conditions.

Boucher later received a plastic apparatus with a mouthpiece on one end. By inhaling on the dispenser, a ball shot up and hit the dispenser, which released some of the drug into the air flow. Boucher was better able to control the flow of medicine with this device.

Frequently, Boucher was forced out of Berkeley and to the dry desert air of 29 Palms. Just outside of Palm Springs, Boucher had to spend a month or so there at a time to help his asthma. James White remembers that his father did not shave on his trips. Phyllis would see the bearded Boucher and refuse to kiss him until he was clean-shaven again.

Epinephrine is a vasoconstrictor that is often associated with hypertension, and Boucher suffered from that disease as he grew older. Boucher took frequent trips to the Pill Hill area of Oakland to receive treatment for his hypertension, although there was no record of Boucher receiving medication for his condition.

Fred Dannay, half of Ellery Queen, told of his conversations with Boucher.

> Tony and I often commiserated with each other and expressed the opinion that if both of us had been blessed with good health, how much more we could have accomplished! We said this to each other ruefully, jokingly, seriously, and at the times we consoled each other we undoubtedly meant it.[2]

Boucher's intelligence seemed to destine him to be interested in books and writing. Among his earliest memories were the Frank L. Baum *Oz* books, provided to him by his mother. Despite his illnesses, Boucher easily kept up with his classmates. He was so bright, in fact, that he was included with a group of children for a Stanford University study of genius.

Boucher's asthma left him weakened and thin during his youth and he was sent to the Ross Sanitarium for several months in 1921 and 1922. Boucher was put on strict bed rest. His family and friends visited him often, and the rest of his hours were spent reading. The precocious pre-teen read works as varied as "She Stoops to Conquer" and "The Last of the Mohicans" before he was released back to his family, stronger and at a healthier weight.

Boucher read voraciously, encouraged by poor health and his mother's desire for his education. In a move that would serve him well in the future, Boucher taught himself to speed-read by age fourteen. This allowed him to read more books quickly. He read everything from classics to mainstream fiction and genre fiction.

Early in life, he'd shown aptitudes for architecture and science, but slowly his interests turned to literature. At the age of 15, Boucher sold a story to *Weird Tales*, which fueled his desire for a writing career. Even with this early success in science-fiction and fantasy, Boucher abandoned the genre early. To his taste, the field in the 1920s had too many poorly written stories with absurd plots.

While asthma is a lifelong condition, by his teens Boucher was strong enough to attend school regularly. He attended three years of military school at Hitchcock Academy in San Rafael, California. He graduated from Pasadena High School in 1928. In the yearbook for that year, Boucher was described as "very wise and clever."

As Boucher grew older, his health improved. The energy and enthusiasm that he'd put into reading spilled out into all areas of his life. At Pasadena, he participated in Honor Society and La Hispaniola and served as president of the Philatelic club. He belonged to the Thrift Club, the Nokoma Club, a club devoted to investigating hobbies, and the "X" club, which was described as a society for

Boucher's graduation photo from Pasadena High School, 1928 (courtesy the White family).

scientific experimental research. With all of this extracurricular work, Boucher still managed to graduate in the top 10 students in a class of over 750.

Boucher went on to Pasadena Junior College the following year. A decade after Boucher's graduation, sports legend Jackie Robinson would play football for Pasadena Junior College. Boucher would point out that he thought of Robinson as a football running back more than a baseball player, since Robinson had been one of the top ten backs in the history of West Coast football. Ellsworth Vines, who would go on to win a Wimbledon championship in the 1930s, was a year behind Boucher at Pasadena High School. With so many connections, sports became another of Boucher's many passions, even though he was unable to play because of his asthma. His love of all things football appeared in many of his works, with characters appearing as either players or spectators.

For the rest of his life, Boucher remained a fan of Cal sports. He attended home football, basketball, track and even rugby events. However, his interest never extended to professional sports, mainly following college-level sports.

Boucher followed junior college with two years at the University of Southern California, where he received a B.A. in Spanish, a Phi Beta Kappa Key and a graduate fellowship to the University of California at Berkeley where he received his MA in 1934. Boucher admits "Scholastically, I did as usual. Spent much time on the theatre and writing and — diversions, and came through with something like 2.9 for both semesters."[3]

Boucher spent a great deal of his time at the Little Theatre in Berkeley. He managed to get multiple plays produced during his time there, though none were a smash hit. Of his play, *Duet and Trio*, he wrote, "Thanks to one Betty Keatings, it flopped."

Boucher lived with his mother at the beginning of his graduate work. She suffered from pernicious anemia and was bedridden most of the time. The pair had a housekeeper who managed to keep things together. After the housekeeper quit, Boucher moved into the International House on Berkeley's campus armed with a $600 scholarship, and his mother moved in with family friends.

Boucher's intellect kept shining through at school. He knew eight languages by the time he graduated: German, Spanish, French, Portuguese, Russian, Greek, Sanskrit, and Italian. His major was German, and his minor was Spanish. His multi-lingual talents served him well, as he would use this ability frequently to translate mystery stories into English for publication in the early mystery magazines.

All of these pursuits, ironically, did not make Boucher a popular man on campus. Many of his classmates were jealous of the graduate student who could earn perfect grades in his classes without seeming to study. Boucher acted as though the languages department was just another avocation along with drama and writing. Many of the students derisively called him "Sonny-boy" behind his back.

At Berkeley, he met his future wife, Phyllis Mary Price. She would later recall:

> I met my husband at a student party at my parents' house. My ... parents often entertained students. I remember the first time he came to our house he addressed just one remark to me. He asked whether I knew what became of the cookies.
>
> After he had been to a couple of parties at my parent's house, he invited us all to dinner at an apartment he had near the campus with his mother. At the end of the dinner he made a date with me to go to the theater with him.[4]

Their relationship proceeded slowly, partly because of a significant age difference between them. Boucher was a graduate student when Phyllis began her freshman year at Berkeley, although they didn't start dating until her sophomore year. The Prices were a bit hesitant about the age difference as well. They'd heard from the Berkeley crowd that Boucher had been involved with another co-ed in the past year, which had ended on a sour note.

> My first date with my future husband was the first date I ever had. I never dated in high school. One of the things we talked about was how much we liked the old theater stock companies. That was a great institution, but it had died by the time we met. There was at that time an attempt to revive it in Oakland, and we went to check it out. The theater was called "The Fulton Theater"—it isn't there anymore. It was a bit disappointing: it wasn't like the real old-time stock companies at all. He met me at my house and after the theater we went and had refreshments at a place nearby. The play we saw was called "Gambling, Gambling!"[5]

Phyllis found her first few dates with Boucher cognitively exhausting and wasn't sure if she would continue dating him. However, he persisted and she finally became used to the constant banter and erudite knowledge. Her trick, she would later say, was to just enjoy it without trying to keep up with his mind.

Phyllis was the product of Dr. Lawrence Price, and Mary "Minnie" Bell. Dr. Price had met his future wife on a trip to Leipzig, Germany. He was finishing a graduate degree, wanting to become a German professor at the University of Missouri. She was a gifted graduate student, matriculating at the University of Manchester, who had garnered a number of scholarships for her work. Bell lived in Germany on one of those scholarships when the couple met. After obtaining his doctorate in German in 1912, Price returned to Manchester to claim his bride.

It was a strange life for Minnie in a new country. She wasn't sure what to expect in the land she'd only read about in books. She'd half-expected to be met at the train station by Indians and cowboys. She didn't have long to get used to Missouri. In 1915, Price accepted a position at the University of California; their only daughter, Phyllis, was born that same year.

Although the Prices lived out their days in Berkeley, they traveled regularly. As a professor, Price received sabbaticals. The family traveled to Europe during these years off. Phyllis learned French easily as she attended classes in Strasbourg, and her father attended language lectures at the university.

The Prices returned home to Berkeley in 1922 and bought a house on Hawthorne Terrace on the north side of the UC campus, where many faculty lived. The house burned down once in those all-too-familiar California fires, but the family rebuilt the house just as it had been. The Prices continued to live there throughout their lives, although the house was gone when Phyllis went back to visit it years later.

Boucher and Phyllis Price continued dating until the time of Boucher's graduation. By this time, Boucher and Phyllis had grown serious. Phyllis joked that he'd been seeing many women at the time they'd begun dating, just like the manner in which he managed to direct, write, act and study for a graduate degree. Boucher slowly stopped seeing other women until just one remained. Of one he wrote, "Rae and I have quite definitely and calmly gone our respective ways. It was simply a mistake. Meanwhile Phyllis has afforded me greater peace and content than I have ever known."[6]

Phyllis had not been able to keep that pace. By the time that school was done, she had found herself divorced from all the extracurricular activities normally associated with college. She just couldn't keep up with Boucher's own pace.

Boucher toyed with the idea of further studies. He had applied for a Rhodes Scholarship; Boucher asked Dr. Price to write a letter of recommendation. However, there's no record that anything came of his application.

By the time that Boucher received his degree from Berkeley, he had decided that he didn't want to spend his life in academia. He really didn't feel that he had the patience to become an educator. Combined with academia's disdain for popular culture, Boucher felt that his future rested elsewhere.

A love of theater had bitten him, and with a small amount of money from his mother, he decided to relocate to Los Angeles to write one-act plays. Boucher moved into a small apartment on Fountain Avenue, across from the Cedars of Lebanon Hospital. The following year, Boucher's mother moved into one of the other apartments in the same complex.

Before he left for Los Angeles and the call of Hollywood, Boucher and Phyllis decided to get married at an undecided time in the future. Because of the distance, she and Boucher wrote to each other every three days. The correspondence continued until their marriage.

> Of course your logic as to the abstraction of the exile is perfectly impeccable, insofar as it applies to events which took place simply in three geographical dimensions and hence are removed by geographical distance. But all that took place between us — since Easter at least — has happened in my heart and is still close, still immediate to me wherever I am. Of course we were mad in those last few moments — lunacy is all that was worthy to grace our parting. Lunacy broiders the whole affair — which is not the word I want — and lunacy knows no time, no place, no logic. I shall not view you, my love for you, dispassionately even now, even if I wanted to. Why even the breeze, the cool West Wind that blows here, means you in all your freshness and all your clarity.[7]

Boucher took time off before leaving for Los Angeles in the summer of 1933 to live in St. Helena, CA. Between years, Boucher had to rest at a ranch because of his health. According to his letters, he "retired for the summer to a ranch in the Napa Valley but read, write and rest for two months. The place is foul with dogs (although really very pleasant), and charmingly devoid of people. Or practically so."[8] His time away was spent writing. He completed a 3-act play while he lived there. Additionally, he spent hours reading, anything from Virginia Wolfe to genre fiction.

Boucher moved permanently to Los Angeles in May 1934 to find employment as a writer. Under the byline of A.P. White, he began reviewing theater and music for a small weekly political paper, the *United Progressive News*, which paid little except for the endless stream of theater and show tickets. His mother had joined him in Los Angeles in 1935 and together they went to as many as five plays a week to review. The number of shows he attended only added to his erudite reputation among his friends in Los Angeles. He could discuss almost any aspect of popular culture at length.

On the basis of all that he'd seen, Boucher knew that he could write something better. He wrote over fifty one-act plays over the next two years. A few were read on stage, and even fewer still were produced. Even so, Boucher saw himself as a dramatist who might write an occasional horror piece.

Boucher didn't limit his activities to writing and the theater. Despite his continual bad health (he had developed a cold within two weeks of arriving), he managed to sightsee across the city, seeing Hollywood and Pasadena. Boucher, ever the liberal, even went to gay bars.

> After that we went to Johnny Walker's, the most disreputable joint for pansies and dikes in Los Angeles, seeking a superb friend of Sam's named J. Hale McCillup. He was not there, but we saw a most amusing pansy floor show with a talented male torchsinger and an excellent comedian, who spends his spare time as a waiter. (Every waiter has to be one of those boys, even the maitre d'hotel).[9]

During his Los Angeles years, Boucher blossomed socially. Away from the competition of academia, Boucher was not judged for his wide-range of activities. He was admired for them and considered good company for being able to talk about nearly any subject. Since he only worked sporadically, Boucher was available for soirees nearly all the time.

At the newspaper, Boucher met two of his lifelong friends, Cleve Cartmill and Roby Wentz, who would introduce him to the world of science-fiction. Likewise, he met his future business partner, Francis McComas, during this stay in Los Angeles and stood up at the man's wedding in 1934.

While Boucher was faithful to Phyllis, he stood in for his roommate, Thel, on more than one occasion as a platonic date for girls that Thel forgot. Thel was a friend who worked as a property manager in Long Beach. Boucher was charming and delightful to the women as he substituted as a dinner companion around town.

For some reason, Boucher took up smoking during his time in Los Angeles. Probably no act could be worse for a man with serious respiratory problems, but Boucher smoked until the end of his life. He often used a cigarette holder that held a replaceable filter in it, Boucher's attempt to minimize the damage to his already weakened respiratory system.

In the meantime, he wrote short stories that didn't sell. Boucher tried ghostwriting, for which he earned next to nothing. He'd seen some of his plays produced, but nothing ever sold. He had managed to sell a poem to *Weird Tales* in 1935, but no other works. He tried repeatedly to find a way into the Hollywood studio system with no luck. In the midst of the Great Depression, Boucher couldn't even find a non-writing job to help make ends meet.

In response to Boucher's application to Metro-Goldwyn-Mayer, the film company wrote:

> After reading your play I foresaw this decision. You are clever, almost infernally so, but every scrap of your writing I have seen shows artifice. Every basic situation you contrive is more or less unnatural or at least exceptional. Perhaps this fanciful quality would make a great success in the movies if given the opportunity of production. But what this department asks is evidence of more serious and typical, perhaps more pedestrian, dramatic ability. Therefore you simply don't fit in.[10]

By July 1934, Boucher had begun to get some of the nibbles that would continue to frustrate him throughout his stay in Los Angeles.

> Suddenly prospects are falling on me. Eleanor hopes to get me some translating from Mr. Macnulty. The twins are turning over to me some ghostwriting for the Satevepost. And while I was out last night, Alfred Kelly (friend to Mae Parker Ruzac) phoned. Job translating for Fox, got him an interview with Fox's Spanish supervisor.[11]

Phyllis finished up her degree early and when Dr. Price took a Sabbatical to visit Europe in 1935, Phyllis went along as well. Boucher was dismal about the matter, but points out that a few hundred miles separation is just as "effectively tormenting" as a few thousand miles. Their letters from the time had that urgent air of young lovers. Boucher knew that he had to find a more steady income from his writing, in order to support a bride. Matters were only made worse when the paper was suspended for a few weeks in December 1935. "The temporary suspension seems genuinely temporary, and things seem to be looking up for the new year."[12]

Phyllis spent most of the year in Vienna during this visit, wary of the growing threat from Nazis across the border. Despite the distance, the pair kept up the communications. Boucher continued to write to Phyllis multiple times a week while she was away:

> I wish to Heaven we could be together, even unmarried (despite the phrasing, that is not a proposition). The warmth of your love, spiritually and otherwise, would help no end when I am beginning to wonder if a break will ever come. How I shall struggle through another half year without once touching you or hearing your voice ... I not only need you. I need love, in its most vulgar sense; and I don't want it without you. There are no lips to kiss save those which now drink Beruiger ... in short, my dear, there is no one for me save you, whom I love with all my heart.[13]

By mid–1936, Boucher was at loose ends for a job: the newspaper was late in paying him, the FTP had tied up his application, and he had been turned down for a WPA writing job because he ironically made too much money. His prospects for supporting a wife seemed bleak.

In between looking for playwriting jobs, Boucher wrote a mystery novel,

Boucher and Phyllis Price White on their wedding day, May 19, 1938 (courtesy Lilly Library, Indiana University, Bloomington).

loosely based on characters and places he knew from his time at Berkeley. His sleuth, Dr. Ashwin, was a professor of Sanskrit; most of the action took place at the International House where Boucher had lived. Finally, Lee Wright, an editor at Simon and Schuster, discovered *The Case of the Seven of Calvary* in her slush pile and took it up with enthusiasm. The novel was published in 1937.

On the strength of this success, he wired Phyllis with the good news while she was still in England. When the Prices returned to Berkeley, Boucher proposed to Phyllis Price. Dr. Price was a bit concerned over the rush to marry, but gave his consent.

The engagement ended up lasting almost 18 months. Phyllis went back to school to become a librarian. With Phyllis attempting to complete her degree, most of the planning for the wedding fell on her mother.

Boucher suffered from a major asthma attack in 1937, one of the worst in several years, and his mother slowly nursed him back to health. The relative good health of the past few years was ending.

At long last, Boucher and Phyllis were married. The couple wed on May 19, 1938. A small wedding was held in Newman Hall on the Berkeley campus with the reception at the Price's home. She officially became Phyllis White, though she frequently answered to Mrs. Boucher.

Boucher continued to write as the big day approached. In a letter to author Stuart Palmer, Boucher writes: "The wedding is tomorrow. The honeymoon is two weeks or so, then another week or two in Berkeley, and so back to Los Angeles around the middle of June."[14]

After honeymooning in Monterey, the couple settled into the Los Angeles apartment where Boucher continued to work on a variety of mystery novels. After he had worked on it for nearly a year, his second novel was deemed unpublishable. Phyllis helped to support the family with part-time library work in the Los Angeles and Glendale library systems.

Phyllis worked as a librarian for several years before giving birth to their first son, Lawrence Taylor White, on Christmas Day, 1940. The apartment house where they'd spent almost 18 months didn't take children, and so the growing family moved to a new apartment on Fernwood Terrace.

The full role of breadwinner now fell to Boucher. He sold six more novels, but had difficulty in selling other projects to the New York publishers. He could never find a home for his children's books or cookbook proposals. He chose to switch to shorter fiction in order to make money faster for his new family. Novels could take six months to a year to write with another year passing before royalties were realized on the book. Short stories took considerably less time to complete and could be in print in a matter of months.

In 1940, Boucher's friend from the *United Progressive News,* Cleve Cartmill, invited him to a meeting of the Mañana Literary Society. The group contained the brightest of the science-fiction writers of the day, including Robert Heinlein and Ed Hamilton. Boucher, who had maintained only a fleeting fascination with supernatural fantasy to that point, had not kept up with the changes in the science-fiction community. The group opened Boucher's eyes to what science-fiction had become since his sale to *Weird Tales*. The group met regularly to discuss works, talk about their own ideas for stories, and enjoy each other's company. The group made an impact on Boucher and slightly fictionalized version of the members made appearances in Boucher's *Rocket to the Morgue*.

In the summer of 1941, Boucher and Phyllis hitched a ride to New York with some of his MLS friends. The couple traveled across country, stopping in Las Vegas, the Petrified Forest, Nashville, and Washington D.C. before arriving in New York City. They stayed with an assortment of relatives in order to save on hotels costs.

Boucher wanted to network in hopes of making personal contacts to further his newly resumed science fiction career. He met frequently with his two editors, Lee Wright and Marie Rodell. In the days before email and fax, the West Coast was considered too far from the locus of New York publishing for much consideration to be given to a writer. Boucher still wanted to write plays and screenplays in Los Angeles, but was unable to get work as a scriptwriter in Hollywood.

In late 1941, he suffered a debilitating asthma attack that lasted several months. Boucher went to 29 Palms, outside of Palm Springs, with his mother to recuperate, and Phyllis, pregnant with their second child, returned to her parents' home in Berkeley along with Lawrence. A weakened Boucher returned to Berkeley in 1942, shortly before the birth of their second son, James Marsden White. The growing family rented a house on Ellsworth Street in Berkeley.

> [I]t's been a good fifteen years since I've had asthma to anything like this degree. Result. We're in a terrible flux. I moved to my mother's apartment and immediately got much better. We're giving up this house. Phyllis and Larry are going to Berkeley with her parents.[15]

The start of World War II only exacerbated the situation with finding markets for fiction. While Boucher continued to write science-fiction stories, the Mañana Society took a break due to World War II. Many of Boucher's friends enlisted or were drafted, but Boucher's family status kept him from serving. "Also trying to coax my draft board into finally establishing my 4-F status so I can take a War Dept civilian job, but they keep insisting I'm 1-A until they make up their minds about fathers over 30. Did you know I was doubly a father by now? Jamie was born in April 42, and the pair of them are by now magnificent hellions."[16]

Boucher with Phyllis, Lawrence and James (courtesy the White family).

Boucher managed to find work. For a while, he taught at the University of California, Berkeley. Boucher had forsworn the academic path when he'd gone off to write in Los Angeles. While never pedantic, Boucher had the knowledge and credentials for teaching at the university level.

He requested that his friend, Lenore Offord, teach when his health or schedule did not permit. He had met her in 1941, and the pair had quite a bit in common. Both lived in Berkeley, and both were heavily involved in mystery and science fiction writing.

When the reviewer for the *San Francisco Chronicle* went to war, Boucher took his place reviewing mystery fiction. Boucher had long encouraged his agent to find him a job reviewing genre fiction, but in the end, Boucher had located the position himself. His agent had written to him

> Also the mystery reviewing business doesn't look too promising at the moment. I have approached *Esquire* and *Atlantic* as the two best bets. *Esquire* feels that Billy Phelps' coverage is sufficient and they don't want to particularize further, and *Atlantic* is just not hot enough on the idea.[17]

At the *Chronicle*, he earned the first of his Edgar awards from the Mystery Writers of America for mystery reviewing. Boucher was exempt from war service because of his poor health. In September 1944, he wrote to a friend, "If the armed forces have any sense at all, this should mean that I shall have at least a nice permanent 4-F classification."

Boucher began his involvement with politics around the same time as well. He began by obtaining absentee ballots for the soldiers who were overseas, still allowing them to participate in the democracy they were defending. He wrote to Mick McComas in 1944, "...I am incurably an optimistic idealist, thinking that Swift probably is right, but Saroyan ought to be."[18]

He began working with Democratic politics in California. He served as president of the Berkeley Democratic Club, and two terms on the State Central Committee, but had to step down on the advice of his doctor.

In 1945, his luck on the writing front changed. He attended a reception for Basil Rathbone and Nigel Bruce, the wildly popular actors who played Sherlock Holmes and Dr. Watson on the radio. Boucher ran into Mary Meyer, who he knew from the Little Theater at UC Berkeley. Meyer

Boucher and Phyllis out on the town (courtesy the White family).

was now married to Denis Green, one of the two writers for *The New Adventures of Sherlock Holmes* for Rathbone and Bruce. At the reception, he learned that Leslie Charteris, the other half of that writing team for the radio show, wanted out.

The show had gone through a number of writers in its short history. Edith Meiser had written the first four seasons. She had been replaced by the team of Denis Green and Leslie Charteris, who wrote for the show under the pen name of Bruce Taylor. Now Charteris wanted to leave as well.

Charteris was tired of writing and claimed to have run out of ideas for the show. Boucher was approached about taking over for Charteris' duties. He accepted and started writing four to five pages synopses for the Sherlock Holmes show, which were mailed to Denis Green, who converted them into half-hour scripts.

In the meantime, he also started writing episodes of the Ellery Queen radio show as well. Fred Dannay who also published many of Boucher's short stories in the new magazine, *Ellery Queen's Mystery Magazine*, needed to take some time off from the series. The other half of the Ellery Queen writing team, Manfred Lee, worked with Boucher on the radio programs. Like with the Holmes series, Boucher wrote up the synopsis for the work and Lee added to that skeleton.

If this wasn't enough writing on a weekly basis, Green and Boucher were also asked to write a new radio program with an original character. They came up with *The Casebook of Gregory Hood*, a San Francisco–based antiquities expert who found current day crimes in the artifacts that he sold. The show had originally been planned as a summer replacement for *The New Adventures of Sherlock Holmes* in 1946, but continued for the next year when the radio network had difficulty in reaching an agreement with the Conan Doyle estate.

With his now busy schedule, Boucher was traveling to Hollywood every six weeks and to New York City every six months. The pace was grueling, but he enjoyed it tremendously. For the first time in his life, he was doing well financially. On the strength of his newfound income, he and Phyllis purchased a new home in Berkeley at 2643 Dana.

As fate would have it, four of his five major writing jobs ceased at approximately the same time. Tax laws for radio program were revamped and government funds could no longer be used to subsidize programming. As a result, all of the radio programs began looking for cheaper writers to do the shows. Edith Meiser, who had written the first four seasons of the series, stepped back into her role as the main writer for *The New Adventures of Sherlock Holmes.* Green and Boucher were summarily dismissed. The Gregory Hood show was cancelled, and the Ellery Queen series became sporadic in its last years. His radio career was all but finished. If that was not enough, Boucher's reviewing job for the *San Francisco Chronicle* ended. Boucher had been filling in for the regular mystery reviewer who returned from World War II at about the same time that his radio jobs ended.

Boucher was still reviewing for *The New York Herald Tribune*, where he reviewed science fiction works under the pen name of H.H. Holmes. This was the same pseudonym that the two Sister Ursula mysteries had appeared under. Holmes was not a homage to the great detective, but was in turn the alias of a legendary Chicago murderer.

At the height of his busy period, Boucher had been developing and writing the equivalent of plots of three short stories or novels every week for the better part of two years. His health suffered for it and again he had a bad asthma episode. He spent several months back at 29 Palms, while the family worried about how to make the payments on the Dana Street house.

In 1949, Boucher and friend J. Francis McComas launched *The Magazine of Fantasy and Science Fiction*. The magazine had been in the planning stages for years, but the publishers were wary of the ever-changing pulp magazine market. The magazine began as a quarterly and moved to monthly as it proved successful. Phyllis remembers giving a multitude of parties in the early days of the magazine, while being worried that the electricity might be turned off at the same time. Boucher continued to edit the magazine, first with McComas and later by himself, until 1958. He was extremely proud of the fact that he'd shown the New York crowd that authors and editors didn't have to live in New York to prosper.

Boucher's reviewing career was revived around the same time that the magazine began to do well. His position as the primary mystery reviewer for *The New York Times* came about innocently enough. His co-writer for the Holmes radio show, Denis Green, heard that *The New York Times* editor was looking for a reviewer. Boucher had always felt that he was hindered in many ways by living on the west coast, but the editor had announced that he would go all the way to California to find a good reviewer. Green suggested Boucher, and Boucher was asked to write for the *Times*. At first, Boucher was one of a stable of reviewers for the paper, but he soon made a reputation for himself. By July, 1951, Boucher had moved into the primary position.

Boucher's speed reading paid off in his new position. His family estimated that he could read a book with full comprehension in 2 to 3 hours. He would then set about writing details about the characters and plot on a

3" × 5" card. Boucher designed his own code system to make the process go faster. He used designations such as "OH" for "Our Hero." He then wrote his review from his notes on the card.

Even with all the critical acclaim, Boucher was still struggling financially. "Latest is: A) AP's mother, after a long series of cerebral hemorrhages [sic] is now in a nursing home, to the merry tune of $250 per month."[19] Boucher was now responsible for the support of his mother along with his wife and children, putting more stress on his already weak physique.

Inevitably, illness caught up with Boucher again. "Between the ever-pressure on the TIMES and running F&SF singlehanded I am not so gradually going nuts. I don't exactly have time to spare for illness, but managed to come down with ersipelas [sic], more colorfully known as St. Anthony's Fire, which is quite spectacular & left me with a hell of a slow convalescence. Can't say I really care much for 1954 so far."[20]

Even though his body was weak, his intellect was more than willing. His well-respected editing at *The Magazine of Fantasy and Science* Fiction led to other editing positions. He and McComas edited *True Crime Detective* during 1952 and 1953. From 1962 to 1967, Boucher edited *The Best Detective Stories of the Year* as well. Boucher's well-written criticism

In 1956, he wrote this to Rex Stout. "This is a time at which Everything is Happening, from a death in the family to the Excision of a tumor from my typing hand (which seems just about healed thank God)."[21] Boucher and Stout had communicated in later years about their common interest in politics.

The worst of his frequent medical problems was that Boucher never qualified for a medical plan. So every illness was doubly hard, the lack of income added to the medical expenses involved.

The frequent medical costs and the need for money meant that Boucher rarely never went on vacation with his family. The children remember trips to science-fiction conferences and interviews; Boucher would sometimes take the family and spend a few days following the event seeing the area. Although the Bouchers would eventually get to New York and Europe, all of the trips had an underlying business purpose as well.

While he was soon in demand as a speaker, Boucher's health problems made it difficult for him to attend to these requests. Boucher's asthma problems hounded him all of his life. He could not make morning appointments, because in the first few hours after waking, he found it difficult to breathe. It would take several hours for Boucher to be able to get into a normal breathing pattern every day.

Boucher with Phyllis, Lawrence and James along with his mother, Mary White (courtesy Lilly Library, Indiana University, Bloomington).

Even though Boucher was busy with his reviewing, radio programs, and more, he still found time for hobbies. Boucher had been collected operatic recordings for most of his life, a collection that counted over 9,000 entries by the time of his death. That collection became the cornerstone for his radio show, *Golden Voices*, which aired Sunday nights from 1949 until his death. Boucher selected the records, wrote his own commentary, and played the selections himself. His work on the radio led to television appearances, work with the San Francisco Opera, and interviews with some of the singers he admired. Boucher wrote copy for the San Francisco Opera programs and served as the local reviewer for *Opera News* until his death. He and Phyllis were long-time season subscribers to the San Francisco Opera seasons, even donning the formal wear for the first-nighters.

Boucher also offered his time to the Catholic Church following the Second Vatican Council. The church was looking for ways to reform its liturgy and include more lay people. In the 1960s, Boucher managed to find time to be a lay reader at his local parish. His friend, Father Brian Joyce, told of the feelings of awe he had at Boucher's reading of the first Scriptures of the mass. Boucher's life-long love of languages allowed him to translate some of the liturgies from the traditional Latin to English.

Even more surprising is that Boucher still continued a very active social life as well. Boucher was an avid poker player and met monthly for a night of low stakes poker with his friends, including McComas and Poul Anderson. His friends described Boucher as a ruthless and brilliant player, even in the wild-card games that they invented.

His son, James, said that his father did not have the ability to just relax. For Boucher, relaxation involved the use of his brain.

> Poker required a combination of both mathematical quickness and the indefinable skill of being able to "read" an opponent. His one fault at poker was pride, a reluctance to recognize defeat. However, the strength of his other skills at the game allowed him to make it profitable, as well as relaxing.
>
> I had only seen him shoot craps or play blackjack when that was the only action available. His preference was poker...[22]

The group called themselves the "The Outpatients Poker Clinic" referring as a joke to their collective mental health. They started early in the afternoon, broke for dinner, and continued on. Boucher's son, Larry told how his own game would sometimes overlap with his father's in the same house. The poker ritual stopped with Boucher's death.

The Author

> Strictly speaking, I made my first professional sale when I was sixteen; a short ghost story so abominably written that I now feel that the editor who bought it must have had a sadistic grudge against his readers.
>
> —Anthony Boucher, *Exeunt Murderers*, 1st ed.
> [Carbondale: Southern Illinois University Press] 1983

Beginnings

Boucher's desire to write stemmed from the extraordinary amount of genre fiction he read as a child. Asthma had sidelined any notion of physical play. Combined with an ability to speed-read, Boucher made short work of most of the authors of his era and earlier authors as well.

A common stereotype in mystery writing has a budding author beginning writing after reading poorly written novels while recuperating from a serious illness; the fledgling author thinks that he or she could write something better. There is something to this stereotype though. Fred Dannay spent his youth in a sick bed and grew up to become one half of Ellery Queen. Likewise, Margaret Millar spent time reading books by contemporary authors after a bout of depression and began writing.

Boucher desired publication; however, his plotting and characterization skills were slow to mature. His first published work, a few hundred word ghost story vignette, appeared in *Weird Tales* in 1927 when Boucher was sixteen. Even with this early publication, the majority of his writings in his teens and early twenties only collected rejection slips.

While developing his fiction writing skills, Boucher sought inspiration through involvement in the arts. He worked in the Little Theater in Berkeley during this time, acting and directing. His experience in the theater pushed him to write plays. "I was writing unnumbered (and unproduced) plays then, and every so often, a few short stories. And when, in morbid moments, I now go back and reread them, I'm ashamed."[1] Boucher was savage in discussing his early work. Most of those stories and plays exist only in passing in Boucher's correspondence through epithets. His kinder remarks deemed the works "muddied" and "unprofessional."

By 1934, he had moved from Little Theater to write theater and music reviews for the *United Progressive News* in Los Angeles. Boucher's experience as a critic would prove invaluable later when he decided to review mysteries. He also made a number of lifelong friends at the newspaper, including science fiction author Cleve Cartmill.

Despite his harsh self-critiques, a few short works by Boucher were good enough to be published during the era. One of his short stories from his twenties is "Threnody," a mystery. In a 1952 introduction to the story, Boucher discusses about why he still liked it:

> I've had a weakness for [Threnody]; and whatever it is in the absolute it's at least incomparably better, in both plot and writing, than anything else I did around that time.
>
> It's strictly of the period, the '30's. Alexander Wolcott no longer sways mass enthusiasms; Granville Hicks no longer contributes to The New Masses; Corey Ford (damn it!) no longer writes brilliant parodies.[2]

A threnody is a mourning song, an elegy for a dead person. In the story, the narrator writes the elegy for a friend who has passed away. The threnody is included in a book of the narrator's poetry and it becomes an instant hit. The work is mentioned in every possible venue, and the narrator becomes famous. When the subject of the threnody returns alive and well, the narrator decides that he values fame more than he does his friend. On the verge of writing a screenplay based on the threnody, the narrator makes sure that the elegy remains valid.

Even with these small, early successes, Boucher craved larger ones. He continued to write, confident that he would become a novelist. In fact, he vowed that he and Phyllis would not wed until he could support her from his writing income. True to his word, he proposed to Phyllis shortly after his first novel, *The Case of the Seven of Calvary*, was accepted by Simon and Schuster in December 1936 for $250. The couple married in the spring of 1938.

Lee Wright, who accepted *The Case of the Seven of Calvary* over the transom, was the well-known editor of Simon and Schuster's Inner Sanctum mystery imprint. She was known for finding new mystery talent, introducing many mystery authors of that era including Craig Rice, Patrick Quentin, and Gypsy Rose Lee. Boucher had submitted the book to eight publishers prior to sending it to Wright. She would later claim that *The Case of the Seven of Calvary* was the first manuscript from the slush pile that she ever wanted to publish.

Despite his previous publications, Boucher had not wanted representation. In the 1930s, editors from the major houses still read unsolicited manuscripts; agents were not required as they are today. Boucher's previous works had not needed an agent. Most of his material had been short stories and one-act plays. New York agents were not inclined to represent either of those genres; neither would net a sizable commission for the agent. Novels were the most commonly represented works.

Even through the slush piles of unsolicited manuscripts, Boucher's submission had caught Wright's eye. Like many Inner Sanctum mysteries, the dust jacket flap contained information about the author and book. On the back cover, Wright joked about Boucher's terse query letter.

> Dear Sir:
> To be perfectly brief— this is a detective novel called *The Case of the Seven of Calvary*, and I hope you will enjoy it enough to publish it.
> Sincerely yours,
> Anthony Boucher

The joke was on Boucher. Lee Wright was a woman editor, but Boucher had to wait several letters to learn that detail. Indeed he addressed his correspondence to Mr. Wright well into December of 1936, "please reassure me that is Mr. Wright? Lee is one of those terrible ambiguous names, that make one always suspicious of committing a faux pas. And although Dr. Ashwin could doubtless tell the sex from the signature, I can't."[3]

The Case of the Seven of Calvary and all of Boucher's subsequent novels are heavily autobiographical. In *The Case of the Seven of Calvary*, Martin Lamb, the Watson of the story, is a director at the Little Theater in Berkeley, just as Boucher had been. Lamb is a graduate student in the German department, Boucher's area of study as well. The book's setting is a university's foreign language department, similar to the department from which Boucher received his MA. Part of the book's action takes place at International House, where Boucher had lived as well.

The plot involves a Dr. Schaedel, an unofficial Swiss ambassador and promoter of world peace, who is brutally murdered following a lecture at the university. Schaedel's nephew, Kurt Ross, is a student at the International House, and suspicion falls on members of the house.

Despite the fact that Boucher left academia for other pursuits, he lovingly portrayed the university life. His sleuth, Dr. John Ashwin, was loosely based on one of his professors. (The front material reveals that the real professor's name, Dr. Ryder, is the Sanskrit translation of Ashwin.) Ashwin has seemingly lost interest in many of his avocations, including chess and billiards, although he seems to still be devoted to his unofficial goddaughter, Elizabeth. The murder brings Ashwin back from his ennui.

From the first page, the reader recognizes *The Case of the Seven of Calvary* is a different type of detective novel. Using a narrative frame structure similar to the early Ellery Queen novels introduced by friend J.J. McQ, Martin Lamb, the Watson of the case, is retelling the story to "Tony Boucher," who has a speaking role in his own book. The narrative between Boucher and Lamb bookends the tale, and Boucher includes multiple interludes between Lamb and Boucher to break up the story's action.

Boucher inserts himself in the tale, both as character, audience, and author. Boucher, as author, footnotes his novel, speaking directly to the reader. In this manner, Boucher toys with the artificiality of the detective story. For example, while the characters struggle to determine the meaning of the piece of paper left beside the body of Dr. Schaedel, Boucher congratulates the reader on having enough sense to determine the clue from the title.

If Lamb is the Watson and Boucher the audience, Dr. Ashwin is the quintessential sleuth. Ashwin, as the armchair detective, is an archetypal Golden Age detective peppering the dialogue with obscure languages like Sanskrit, a step beyond the normal pithy quotes in Latin and Greek spouted by Wimsey and Vance. Ashwin's library, which the detective rarely leaves, is a testament to his arcane knowledge in such matters as *The Mystery of Edwin Drood*, Conan Doyle, and detective stories in general. Earlier drafts of the novel show an even more erudite Ashwin, giving a cogent solution to the unsolved Edwin Drood case.

Besides having a detective who studies mystery fiction, the book carries a number of inside jokes on specific novels and the genre. The characters participate in this humor. At one point, Dr. Ashwin exclaims, "My dear Martin, this isn't a detective novel. You can't reason things out in actual life with such absolute precision. If a thing is reasonable and yet fantastic, it's not worth considering."[4] Despite the light tone, the murders are taken seriously. Ashwin scolds Martin Lamb for pursuing only an intellectual interest in the two murders.

Boucher also tips his authorial hat to the great detectives of the 1920s and 1930s. Philo Vance and Ellery Queen are not the only detectives that Boucher pays homage to in his first novel. "'You see,' Dr. Ashwin concluded,

'I am well conversant with my Stuart Palmer and my Erle Stanley Gardner, to say nothing of my never-to-be-sufficiently praised John Dickson Carr.'"[5]

Ashwin's deductions also pay tribute to Sherlock Holmes. When Dr. Schaedel is found murdered via an ice pick, beyond the knowledge needed to strike a fatal blow Ashwin deduces the following:

> "Holmes, of course, would begin by deducing from the ice pick that the murderer was a cuckold; but I think that a bit farfetched."
> "A cuckold? Just how —"
> "Because his household still employs an icebox in these days of electric refrigeration, a fact most probably occasioned by his wife's intrigue with the proverbial iceman. Elementary, my dear Lamb..."[6]

Boucher's devout Catholicism shows in *The Case of the Seven of Calvary* through the supposed symbol of the Vignards, a secret Swiss cult descended from the Gnostics. The cult believes in a seven-headed divinity, a "septinity," which is explained via the dialogue and charts. The details of the cult are so vividly explained that Boucher's love of religious trivia vies for supremacy with the plot in places. In yet another wink to the reader, Ashwin ascribes all secret cults as a bit "too early Conan Doyle," a hint to the reader that this matter is a major red herring to in solving the case. Religious elements appear in later works, culminating in the introduction of a nun, Sister Ursula, as the detective in *Nine Times Nine* in 1940.

Boucher's best tribute to the detective story is his creation of a scrupulously-clued plot. In the *Seven of Calvary*, a traditional mystery pits the reader against the armchair detective. Boucher goes as far as to place an asterisk next to the names of the actual suspects in the front papers of the book. A Boucher-Lamb interlude in the next to last chapter issues the Challenge to the Reader, similar to the ones started in the Ellery Queen series nine years prior. The reader is told that all the clues have been presented and is given an explicit chance to solve the mystery before Ashwin. To ensure the fairness of the clues, Ashwin enumerates the clues needed to solve the mystery, and Boucher includes the page numbers where each clue appeared, giving the reader every opportunity to solve the murders.

Boucher received some unexpected benefits from his first novel. Agent Willis Kingsley Wing approached Boucher in 1937, after the author had sold the *Seven of Calvary* on his own. Wing's office expressed interested in his work.

Because of his broad interests, Boucher wanted an agent who could represent him in a number of genres. Boucher sent Wing information about his short stories and one-act plays. Then, as now, most agents do not handle the promotion and publication of short fiction. They are difficult to sell, and the payment for stories makes the agent's ten percent a paltry sum. The one-act plays, however, were received with more enthusiasm. Even with this interest, Boucher held off on hiring an agent, hoping to sell a second Ashwin book before signing with an agency.

Boucher wrote a second Ashwin novel shortly after the first, tentatively titled *The Case of Toad-in-the-Hole*, but it was never published. The extant book resides in the Lilly Library at Indiana University in Bloomington, Indiana.

The setting for this second Ashwin novel is Los Angeles, where Boucher lived and worked as a reviewer from 1933 to 1937. Martin Lamb, in a very autobiographical touch, works as a drama critic for the *Liberal Front Weekly*, a parody of the *United Progressive News*. Coincidentally, Dr. Ashwin has moved from the Berkeley area to take a professorial job at UCLA. Anita Tourian, a secretary for the weekly, accompanies Lamb on his detective work. Boucher doesn't explain the disappearance of Mona, Lamb's love interest from the first novel.

Lamb is producing a new version of his play, *Don Juan Returns*, which was first performed in *The Seven of Calvary*. A drunken, womanizing actor, Sid, is the first to be murdered. The crimes become more shocking to the cast as they realize that the murders are current day re-enactments of historical crimes.

The Maybrick, Border, and Berkeley true crime cases are all replicated with great care. In these cases, Florence Maybrick was convicted of poisoning her husband with arsenic.

At his paying job at the newspaper, Lamb reports to David Landrew, whose brother has recently died. According to the will of George Landrew, his widow has to stay in the house with his corpse for three nights after his death. The widow Landrew is having an affair with Sid. After she invites Sid to spend her first night alone in the house, the actor is murdered the next day.

This homicide brings Lieutenant Jackson, who later appears in the Fergus O'Breen's series. Only in this unpublished book is the truth of Jackson's name revealed. In all of the later O'Breen cases, he is referred to as A. Jackson, nicknamed Andy. In *The Case of the Toad-in-the-Hole*, he reveals that his name is Aramis; his father had been a Dumas fan.

Another name provides a major clue to the solution of the case. The Landrew name is a corruption of Landru, the name of a real-life mass murderer. Henri Landru was a rather obscure figure in mystery fiction until he became one of the two namesakes of the contemporary publisher, Crippen and Landru. Crippen and Landru is familiar to many readers as the publisher of mystery short story collection from Golden Age and contemporary mystery authors. However, readers in the 1930s were unlikely to have heard of the case or the killer.

Like its predecessor, *The Case of the Toad-in-the-Hole* is structured in an unconventional manner. The first of two appendices, in a comment to the reader, decries the way that the people in a murder mystery are abandoned after the solution to the crimes. Boucher gives the reader two more chapters of information about the main characters, closing the story in a more satisfying way. The second appendix is a short reference guide to all of the real-life true crimes alluded to in the book, presenting detailed information on how to learn more about each one of the historical murder cases.

Despite the accolades he had received for his first novel, the second novel was never published. Boucher's last draft of the book was entitled *Phoenix: or Up from the Ashes*, pointing to his concern over the book. The Bouchers, who had married on the strength of the first novel's sale, grew concerned about making ends meet.

After failing to get a contract from Lee Wright, Boucher opted to shop the book around New York. He had hoped to sell his second Lamb novel before taking on Wing as an agent. He tried to sell it to Marie Rodell at Duell, Sloan & Pearce prior to selling her the Sister Ursula series. She kindly wrote about the novel:

> I think it's a brilliant idea and loads of fun — but I'm afraid that it's a connoisseur's mystery. I think it's the kind of book Mr. White will be able to afford to do a few years from now, when we have built up the new pseudonym, but for a starter, I think it has too little general appeal. The average fan is not sufficiently well versed in criminology to get all the clues or understand what a large portion of the action is about, and I do feel that with a first book it is best to play safe, observe the rules and avoid insane murderers.[7]

Her comments mirrored what Lee Wright had told him. The phrase "toad-in-the-hole" is an obscure English disc-pitching game (as well as an English dish, another example of the kind of allusions that would be lost on most readers.) Mystery writer Stuart Palmer put it most succinctly when he wrote,

> *Toad in the Hole* has every fault of its predecessor and as far as I went no new virtues. Probably the story is swell, but if I didn't care to dig on into it, the reader will not.

> Tony, you have got to know the tricks of the trade before you successfully disregard them. You must consider your reader, you must serve your apprenticeship in fiction. Suspense — SUSPENSE ... write it in your hat and write it on your wall. Create real, simple, clear characters and get them into trouble. You can be erudite on page 70, but not on page two.[8]

Boucher didn't give up on Dr. Ashwin easily. He wrote another Dr. Ashwin story, entitled "Death on the Bay," set on one of the ferries crossing San Francisco Bay. A man is stabbed on the boat; Ashwin noticed only five people cross near the victim during the trip and deduces that one of those people must be the killer.

The story is full of the references to other detectives and crimes. If anything, Ashwin is even surer of his talents during this case. He discusses Sherlock Holmes, at one point. "[O]ne of their favorite topics that ineffable master of all detectives (in which category Dr. Ashwin counted himself) since his success with the Seven of Calvary [sic] — Sherlock Holmes."[9]

The story is unique in that the same fair-play spirit exists in the short story as in the previously published novel. The reader is given a "Challenge to the Reader" at the point where all the clues are given. "I know that it is not customary to issue a Challenge to the Reader in a short detective story ... Nevertheless, it can be done, and this is the place."[10] Like *The Case of the Toad-in-the-Hole*, the story was never published.

Boucher published a single short story featuring Martin Lamb, entitled "It Will Have Blood." Lamb has a limited role in the story. He appears only as a minor secondary audience to a murderer's confession. Lamb doesn't realize that this story is a confession; instead, he thinks it's the idea for a new play and encourages the killer to write the script. The resulting play is entitled "It Will Have Blood." The play is produced with murderous results that reflect the supernatural mysteries that Boucher would write about later in his career.

This Martin Lamb story introduces another theme that Boucher explores in his later works and eventually his review columns, the idea that "murder will out," or that the murderer will eventually be exposed through some means. The decades old murders uncovered by O'Breen in *The Case of the Solid Key* and *The Case of the Seven Sneezes* also show this concept.

Boucher had been working on a new series prior to the rejection of *The Case of the Toad-in-the-Hole*. He provided his agent-in-waiting, Willis Kingsley Wing, a novella, entitled *The Clue of the Crumpled Knave*, featuring a new private eye. Boucher still hadn't officially signed with Wing, but allowed him to market Boucher's mystery projects. Multiple magazines rejected the novella because the "surprise" ending was felt to be too trite, and the detective was without depth. Lee Wright suggested expanding this story to a full-length novel, and at that point, Boucher formally asked Wing to take him on as a client.

Boucher hated the process of expanding his work into a novel. He thought it was much less trouble to write something new than to revise to this degree. However, he persevered and when he was complete, he had the start of a new mystery series.

The O'Breen stories

In 1939, Boucher's second published novel, *The Case of the Crumpled Knave*, came directly from the novella with the same name. The book introduces Fergus O'Breen, a private detective both brash and full of the Irish blarney. O'Breen appears in three novels and a handful of short stories. O'Breen's entrance into the case was always hard to miss. "Colonel Rand had never before seen a detective in a tight-fitting yellow polo shirt. It really was not a good idea. It made the young man's lean face seem even leaner and clashed violently with his crimson hair — hair of so brilliant a shade that Rand wondered whether Kay was really entitled to be called a redhead after all."[11] To make matters even more colorful, an equally bright yellow roadster accompanies the ubiquitous yellow shirt. In *The Case of the Crumpled Knave*, O'Breen is new to the detective game, having been a PI for only six months before the start of the narrative.

If Ashwin was developed as the quintessential armchair detective, O'Breen was envisioned as California's answer to Ellery Queen: erudite, brash, and full of himself. O'Breen's conversations are peppered with *bon mots*. He is given to rash pronouncements on the case, only to later have them shown to be incorrect.

Even so, the glib O'Breen is not without insight into his own shortcomings. He gives a brutally honest psychological appraisal in himself in his first outing.

> I've got the fine Gaelic capacity for getting low as all hell; and I've got to keep myself high as heaven the rest of the time to make up for it. Maureen got roped into a psychology section at her club once and began Studying me with a capital S. She played around in her quaint jargon and decided that I was quote an introspective extrovert with manic-depressive tendencies unquote.[12]

Boucher didn't stop at modeling his detective on Queen. The mystery is Queenian as well, a fairly straightforward murder with a dying clue. A man is poisoned in his own home, which is locked from the inside, so that only a handful of people could have committed the crime. Each of the suspects has a motive and no alibi for the time of the crime.

Hammond Garnett, a retired chemist and amateur gamer, is found with the jack of diamonds from one of his many collectors' playing card decks crumpled near his hand. The card's history and the history of this particular knave are investigated by Breen and Colonel Theodore Rand in depth. With each new interpretation, the clue points to another suspect until nearly everyone in the house is under suspicion.

O'Breen is introduced into the case as a friend of Garnett's daughter, Kay, and as the private detective who has been investigating her fiancé's past at the request of the victim. When Kay's fiancé, Richard Vinton, is arrested for the crime, Kay fears that the police won't investigate the case further to find the real killer. She hires O'Breen to find the culprit. The police element is portrayed in the person of Lieutenant Jackson, who once played basketball at USC against O'Breen, "the fighting forward," in a game where Fergus scored 13 baskets. As a result, O'Breen is allowed access to police information in the case.

O'Breen starts his quips early with Kay Garnett, making light of the many levels of their relationship:

> "Maureen gave me pretty much the same idea from the times she visited you, Kay."
> "I thought, Mr. O'Breen, that you'd decided on Miss Garnett."
> "Look. That's too much trouble. Suppose I just call you Client. That's easy, and still it's formal. Well, almost formal anyway."
> "Very well ... Detective." She tried hard to smile.[13]

Even though O'Breen's major influence is plainly Ellery Queen, Boucher alludes to many of the crime writers of his era. He mentions Agatha Christie and G.K. Chesterton. Boucher gives the readers a sly nod by introducing Colonel Rand, whose quirks and worldview are strikingly similar to those of Agatha Christie's military characters.

Colonel Rand was ostensibly visiting to play as the fourth in a game of four-person chess. He appears after receiving a telegram from Garnett, announcing his own death and imploring Rand to keep an eye on "Hector." As is typical for a detective novel with a dying clue, "Hector" turns out to have as many meanings as the Jack of diamonds, including being a name for the playing card itself.

The book references any number of mysteries and mystery writing conventions. As O'Breen points out in the novel, "'You see, she's read too many of those novels where the person who Knows Too Much is the second victim.'"[14] Boucher even brings in S.S. Van Dine rules for mystery writing when O'Breen is frustrated:

> Fergus frowned and viciously uprooted an innocent tuft of grass. "Which makes this," he announced, "beyond any doubt the Goddamnedest first murder case that any promising young detective ever tackled. It's got everything in it but a sinister Oriental, and I expect him to open the door when we get back to the house."[15]

Even though the character of Fergus O'Breen was based in part of the long-running Ellery Queen series, *The Case of the Crumpled Knave* doesn't lead the reader to assume O'Breen will be making more appearances. At the end of the novel, O'Breen lays out a plausible solution to the murders, pointing to one character as the criminal. After putting his cards on the table, Colonel Rand clears his throat with a "harrumph" and then proceeds to present an alternate solution — the correct one. O'Breen shuffles off, having been outshone in his first murder case.

Boucher did not intend to write an O'Breen series. Instead, he wrote a short story with Colonel Rand as the sleuth. While *The Case of the Crumpled Knave* had not contained any supernatural elements to it, the Rand case, "Murder of a Martian," contained supernatural elements that would also appear in the later O'Breen tales. The story is about a murder at a "Martian" exhibit at a fairground. Someone murders one of the girls dressed up as a woman from another world. Colonel Rand, a visitor to the fair, solves the crime.

Even after his less than stellar debut, O'Breen reappears not only in two more detective novels but also in Boucher's unique blend of science fiction, fantasy and mystery short stories. Many of these tales have O'Breen facing time travelers, extraterrestrials, and spirits better suited for a horror or a science fiction story than a straight mystery tale.

Many of the Golden Age writers, like Father Ronald Knox and S.S. Van Dine, had written extensively on the ethics of fair play with the reader. In traditional mystery stories, any supernatural event had to be explained away logically by the end of the work. Ghosts had to be humans in sheets. Puncture wounds in the neck required needles, not Nosferatu.

As a fan of mystery fiction, Boucher knew them all. He just chose not to play by those rules. "Fergus grinned. 'Look. Dorothy Sayers said someplace that in a detective story the supernatural may be introduced only to be dispelled. Sure, that's swell. Only in real life there come times when it won't be dispelled. And this was one.'"[16]

In "The Compleat Werewolf," O'Breen meets a lycanthropic professor of languages with a penchant for cursing in Middle High German, another Boucher touch. Boucher's father-in-law, Dr. Price, had been a professor of German at University of California Berkeley. "The Compleat Werewolf" is about Professor Wolfe Wolf who discovers that he can become a werewolf by uttering an incantation. The difficulty lies in that he must speak the same word to return to human form, but he cannot pronounce it as a wolf. O'Breen shows up late in the story and later recruits the professor to use his unique skills in working for the FBI.

The plot of "Elsewhen" revolves around a crime committed with the help of a time machine. Harrison Partridge discovers a way to travel through time, but the machine he invents can only move the person forty-two minutes into the past or future. This limitation is put to use when Partridge decides to create an alibi for himself in a murder case. O'Breen is brought in to solve the murder and discovers the time machine and Partridge's scheme.

O'Breen investigates another form of time travel in "The Pink Caterpillar." Fighting in the South Pacific during World War II, O'Breen runs across a supernatural phenomenon. Norm Harker, a character possessing the same name as the protagonist in *The Case of the Solid Key*, is telling the story to O'Breen and another soldier named Tony, presumably Boucher although he did not serve in the war. The *tualala*, an island tribe's medicine men, have the ability to travel one hundred years into the future and return with any particular item requested. The characters speculate what goods from the future would be valuable today.

With that foundation, O'Breen starts telling the story of a man who died of a heart attack in Mexico. His mail and papers listed him as a physician, although he did not have a medical degree. O'Breen has to determine the source of the discrepancy before the insurance company will issue a payout. He discovers that the man possesses a skeleton, which is why he is assumed to be a doctor. The skeleton turns out to be from the *tualala*, and O'Breen learns why the man insisted on keeping it.

In "The Chronokinesis of Jonathan Hull," O'Breen appears in the story, but does no detection to speak of:

> This isn't, properly speaking, Fergus O'Breen's story, though it starts with him. Fergus is a private detective, but he didn't function as a detective in the Jonathan Hull episode. It was not the fault of his Irish ingenuity that he

provided the answer to the mystery; he simply found it, all neatly typed out for him. Typed, in fact, before there ever was any mystery.[17]

Through his scientific work at a paranormal research institute, Hull discovered a way to go against the natural flow of time and live backwards, which he calls chronokinesis. Hull and another man are the only two people to do this, which makes them reliant on each other, despite their animosity. This unhealthy relationship leads to murder and the discovery of the body in Fergus's room.

"Gandolphus" features a disembodied extraterrestrial murderer. Charles Harrington, a religious scholar, is trying to debunk the story of Saint Gandolphus the Lesser. Harrington starts finding signs that another person has visited his apartment. As a result, he contacts Fergus O'Breen to put a stop to the nocturnal disruptions. The visits become increasingly upsetting until murder ensues. Following the murder, the alien spirit jumps into the body of the investigating police officer. O'Breen determines that both men have been invaded by an alien who wants to experience emotions and new events to report back to its home planet.

While trying his hand at mystery short stories, Boucher continued to write detective novels. His next book, *The Case of the Baker Street Irregulars*, features an O'Breen, but not Fergus. Maureen O'Breen, Fergus' sister, who had been mentioned in early works as the publicist for Metropolis Pictures, appears as the love interest for one of the Irregulars, Professor Drew Furness. *The Case of the Baker Street Irregulars* is a panegyric to Holmes.

Fitting for a novel about Doyle and a novel by Boucher, the author points out on more than one occasion that many of the Golden Age detectives owed a debt of gratitude to Holmes. "'You are probably thinking,' Dr. Bottomley interrupted, 'of *The Green Murder Case*. Out of charity to the dead, let us say that it is an unfortunate example of coincidence in plot device. There snow served in the place of water for the concealing agent; here it is bushes.'"[18]

The detective puzzle is not as complex as some of Boucher's other books, but its light-hearted references to the Holmes series are fun. The story is a classical detective novel with a closed setting, in which only the Baker Street Irregulars had the opportunity to commit the murder.

The novel starts from the viewpoint of the head of Metropolis Pictures, F.X. Weinburg. Stephen Worth, who has expressed his disdain for all things Doyle, has been contracted by Metropolis to write a screenplay for "The Speckled Band," one of the best-known stories from *The Adventures of Sher-*

lock Holmes. After a rousing reaction from Holmes fans across the country, Weinburg attempts to fire Worth, but is contract-bound to keep him involved in the picture.

Weinburg's solution is to invite five of the country's best Holmesian scholars, all members of the Baker Street Irregulars, to participate in the project as creative consultants. He hopes to rein in Worth and make a movie that is true to the story. Metropolis tries to accommodate the quirky needs of these scholars. Like Holmes' address, the Irregulars' house is renumbered for the occasion as 221B; however, the street remains Romauldo Drive. Weinburg and Maureen O'Breen even find an austere housekeeper named Mrs. Hudson to watch after the men.

Even though Fergus O'Breen is not part of the action, his police sidekick, Lieutenant Andy Jackson, plays a role. The reader learns that he's the brother of Paul Jackson, one of the movie stars at Metropolis. Both Jacksons attend the get acquainted party for the Irregulars. Worth is murdered following the party, and, of course, all the Irregulars are considered suspects because of their animosity towards Worth.

The tale is told in a repeating manner. After the opening action, the same events are recounted from the viewpoint of each of the five Irregular suspects. In the days after the murder, each suspect is involved in a unique, bizarre adventure. The tales are given to the reader as police records, set apart in typewriter-like font, so that the reader knows that this account is in the words of the suspect. These accounts slow down the pace of the book, but are fascinating pastiches of Doyle's style and plotting.

Each adventure has two distinct features. The first is a remarkable similarity to one of the cases in Sir Arthur Conan Doyle's Canon. The clues include a dancing-men cipher, five orange pips, *Rache* scrawled in blood on Worth's wall *à la The Sign of the Four*, a gun whisked away on a string as in "The Problem of Thor Bridge," a severed ear in a cardboard box, and more. Even Ricoletti of the clubfoot from "The Musgrave Ritual" is involved in the plot, although there is no sign of the Giant Rat of Sumatra or pygmies.

Maureen O'Breen is very much caught up in the odd goings on at the house, the everywoman looking in at the idea of fandom. "In a way the orange seeds helped. They were the final touch of unreality. No one could feel the actual tragedy of death in a world where people drew dancing men for murder threats and sent dried orange seeds by special messenger."[19]

The Irregulars are in their element with these fiction-based clues. The detailed knowledge of the Canon is such that the characters are able to decipher the "dancing men" message, even knowing that Doyle had used the same "dancing men" figure to represent "P" and "V."

Some clues inserted in these Holmesian adventures are not from the Canon, and this evidence dumbfounds the sleuths at 221B. When the Irregulars are removed from the familiarity of the Holmes stories, Boucher shows them as lost children, unable to find solutions. In fact, it is Maureen O'Breen who decodes the typed list of numbers found at the scene of the crime.

The second part of each Irregular's adventure is the revelation of another Irregular's dark secret. In the chapter titled, "The Adventure of the Tired Captain," Professor Drew Furness' problems with his senile aunt are revealed to one of the other Irregulars, Each of the residents of 221B has their secret revealed in turn, and Andy Jackson has to determine which mystery provided the actual motive for killing Worth. Despite these secrets being the motive for murder, Boucher never explains how the dead author could have uncovered so much dirt on the Irregulars, in just the few days before their arrival in Los Angeles.

In a classic detective ending, Jackson brings all the suspects together and systematically rules them out, until only the murderer remains. The love interest prevails as Furness and Maureen O'Breen announce their intention to marry in the final pages of the story.

O'Breen's next two novel-length adventures, *The Case of the Solid Key* and *The Case of the Seven Sneezes*, are conventional detective stories with a more competent Fergus O'Breen. In books where the plot commanded the most attention, O'Breen develops into his role as a competent detective. Both novels feature ambiguous clues that give widely different solutions depending how the reader interprets them. Some of these clues focus around "impossible crimes," adding layers to the plot on how the crime was committed.

In *The Case of the Solid Key*, Boucher works with another difficult plot in the mystery genre, the locked room mystery. He would later re-use the impossible crime motif in his Sister Ursula books.

The titular key is solid, because most of the recognized methods for locking a room from the outside involve the hole used for a keyring. A string attached to the keyring hole can pull it from the room after knocking it to the floor. Another method is to turn the key in the lock via the keyring hole. In *The Case of the Solid Key*, Boucher reduced the possible solutions to the locked room; therefore, he has fewer solutions to explore in the course of the novel.

The setting of the book is again a small theater, which reminds the reader of Boucher's first novel, *The Case of the Seven of Calvary*. However, in this book, the theater is not lovingly portrayed. The entire company is a scam perpetrated by Rupert Carruthers, who uses the hopes of actors and playwrights to bilk as much money as he can from them. Norm Harker, a writer fresh from Oklahoma, stumbles upon the theater and wants to break into Hollywood and the legitimate theater. He befriends an undercover Fergus O'Breen before the apparently accidental death of Rupert Carruthers. Both have an interest in true crime, especially the unsolved Randolph case a decade earlier.

Unlike the later Sister Ursula books, the locked room portion of *The Case of the Solid Key* is diminished for this book. Despite the supposedly impossible nature of the crime, the characters only look at the locked room as an inconvenience rather than something inexplicable. The reader quickly sees that the murder could easily have been facilitated by one of the many ways that locks can be manipulated. The solid key eliminates many of them, but the answer to this case lies in merely determining which of the methods could be used with a solid key:

> "That leaves us," said Norman, "one door safely latched on the inside."
> "That doesn't necessarily signify. There's ways and means.... For instance, you could turn the key in the lock with pincers from the other side."
> "But that would leave scratches on the end of the key. I had a good look at it, and it wasn't scratched."[20]

This focus on the mechanics of the locked room makes the mystery feel rather staged. In order for the "impossible" crime to be committed, the key was made especially for this door. This early revelation signals to the reader that the locked room is not impossible, but merely a smokescreen to fool the police. The accident theory is eliminated by O'Breen, leaving the reader to figure out the how of the crime as much as the why. He meets Lieutenant Andy Jackson again in this case, who serves as a foil for his own deductions.

Again Boucher mentions a variety of mystery authors and characters in his own work:

> "Only of course, the climax of it all is an accident."
> "I'll admit," said Jackson, "that Rupert Carruthers was asking for murder. On purely psychological grounds, maybe that looks like a murder case. But the physical evidence is too strong the other way."
> "Too strong is right. It's so strong it smells. No natural death could ever be so congoddamnedclusively natural."
> Jackson grinned. "You've been reading Chesterton again. Bad influence."[21]

The Case of the Solid Key was another case that did not end with O'Breen solving the crime in the typical Golden Age tradition. He presents an inaccurate solution to the case that covers some, but not all, of the vital clues to the insurance company which had insured Carruthers' life. As O'Breen concludes the presentation, he realizes the errors in his own case and finally knows who the real killer must be. However, he is conflicted about the solution and unhappy when Lieutenant Jackson leads away the killer.

The book does have a surprise ending, at least for a Boucher mystery. The couple who had been kept apart by the mystery and circumstance is actually re-united in this case. Even Maureen O'Breen and Drew Furness, her romantic interest from Boucher's previous novel, *The Case of the Baker Street Irregulars*, make an appearance in this novel.

For some time, it appeared that *The Case of the Solid Key* would not be published. Both Boucher's agent Wing and editor Lee Wright found the novel too discordant between the love story, the necessary characterizations, and the locked room puzzle. While the first half of the novel was a story of a young Oklahoman playwright trying to make good, the murder takes the forefront as soon as it occurs. The financial and personal problems of Norman Harker are shoved offstage and are dealt with in between scenes and clues. The book needed alterations. Boucher spent the better part of two months to balance the two battling elements and create a book that Simon & Schuster was interested in.

The book was originally thought of as a vehicle for that perennial Watson, Martin Lamb. For some reason, Boucher changed his mind. Instead, Boucher inserted a new character, Norm Harker, because of the love interest in actress Sarah Plunk.

There would only be one more novel-length O'Breen case. In *The Case of the Seven Sneezes*, the mystery revolves around an old Hollywood murder, harkening back to the never-solved William Desmond Taylor case, which of course Boucher includes in the book.

> His sister's eyes lit up. "Murder? Oh, Fergus, are you going to find out who killed William Desmond Taylor?"
> "Hardly. Not, this is earlier and much more obscure. The Stanhope case. You wouldn't know it."[22]

The book opens with a nameless client who wants to hire O'Breen to discover the truth about the twenty-five year old murder. O'Breen rejects the case because his visitor wants only to learn the truth and not to report any findings to the DA. The high-profile case included Hollywood *ingénues* and up-and-coming businessmen as suspects. O'Breen gets some help in the early pages of the book from his sister, Maureen. She identifies her brother's mysterious visitor as Lucas Quincy, the fiancé of the murdered woman, and she also introduces her brother to Stella Paris, a fading silent picture star and another suspect in the old murder.

In this book, Fergus O'Breen is imbued with an allergy to cats. This new twist is recognition of Boucher's own allergies and asthma. "'Trust the O'Breens to have a unique and screwy type of hay fever all their own. Seven sneezes. Mystery number and stuff. But where's the cat? I haven't met him yet.'"[23] In both the older mystery and the current rash of murders, the killings were presaged by the death of a cat by throat slashing. O'Breen's allergies give him the first clue that the crimes have started again, when he has a sneezing attack and finds the grave of a recently murdered kitten.

Boucher weaves in some deft touches, making both the previous case and the current crimes sit on the cusp of war in Europe. In 1915, the ocean line *Lusitania* was torpedoed by a German sub, and Jay Stanhope, one of the characters in *Seven Sneezes*, was lost at sea when the ship went down. The first crime takes place shortly after the sinking of the *Lusitania*. The day before the Brainards' wedding, Jay Stanhope's sister, Martha, is brutally murdered; her throat slit two days before her own wedding. The wedding party managed to construct a plausible alibi for the events; the police investigation discovers nothing. So the group is all released to live the next twenty-five years in relative peace.

The two sets of crimes are neatly paralleled by the events of the world and the changes in the characters over the years. In 1940, World War II began with the invasion of the Netherlands, an event that occurs on the twenty-fifth anniversary of the murder. An early version of the novel shows the cast of characters back in the days just prior to World War I, but the prologue was cut from the second draft of the novel.

The entire cast of characters goes to Blackman's Island to celebrate the silver wedding anniversary of the Brainards. O'Breen attends as the guest of Stella Paris. Mr. Brainard wants to throw him off the island, but he's prevented from doing so. The murderer sets the only boat adrift, which strands the party without communication to the outside world.

Boucher sets up a neat, closed setting murder, similar to those written by Ellery Queen and Agatha Christie. The isolated setting means that the cast of suspects is firmly established. Only certain people could be guilty, and that set of people is all present and accounted for at the scene of the crime. By limiting the suspects in this way, the reader is given a fair chance of discovering the solution. The author cannot introduce a murderer in the last pages or pin the crime on a least likely person.

Even with the domestic tableaux, O'Breen is still a professional private eye. He is paid to participate in the solution to this crime.

> Fergus could feel his fist clenching. He envied these tough and two-fisted investigators you read about who shoot out a straight right to the jaw whenever some dope cracks wise. The hell of this business when you're in it is that you can't afford to have a temper. You've got to take what's handed out to you and hope you can make up for it when the time comes for the bill; and Fergus had already decided that, failing Lucas Quincy, Horace Brainard was going to sign one honey of a check before this party was over.[24]

In his final novel-length case, O'Breen does manage to solve the crimes on his own. In order to earn any pay from the case, O'Breen had vowed to solve the latest murder and rescue the group from the isolation of the island. He follows a very labyrinthine set of clues to come up with the responsible parties. Like O'Breen's other mysteries, the solution of the case is presented in stages, each new solution scaffolding on the last to create a complicated structure. No less than three separate solutions are given for the murders. Each explanation is needed, because different people committed each of the crimes. Four people, working independently, are responsible for the crimes. The final solution to the crime is revealed on the last few pages.

The solution is similar to *The Case of the Crumpled Knave*, in that the same version of the least likely ploy is used. While in many books the criminal could be divined by the romantic pairings, this does not happen in Boucher's books. True love does not run smooth; the young lovers are separated by the crimes, not brought together.

The Sister Ursula stories

Boucher's first two detectives stemmed from his love of the mystery genre; his third sleuth, who first appeared in 1940, developed from his lifelong devotion to the Catholic faith. Sister Ursula, who is introduced in *Nine Times Nine*, is a more mature, complex character than Boucher's other sleuths. Ursula, whose father was a police detective, had planned to join the police as well before illness ruined her plans. Joining the convent had been a second choice, but one she followed just as passionately as crime-solving.

Unfortunately, the detecting nun only appears in two novels and a handful of short stories, but her fans remember her fondly. The naming of the fictitious Catholic order, the Order of St. Martha of Bethany, is one of Boucher's many subtle jokes. The nuns are helpmates to women throughout the Southern California area. As Sister Ursula explained:

> He gestured at the face of an elderly woman, wearing the headdress of the order, embroidered on the banner.
> "[T]hat is our founder—Blessed Mother La Roche. Sister Perpetua just finished embroidering this. It's to stand by the altar Saturday—her feast day, you know."
> "Is she a saint?"
> "No. Not yet. Of course, we are prosecuting her cause most vigorously. It is the dearest hope of our life to live to see Mother La Roche canonized."
> "When poor women are sick or in childbed, they can often find a charitable agency to supply them with nursing care, but meanwhile the household goes to pieces. There's no one to do the housework and look after the other children. That's one of our jobs. That is why we're called the Sisters of Martha of Bethany. You remember perhaps? Lazarus had two sisters, and Martha complained because Mary spent too much time listening to Our Lord and too little running the house. Mother La Roche thought there was a good deal to be said for Martha."
> "We take the usual triple vows of poverty, chastity, and obedience; but we aren't subject to canon law. You see, we've never asked approbation from the Holy See. Mother La Roche wished this community to be a lay one, with only private vows. In the strictest sense, I suppose, we're not nuns at all."[25]

Like Miss Marple and other amateur detectives who look into human nature to solve crimes, Sister Ursula uses her own knowledge of the Catholic religion and her faith to find the criminal elements.

> "I don't blame you for sounding doubtful. But you see I am not inexperienced at detection. The Mother Superior was quite astounded when I proved what had been happening to the sacramental wine. And then there was that little business of vandalism when someone slashed the missal which Sister Perpetua was illuminating. In fact, Sister Immaculata always calls me—
> "I think," she said slowly, "that everyone has a particular Deadly Sin—one out of the Seven to which his moral self is peculiarly susceptible. Mine is Pride."[26]

In *Nine Times Nine*, she recognizes the motive for the murder by her knowledge of human nature espoused in the Bible. While Sister Ursula might be proud, her skills are proof of her superior skills in solving locked room murders.

Not only was the detective a change from his earlier works, Boucher published these works under a pen name. Boucher's two Sister Ursula novels appeared under his pseudonym H.H. Holmes. Unlike the O'Breen novels where he was under the tutelage of Lee Wright, Marie Rodell from Duell, Sloan, and Pearce published the Sister Ursula books. The name change was requested by the publisher to keep the two series distinct in the readers' minds.

While many readers assumed that Holmes was a play on the name of the Great Detective himself, Boucher used the alias of a notorious Chicago mass murderer. H.H. Holmes, who confessed to more than 27 murders by the time of his trial in 1896, was a alias for Herman Mudgett (whose name Boucher also used for some original verse.) Boucher used the H.H. Holmes name to write book reviews for the *New York Herald Tribune* in addition to the Sister Ursula novels. Holmes was recently immortalized in the book, *The Devil in the White City: Murder, Magic and Madness at the Fair that Changed America.*

The pseudonym was not a true secret. Boucher left clues to his identity in the Sister Ursula books. *The Case of the Baker Street Irregulars* is mentioned in *Nine Times Nine*. Even more telling, Boucher appears as himself in *Rocket to the Morgue.*

The pseudonym and new publisher were not the only changes in Boucher's work. His earlier novels had focused on fictionalizing true crime cases with mentions of every criminal case from Landru to William Desmond Taylor. In his later books, Boucher turned his sights to the strictures of the mystery genre, mainly unique plot devices. The Sister Ursula books featured impossible crimes. Boucher put as much of his intellect into these plots as he had the earlier use of the fact-based crimes.

Not everything about these later novels was new. The two Holmes novels recycle plot devices from earlier Boucher novels, just more successfully. The Sister Ursula novels are locked-room mysteries with extremely original solutions. Boucher had flirted with a locked room puzzle in *The Case of the Solid Key*, but the means were explained early and took a backseat to the mistaken identity romance.

As with his earlier books, Boucher still includes elements of religion, cults and Hollywood. The protagonist in the case is no less than a nun. The cult in the story is led by a mysterious yellow-robed prophet named Ashavar. Lieutenant Marshall's wife, Leona, is a former model and burlesque performer.

Despite the use of a complicated locked room mystery in *Nine Times Nine,* the plot is relatively simple. Wolfe Harrigan, a devout Catholic who debunks religious cults, is discovered murdered in a locked room in his home moments after the cult leader was seen in the room with him. All of the windows and doors to the room were either locked or under constant observation, leaving the cult leader as the sole suspect. The cult leader, Ashavar, had been under investigation by Harrigan; as a result, Ashavar had placed a curse called the Nine Times Nine on Harrigan. Suspicion for the crime immediately falls on Ashavar even though everyone in the family had ample motive.

The "Children of Light" cult leader is larger than life and yet elusive:

> He dominated the stage and the whole auditorium. But it was even harder to guess what he actually looked like than it had been with Sister Ursula. His face was obscured by a black, spade-shaped beard, along with the Assyrian style. And his body was completely enveloped by the famous Yellow Robe.
>
> There was nothing of gold or saffron or lemon or chrome about the robe. It was absolutely and blatantly yellow, a pure simple, and hideous declaration of a primary color. It displayed no embroidery, no cabalistic signs, no sense of style in its designing. It was just that — a yellow robe.[27]

The "Children of Light" cult is shown to be made up of everyday people, hoodwinked by Ashavar, who claims to be the "Wandering Jew," a contemporary of Jesus Christ. Wolfe Harrigan, the murder victim, is a devout Catholic who has made it his life's work to expose charlatans. In this case, Harrigan suspects a power directing Ashavar who has greater goals for the cult. Ultimately, like the cult in *The Case of the Seven of Calvary*, the cult itself is just a red herring for the reader.

Beyond the well-rounded heroine and cult leader, Boucher's sidekicks are more fully realized as well. Lieutenant Marshall, the investigating police officer, is a former football player and scholar turned police detective, "six-feet-two in height, a hundred and ninety pounds in weight, ruggedly homely in features, and already a trifle gray in hair."

Marshall's wife, Leona, is a former burlesque performer and model who has given up her career for domestic bliss with her husband. Even with her beauty, she is an intellectual, who quickly sums up parts of this rather complicated case. In her summary of the novel, Boucher's editor Marie Rodell calls the scenes with Marshall and his wife some of the best of the book. The human elements are meshed effortlessly with the rather demanding puzzle elements. Unlike the O'Breen novels, only one solution is presented, a more emotionally satisfying ending. Matt Duncan, Harrigan's secretary, and Concha, Harrigan's young niece, fall in love and plan their life together.

Even with the romantic entanglements, the main thrust of the book is the complicated means of murder. Locked room mysteries are the pinnacle of the Golden Age, a puzzle that cannot have happened and yet must be explained. Called "impossible crimes," the murder appears to have taken place in a hermetically sealed space where no one could enter or exit. While the investigation of the case may turn an eye towards motive and opportunity, it is the means of entrance into the locked room that consumes most of the book.

Locked room murders are as old as the mystery story itself. Many experts consider Poe's "The Murders in the Rue Morgue" to be the first locked room mystery. Others are inclined to credit later works since the killer in Poe's tale had not intentionally created a locked room puzzle. Doyle had Sherlock Holmes battle a locked room in "The Speckled Band." Boucher had referenced that Holmes case in *The Case of the Baker Street Irregulars* and would later adapt it for radio. By 1900, authors such as Israel Zangwill in *The Big Bow Mystery* and LeFanu had created full-length works that included more proper locked room mysteries.

The Golden Age, usually defined as the period between World War I and World War II inclusive, was a showcase for the locked room mystery, where plot counted for so much. Most every Golden Age author tried their hand at a locked room. S.S. Van Dine used them in *The "Canary" Murder Case* and *The Kennel Murder Case*. Ellery Queen came up with a unique variation in *The Chinese Orange Mystery*. Clayton Rawson and his character The Great Merlini dabbled in locked room mysteries as well.

Undoubtedly, the king of locked room mysteries was John Dickson Carr. In his works, people were found dead in sealed rooms, people were discovered in homes where the snow had not been sullied, and fully clothed men dove into swimming pools to vanish. Between 1930 and 1972, Carr wrote locked room murders, trying new tricks with existing methods and creating new methods of his own. Carr included elements of the supernatural around the impossible crimes to suggest that the murderer had been helped by the paranormal.

The locked room still appears in some stories today, but not as often as in the Golden Age. Ed Hoch and Jon Breen both currently write locked room mysteries in the short story format. French author Paul Halter writes novel-length locked room murders, but unfortunately, many of his novels have not been translated to English.

Boucher's locked room mysteries are heavily indebted to those who had gone before. Chapter fourteen of *Nine Times Nine* features a discussion of the locked-room problem in the mystery genre, and specifically in terms of John Dickson Carr's well-known examination of locked rooms that appeared in his novel, *The Three Coffins*. As *The Case of the Baker Street Irregulars* had paid homage to Doyle's Holmes, *Nine Times Nine* offers deference to Carr's Dr. Fell. In fact, the book itself is dedicated to Carr. Boucher was careful with the details and got Carr's written permission to use the rather lengthy excerpt before its appearance in *Nine Times Nine*. In a letter to Boucher, Carr wrote, "My curiosity is roused by your locked-room. If you can find a new way of doing it, many congratulations."[28]

Boucher, with his incisive manner, paraphrased Dr. Fell's lecture in a succinct manner through the characters of Lieutenant Marshall and his wife Leona. The Marshalls are not familiar with impossible crime and must research mysteries to get ideas on how Ashavar might have killed Wolfe Harrigan. Lieutenant Marshall explained it this way:

> "A guy named John Dickson Carr, and he damned near makes me change my mind about mystery novels.... We aren't interested in the literary excellence of Mr. Carr's *Three Coffins*; we want to know how a murderer gets out of a locked room....
>
> "Now Carr's detective, Dr. Gideon Fell — a splendidly ponderous old man who sounds like G.K. Chesterton with a drop of walrus blood — starts out by specifying that you must have a validly locked room, "hermetically sealed," as he calls it.... Now for his theories of classification:
>
> "'First!' he says. 'There is the crime committed in a hermetically sealed room which is really hermetically sealed, and from which no murderer escaped because no murderer was actually in the room.'"
>
> "...A guy named Stuart Mills 'saw the murderer' in this book, too, and still the explanation fitted under this head. Let's go on to the more detailed listings:
>
> 1. It is not murder, but a series of coincidences ending in an accident which looks like murder.
>
> "...Then Point Number One, Accident, is out. Next:
>
> 2. It is murder, but the victim is impelled to kill himself or crash into an accidental death....
>
> "Point Number Two, Suggestion, out. Next:
>
> 3. It is murder, by a mechanical device already planted in the room, and hidden undetectably in some innocent-looking piece of furniture....
>
> "Point Number Three, Mechanical Device, out.
>
> 4. It is suicide, which is intended to look like murder....
>
> "...we can prove that the corpse did not use the weapon. Point Number Four, Suicide, out.
>
> "The next one is tricky:
>
> 5. It is a murder which derives its problem from illusion and impersonation....

"Well, then, the light arrangement kills visual illusion; and if the illusion was anything solid, we're up against the same problem as with a murderer. So Point Number Five, Impersonation and/or Illusion, out. Next:

6. It is a murder which, although committed by somebody outside the room at the time, nevertheless seems to have been committed by somebody who must have been inside....

"All right. Point Number Six, Murder from Outside, out.

7. This is a murder depending on an effect exactly the reverse of number 5. That is, the victim is presumed to be dead long before he actually is....

"Right. Point Number Seven, Murder After the Fact, out. And that, my dear Watson, ends the list of situations in which no murderer was actually in the room. Are you quite satisfied that none of them applies?"

"I was to start with. We know the murderer was in the room...."

"All right. Now the grumpy and splendiferous Dr. Fell gives us his list of the ways a murderer can hocus a door after his escape, to make us think it was locked on the inside. He starts:

1. Tampering with the key which is still in the lock....

Several pretty examples with pliers and string... Right. That's out. Next:

2. Simply removing the hinges of the door without disturbing the lock or bolt....

"It couldn't be done on the French windows..."

"So Point Number Two, Hinges, is out. The next two are:

3. Tampering with the bolt. Strike again...

4. Tampering with a falling bar or latch....

We went over all the bolts and latches in that room and disproved those possibilities. There remains:

5. An illusion, simple but effective. The murderer, after committing his crime, has locked the door from the outside and kept the key....

He then reintroduces the key to the room after it's been broken into, in such a way that we police, who seem to swallow anything, think that it's been there all along.... Exactly. Well, my friend, there, according to what Leona assures me is the foremost fictional authority on the subject, is your list of all the possible solutions to a locked room. And where are we?..."

His wife, Leona, explained it a bit more succinctly. "The Locked Room (my, I wish I could bumble like Dr. Fell) falls into three categories:

A: The murder was committed before the room was locked. B: The murder was committed while the room was locked. C: The murder was committed after the room was broken into."[29]

Yet even as Boucher listed the ways that a man could be murdered in a locked room, the reader suspects that he has produced a new method of the locked room murder, something that had not been tried before. After the comprehensive discussion of locked rooms in *The Three Coffins*, readers and authors generally assumed that all the methods for perpetrating a locked room mystery had appeared in some mystery tale. Robert Adey, in *Locked Room Murders*, calls Boucher's addition to the possible solutions set forth by

Carr in *The Three Coffins* as excellent. In all fairness, Boucher's locked room is accomplished by a melding of two of Dr. Fell's lecture points, but that does not diminish its ingenuity in any way.

In the end, Sister Ursula solves the crime without the aid of Carr or his novels; Lieutenant Marshall and his wife are the ones who seek out mysteries to help in the investigation.

Stuart Palmer summed up the response of most critics when he said,

> You'd better kill off Boucher and stick with this guy Holmes. He writes better.
>
> Incidentally, Holmes' real name was Herman Mudgett, and you will always be Herman to me from now on. Or are we thinking of different Holmeses?"
>
> A fine thing giving Boucher a plug in *Nine Times Nine*.[30]

Two years after his success with *Nine Times Nine*, Boucher published a sequel, *Rocket to the Morgue*. The book included large amounts of autobiographical data on everything from Boucher's own double-jointedness to his science-fiction writing friends to semi-fictional characters that included Anthony and Phyllis Boucher.

Boucher borrows heavily from his other books as well. Sister Ursula and Lieutenant Marshall, her police counterpart from their previous encounter, solve a locked room murder that touches upon the early science-fiction market. Many of the characters from the previous novel are present, requiring that the books be read in order as not to give away too much of the plot of *Nine Times Nine*.

Matt Duncan (and his new wife Concha) are now friends with the Marshalls who have a daughter named Ursula. Matt is still trying to earn a living as a writer and had been commissioned by the family of Fowler Foulkes, the author of the original Dr. Derringer works, to write a series of new adventures featuring the intrepid sleuth. The estate of Fowler Foulkes had agreed to the sequels, but at the last minute asked for all of the earnings from the stories in return for its portion of the rights. The Foulkes estate, through son Hilary, has battled with a number of authors, who are all considered suspects when Hilary's life is threatened through a series of near fatal attacks.

In *Rocket to the Morgue*, the locked-room puzzle is weaker. Sister Ursula, Sister Felicitas, and Mrs. Foulkes all have their eyes on the only open door when Hilary is stabbed in the back. Sister Ursula instructs Marshall to look for the "invisible man" in this case. The suggestion turns out to be one a matter of character, rather than a science fiction gimmick from H.G. Wells.

Indeed, in the solution of the case, the character who is least self-fulfilled turns out to be the murderer.

This book is Boucher's most popular mystery. A favorite among science fiction fans, it's set against the backdrop of the penny-a-word science fiction writing, which Boucher knew so well.

This would be Boucher's last novel. Boucher did not desert science-fiction after the mystery novels. He wrote science fiction short stories after *Rocket to the Morgue* and later founded and edited *The Magazine of Fantasy & Science Fiction*.

Part of the fun of the novel is identifying the real-life inspirations for the characters. In an afterword written for the paperback edition, Boucher disavows any direct portrayals of real people in his characters in the book. This is not exactly true. Anthony Boucher appears as a character as does his wife, Phyllis, although the book originally appeared under his "H.H. Holmes" pseudonym.

Even with the disclaimer, several science fiction authors and editors can be recognized, some under their own pen-names. Boucher dedicates the book to the Mañana Literary Society and features the science fiction writing group in the book. The Mañana Literary Society was the weekly gathering in Robert Heinlein's Hollywood home. Science fiction author Jack Williamson described it as such:

> Tony Boucher and Phyllis. Mick and Annette McComas. Sometimes I was allowed to bring Ray Bradbury, thought he was still so brash and noisy that Leslyn didn't always want him. Henry Kuttner and C.L. More were there now and then. Leigh Brackett, Art Barnes. Sometimes such visiting notables as Willy Ley and de Camp and Hubbard. I remember a fetching redhead named Marda Brown.
>
> He [Boucher] put our society into his 1942 novel *Rocket to the Morgue*. Heinlein is there as Austin Carter, a chief suspect. Hubbard is D. Vance Wimple and [John W.] Campbell is Don Stewart. Ed Hamilton and I are combined into Joe Henderson.[31]

One of the most discussed characters in the book is the overbearing Hilary St. John Foulkes. Most people believe Foulkes is a thinly disguised version of Arthur Conan Doyle's outspoken son, Adrian Conan Doyle. The character is the widely unpopular heir to one of the great literary estates of the 20th century. Like Sherlock Holmes, Dr. Derringer is an adventurer who solves impossible things. The character actually spouts the aphorism, "eliminate the impossible. Then if nothing remains, then some part of the 'impossible' must be possible."[32] This is a quotation remarkably close to Holmes' own axiom.

One reason for the negative portrayal of Adrian Conan Doyle could be the discussions being held in the early 1940s over the publication of a collection of Holmes pastiche stories. Two years following the publication of *Rocket to the Morgue*, Adrian Conan Doyle would squelch the distribution of *The Misadventures of Sherlock Holmes*, a collection of pastiches edited by Fred Dannay who was half of Ellery Queen. Doyle threatened lawsuits and demanded a financial settlement as well as pulling the book from the market, feeling that pastiches would ruin the purity of the Canon. Ironically, the collection included a story, "The Adventure of the Illustrious Impostor" by Boucher himself.

Dannay wrote to Boucher: "Where I expected a letter of thanks and appreciation from the Doyles, I'm getting a — lawsuit. All stories had been previously published without reaction to them."[33] Doyle listened to suggestions that the estate would be better served by suing each author, Boucher included, rather than Queen, but ultimately the book was pulled from the market instead.

Doyle tried to enlist the help of the Baker Street Irregulars in removing the book from the market, as many members felt that the pastiches were not in keeping with their celebration of all things Holmes. In the eyes of many members, the stories were not part of the Canon and not worth the interest.

Dannay finally agreed to remove the book from the market. He had erroneously put a copyrighted Holmes story in his collection, *101 Years of Entertainment*, thinking it to be in the public domain. Doyle threatened legal action against Dannay, but offered to drop the matter if Dannay pulled *The Misadventures of Sherlock Holmes* from the market. Dannay decided that *101 Years of Entertainment* would be the better book to keep in print, even though *The Misadventures of Sherlock Holmes* had been through five printings so far. The limited distribution of the book makes it a collector's item today. Following that debacle, John Dickson Carr and Adrian Conan Doyle would co-author a series of pastiches, entitled *The Exploits of Sherlock Holmes*, some ten years later, but those stories did not have the forbidden allure of the *Misadventures* collection.

Not only does *Rocket to the Morgue* depict the pitfalls of mystery fandom in the 1940s, the author also borrowed conversations held at the Mañana Literary Society surrounding the idea of blurring the boundaries between mystery and science-fiction. Chapter three of *Rocket to the Morgue* contains a heated discussion over the continued segregation of science fiction and the detective story, pushing *Astounding Stories'* editor John W. Campbell's belief that the genres could not be commingled. The Campbell character, Don Stewart, is visited by Lieutenant Marshall and gives a soliloquy on how the rules of science fiction would alter any attempt to have a locked room mystery. Stewart suggests that a time machine could be used to alter the alibis, a device that Boucher would use later in his O'Breen short stories. The murderer could disassemble and reassemble himself atom by atom in the locked room. The character also discusses a method by which the character could enter the fourth dimension, enter the room, and leave by the fourth dimension again.

Despite the fun that Boucher seems to have had in writing *Rocket to the Morgue*, not everyone was thrilled with the end result. Marie Rodell had this to say about *Rocket to the Morgue*—"It is less the fact of "self-murder" that bother me than what seems to me to be cheating in the locked room setup. The given in a locked room setup is that someone get in and/or out and attacked the victim, in spite of the seeming impossibility of doing so; your reader, confronted with such a setup, baffled as all get-out, impatiently waits for the moment when you, the author, will show him how it was done—and lo! it was not done at all."[34] Boucher borrowed from his own life for the less than fulfilling denouement. Indeed, it is Boucher's claim that he can disprove any mystery novel that says a particular knife wound could not be self-inflicted that helps solve this case. Boucher was extremely double-jointed in his shoulders and elbows.

The final chapter finishes with a somber note to a fun-filled romp through the science fiction community of the 1940s. Boucher sets the final chapter on December 6, 1941, the day before Pearl Harbor's attack. The seemingly innocent conversation between the characters is laced with the knowledge that in a few hours the United States will be at war following the Japanese attack.

Although *Rocket to the Morgue* successfully combined mystery and science fiction, no other similar works were forthcoming. No author could combine science-fiction fandom and a great mystery. No other book would give such a detailed portrayal of science fiction authors and fandom until Sharyn McCrumb's Edgar-winning *Bimbos of the Death Sun* published in the 1990s.

Rocket to the Morgue was one of the few Boucher titles to be reprinted during his lifetime, perhaps because it was named a Haycraft-Queen cornerstone book. Most of the reprint markets required sales of 5,000 hardcover copies or more, and the Boucher books tended to land in the 3,700 copy range. *Seven Sneezes* was reprinted in a Dell mapback edition a full 5 years after its initial publication.

Readers were fortunate enough to have a few short cases involving Sister Ursula as well. *Exeunt Murderers*, a collection of Boucher's short stories edited by Mike Nevins, has two short works featuring Sister Ursula. "Coffin Corner" is the story of a young football hero, Coffin Corner Cassidy, who wants to clear his name before going off to fight in World WarII. The plot is similar to "The Punt and the Pass," a Nick Noble story, but the solutions are widely divergent. In each story, two football stars are accused of murder with the evidence pointing equally to either one.

In "Coffin Corner," Cassidy confessed to a murder years ago in order to clear his friend and teammate of the crime so he could play on the day of the big game. Cassidy was acquitted, but the murder was never solved. The crime left a mark on both men's records that needed to be expunged in order for one to be accepted into the air commission. Sister Ursula solves the problem easily and sends the murderer off to the priest for confession at the end of the tale.

The other story, "The Stripper" is about a serial killer who kills while undressed. Boucher originally entitled the story "Quasimodo," but the editors went with a more provocative title before publication. "The Stripper" is a progressive story for its era. This Sister Ursula vehicle looks at a serial killer and the psychology of a man who kills while naked. The suspect is identified as a neighbor of Harvey Flecker, who shares a boarding house with three other people. A good part of the story is told in italics from the killer's perspective. The result is a thrilling story of a man who kills without motive or reason.

A third Sister Ursula story was not included in that collection, but is every bit as worthy. "Vacancy with Corpse" is almost novella-length. Homicide detective Ben Lattimer is romantically involved with Liz Cain, who finds a dead body in her house. The Cain family had opened up their home to workers in the war effort who needed a place to stay. The little man staying with them is only there an hour or two before he is found murdered in his room. Sister Ursula is introduced to the case through Sherry, Liz's cousin, who had previously dumped Ben when she decided to take the veil.

Other mystery short stories

As Boucher became more involved with science-fiction, radio plays, and editing, his mystery output dropped dramatically. He went from producing a novel a year to merely two or three short stories each year. His few mysteries were quickly snatched up by Ellery Queen (through his friend, Fred Dannay) or in a variety of science fiction magazines that published so many authors in the 1940s and 1950s.

One of Boucher's earliest efforts was the Holmes pastiche, "The Case of the Illustrious Impostor," which was featured in short-lived *The Misadventures of Sherlock Holmes*. Boucher's story is one of the shortest in the book. Holmes has been brought forward to World War II and reflects with Watson the curious case of Rudolf Hess in British custody. Holmes thinks that the man is a fraud, part of a Nazi plot to confuse the Allied efforts.

Boucher developed a series of short stories about Nick Noble, a retired police detective who was forced out of the police for his alcohol problems. Impossible cases are brought to Noble for a solution, which he provides in a day or less.

The characterization of Noble is rather weak. Noble was thrown off the LA police force, taking the fall for his corrupt captain. He lost his salary and health insurance at a time when his wife was very ill and ended up losing both career and family. As a result, he became a wino of the worst variety. Seen only in the bar Chula Negra, Noble swills cheap sherry and brushes nonexistent flies from his face. "He was a wizened man whose sharp nose seemed trying to push out of his dead-white skin. His hair and heavy eyebrows were white too, and his eyes so pale a blue as almost to match them."[35]

Boucher remembered this about the creation of the stories featuring Noble:

> I can recall why I started the series: because Ellery Queen had just opened up a fine new market. I can recall where I got the name Screwball Division: it was a translation into American of Carter Dickson's Department of Queer Complaint. I can recall the model for the Chula Negra: a little Mexican café on Second Street in Los Angeles, where the staff of a political weekly used to gather to talk about the stories we were going to write and eat the best lengua en mole and drink sherry (which the waitress always called cherry) at ten cents per water-glassful. But I absolutely cannot recall how I ever conceived the wino-detective Nick Noble.[36]

The first Noble case was "Screwball Division" and introduced Noble and his police sidekick Detective Lieutenant Donald MacDonald of the Los Angeles Police, Homicide Division. Noble is called on for help after three men are killed in three separate locations at the exact same moment in time with the same weapon. Once again, Boucher introduces an element of religion into the story, as one of the victims is a priest. A cult called the People for the Kingdom is involved in the case as well, harkening back to *The Case of the Seven of Calvary* and *Nine Times Nine*.

In another Noble case, "QL.696.C9," the story is prescient of today's Patriot Act with its discussion of librarians working to report suspicious lending activities of its patrons. When the librarian is murdered before she can pass on her most recent findings, Noble is called in to figure out the meaning of a strange dying clue. In a true armchair detective solution, Noble is able to determine the murderer without even leaving his seat at Chula Negra.

In "Black Murder," Boucher draws on the Sherlock Holmes case, "The Bruce Partington Plans" when a naval inventor is found poisoned before he can complete naval plans that are needed for the war effort. Noble shows that the poisoning was accidental, but before the police can breathe a sigh of relief, the inventor is found murdered with his throat slit and a swastika drawn on the wall. Noble discusses the history of the Nazi symbol as he solves the case easily.

The death of a Russian count is the mystery in "Death of a Patriarch." In a nod to the Communist threat of that era, the "red threat" is suspected of the crime until the police find a dying clue, the initials "CP." The nephew is blamed for the crime. Before he can clear himself, the communist party members kidnap him, and Nick Noble has to come to the rescue, in a rare appearance outside of the Chula Negra. The dying clue again comes down to the study of language, one of Boucher's passions.

Fred Dannay and Boucher scratched "Death of a Patriarch" from *Ellery Queen's Mystery Magazine* after three of the magazine's readers didn't like the story. Dannay was sorry to see the story go. He wanted an exclusive arrangement with Boucher for all of the Nick Noble stories to appear in *Ellery Queen's Mystery Magazine*.

Instead, Boucher requested to substitute "Rumor, Inc." for the declined story. "Rumor, Inc." also uses the war background as a setting for crime. MacDonald is on the phone with a woman suspected of funneling military secrets to the enemy. He hears her address her killer as "Mr. Patrick" before she is gunned down. Noble has to solve a case that has not one, but three Patrick cousins who might be the killer.

Besides Boucher's interest in politics and world conflict, his other interests appeared in his short stories as well. As the war wound to a conclusion, some of those interests started playing a greater role in his fiction. In "The Punt and the Pass," Professor Cross is murdered during an elevator ride with two football players. Both of them had the means, motive, and opportunity, and Nick Noble has to find out which one stabbed the professor.

Opera was introduced in "Like Count Palmieri," a reference to *Tosca*.

Noble runs into Mr. Matteson, an operatic recording collector like Boucher himself. Matteson has found a rare recording of Lena Geyer singing Rossini's *Cenicienta* (Cinderella). He tries several methods to obtain the recording from the bar's owner to no avail. Noble actually stops him from stealing the recording. When Matteson's partner is murdered, Noble is asked to solve the crime.

In this story, Boucher shows a spirit of racial tolerance and gently chides others for using stereotypes. Lieutenant MacDonald is the voice for this tolerance. "'Now Wilson's a Negro, but he'd be a great disappointment to fiction writers. He didn't think it was a ghost, nor start rolling his eyes in terror, nor mutter "Feet, do yo' stuff!" nor any of the other things that make nice comic relief. He very sensibly and capably rolled off the bed and under it.'"[37] This type of reference to minorities is a far cry from the works of mystery authors like Leslie Ford who wrote in the same era.

"Crime Must Have a Stop" is a different type of story for Boucher. MacDonald introduces Steve Harnett, the writer for Pursuit, an adventure radio program, to Lynn, a radio actress. They soon become a Hollywood couple, even though Steve is already married. MacDonald feels guilty for his small part in the matter. When both Lynn and the wife are found murdered, MacDonald has a personal stake in finding the solution to the case. The solution hinges on a printing-related clue and a quotation. Dannay was only able to offer Boucher $200 for the story as the magazine was still having financial issues, but suggested it for the annual contest. "Crime Must have a Stop" won 3rd prize in the *Ellery Queen's Mystery Magazine* Fifth Annual Detective story contest.

Boucher's discussion of right and wrong is highlighted in the story when MacDonald confronts Steve about the affair. "'You always were a sucker for quotations. Lends authority, doesn't it? Takes away your own responsibility for what you're saying."[38]

In one of the last Noble cases, Boucher uses the true crime case of Raymond Fernandez, the Lonely Hearts killer for inspiration. "The Girl Who Married a Monster" asks the question "Why would a woman marry a known Bluebeard?" Luther Peabody is the widower of at least five women who met with untimely, "accidental deaths." When Doreen decides to marry Peabody, Doreen's cousin Marie asks for help from Lieutenant MacDonald. Boucher brings in Fergus O'Breen in a one-line appearance, where O'Breen is staking out Peabody's house.

Boucher also wrote non-series mystery short stories as well. In his introduction to the short story "Mystery for Christmas," Boucher discusses the collaborative process that he found in mystery writing. Even after publishing multiple novels and a handful of short stories, Boucher wasn't too proud to take assistance in creating new works. He submitted a number of works to Fred Dannay when Dannay was starting *Ellery Queen's Mystery Magazine*.

> It's fitting that a story dealing with teamwork between two detectives should itself have been produced by teamwork — that type of teamwork so valuable to writers and so little known to reader, which can developed between an author and a truly creative editor. In 1942, when I'd begun selling my first detective short stories to *Ellery Queen's Mystery Magazine*, Queen asked me if I had any unsold shorts cluttering up my files; maybe something could be salvaged from them. Of course I did (is there any writer who doesn't?). I sent him a batch of unpublished and (I'll admit now) unpublishable stories; and the one in which Queen saw possibilities was this, at the time called The Mickey Mouse Mystery. Now Queen is, God bless and keep him, the kind of editor who can not only tell you what's wrong but show you how to make it right; he indicated a completely new angle from which to approach the story — and that entailed, again fittingly, the introduction of the character of Mr. Quilter and the productive the-whole-is-more-than-the-sum-of-the-parts teamwork between him and young Tom Smith.
>
> Just to balance things a little, this story also brought about the one occasion on which I've been able to catch Queen with his editorial slip showing. He wanted to run it in the issue of *Ellery Queen's Mystery Magazine* appearing just before Christmas in 1942, and said that we should therefore retitle it Murder for Christmas. I wrote back that this was fine (aside from the fact hat the title had, like almost anything a mystery writer can think of, been already used by Agatha Christie); there was only one small point against it — the story contains no murder.[39]

The renamed "Mystery for Christmas" is one of Boucher's weaker efforts, in a work that vaguely reminds the reader of some of Agatha Christie's works based on the characters of Harlequin and Columbine. A necklace is stolen from a masquerade party. The characters are all dressed as Disney characters; the ultimate clue not surprisingly stems from knowledge of the German language.

In 1941's "Design for Dying," a mystery novelist, John Bennington, unwittingly hatches a plot for his own death. His secretary, Ronald Markham, plans to use the perfect murder plot designed by the old novelist for the man's death. Markham learns at the last minute that the plan had its flaws and is arrested for murder.

Boucher used another last minute surprise in his story "Transcontinental Alibi." In the story, Hugh Wimperis murders his law partner, Sidney Steiner, using Steiner's murder mystery manuscript. Steiner, suffering from sinus problems, had returned to Berkeley on a flight to deal with Wimperis' embezzlement. Rather than face ruin, Wimperis kills his partner and sets about making the time of death seem later so that he had an alibi at the time of the crime.

When a radio program calls Steiner's house, Wimperis impersonates Steiner, thinking that it gave him an impregnable alibi. Instead, the reader learns that flying with sinus problems had rendered Steiner temporarily deaf, so that answering a phone, much less hearing it, would be impossible.

Boucher put his spin on an urban legend in his story "The Way I Heard It." At a party at Martin Lamb's home, a few revelers begin telling a story that each had heard about a phantom hitchhiker, interrupting each other in turn to correct a detail or make a minor change. The ending of the story throws a twist to the reader in spirit of O. Henry. Fred Dannay and a few other editors had trouble with the story because of the frequent interruptions; the story appeared in *The Acolyte* in 1944.

In "Code Zed," Boucher creates another of his many World War II mysteries. Like many of the short pieces, this one deals around the war and the espionage efforts. Two Englishmen are preparing to torture a German spy to get the secret to Code Zed when the FBI arrives. The results are surprising. Vincent Starrett reprinted this story in a later spy anthology.

In "The Ghost with the Gun," the story is told from the first person point of view of a Homicide detective in the Berkeley police force. A man wearing a ghost costume on Halloween shoots Ben Flaxner, a former Chicago mobster, at close range. "'This is maybe the smartest killer I've ever run up against. He picks the one night in the year when he can go around completely disguised without bothering anybody. Then he ditches the sheet and the mask and there's not a thing to tie him to the crime.'"[40] The story gives a great description of the small college town during the war. The story is more hardboiled than most of Boucher's work and closer to a real private eye case than some of the O'Breen cases.

As the war ended and Boucher went in different directions with his fiction, some of the social issues of the day came through in his work. Boucher discusses the idea that every person has a possible murder in them in "The Catalyst." It's only when certain people or circumstances crop up in their lives that the murder moves from the possible to the real. The catalyst is the person or circumstance that creates the murderous situation. The story hinges on a clue based on a duodecimal code that the victim uses; it resembles the many dying clues about language that Boucher used in other stories.

"The Retired Hangman" uses a background of capital punishment for this murder case. The titular character discusses the changes in capital punishment from hanging to the gas chamber and the electric chair. The case deals with Willis Wythe, whose sentence was commuted after the gallows malfunctioned three times in a row. The murderer's escape from justice bothered the executioner even after his retirement, and the case deals with that premise.

Boucher uses a more political background for "The Smoke-filled Locked Room." A politician, an ex-governor, is murdered during a caucus to establish a constitution for California. Many of the progressive movements have banded together for its creation. The story is less a locked-room than a watched one. In the same vein as *Rocket to the Morgue*, the politician is slain in a room with only one entrance that was watched from the outside by his mistress. The case has a different solution from *Rocket to the Morgue*, but it is still an interesting twist on the locked room mystery.

"The Statement of Jerry Malloy" tells the story of the age old love triangle with two men and a girl. The story is flash-fiction, just over 1000 words. The story has a final twist that is reminiscent of the O. Henry stories.

"A Matter of Scholarship" deals with the literary conundrum of popular fiction versus scholarly work. Even though Boucher was a passionate defender of popular fiction and its place in modern society, the scholar wins out in the end.

In one of Boucher's last stories, "The Ultimate Clue," the story itself is structured like the dying clue of a football coach who suspects that either the quarterback or the receiver has thrown a big game so that the bettors could make a tidy profit. The story is told in first person, but the protagonist is identified as O'Breen. The dying clue is a missing half-page of a biography of the legendary Knute Rockne. The last page of Boucher's story is written to look like the dying clue. Not only is there a tie-in between the case and the physical layout of the story, the solution is given in the last few words of the story, a difficult maneuver in writing detective fiction.

Boucher continued to work on a variety of longer projects as well. He had a juvenile mystery, entitled Palace, which was never placed. He also talked to Lee Wright about a cookbook project that never got off the ground.

Boucher wrote a costume mystery, *The Hard Way*, in 1942. Per Boucher's instructions, the book was submitted blindly to several publishing houses. The book was panned by all of the editors, including Lee Wright, who said that the author was just not a storyteller.

The year 1942 marked the end of Boucher's mystery novels; the future rested in a number of other endeavors.

The Editor

> Editorial policy: very broad. We're willing to go as far off formula as any writer wants, provided he makes a good story.
> Letter from Anthony Boucher to Ted Sturgeon, April 14, 1949.
> William A.P. White collection. Lilly Library,
> Indiana University, Bloomington.

By the early 1940s, Boucher wanted to widen his vistas in writing. He had written mystery novels with some success for six years, but the market was not paying as well as he wanted — and certainly not often enough.

Boucher had always been a man with diverse interests, and for the next ten years of his life, he indulged those interests. He wrote synopses for a number of very successful radio series, including shows based on the characters of Sherlock Holmes and Ellery Queen. His involvement with *The New Adventures of Sherlock Holmes* led him to co-found a West Coast chapter of the Baker Street Irregulars and participate in the founding of Mystery Writers of America.

Boucher also wrote science-fiction short stories. Boucher had wanted to edit his own magazine, but he'd been frustrated by his distance from the hub of publishing, New York City. He edited anthologies to supplement his income; he later founded *The Magazine of Fantasy and Science Fiction*, one of the best-written and enduring science-fiction digests ever published.

While some of the interests revolved around new stories, Boucher increasingly found himself drawn into other areas of the creative process. He wrote reviews for *The Magazine of Fantasy and Science Fiction* as well as newspapers around the country. These activities led Boucher more and more into the role of critic, which would be his primary creative outlet for the last two decades of his life.

Science-fiction writings

As a teenager, Boucher had abandoned science-fiction. He had complained that the genre, younger than mystery, had too many dull, poorly written stories. It was at that early age, during the Golden Age of mystery, when he'd switched to reading mystery fiction. While he never gave up his love for mystery, Boucher found time as an adult to begin reading science-fiction and fantasy again.

Boucher told friends. "'Around 1940 ... I rediscovered it [fantasy and science-fiction] and realized that the field had matured incredibly.... I began to read *Astounding* and *Unknown* with — well, this time avidity is a mild word; and pretty soon I began to write for them, too.'"[1]

By 1942, Boucher had a wife and two small children. He wanted to make money faster than was possible in the slow process of writing novels. He gravitated towards the more lucrative field of short stories. Shorter works could be written in a fraction of the time and make more money in total than the same time spent on writing a longer piece of fiction.

Boucher started writing science-fiction again in the early 1940s. The proliferation of science-fiction magazines in the 1930s made an opportunity for Boucher to write more and be paid quickly; there were no similar outlets for mystery fiction. Boucher was devoted to his craft and made efforts to put out quality science-fiction, unlike the work he'd read as a boy.

To further his aspirations, he joined the Mañana Literary Society to work with other science-fiction authors. The group met weekly in the Los Angeles area at the house of then up-and-coming science-fiction author, Robert A. Heinlein. The group talked about their current works in progress, the stories that would be written "mañana." They drank and discussed any subject in the galaxy. The group contained some of the brightest authors and editors of science-fiction over the next twenty years, including John. W. Campbell, Cleve Cartmill, and future Scientologist L. Ron Hubbard. Boucher was able to make the trip south on occasion to bounce ideas off the other writers and enjoy the camaraderie.

Judging from the number of science-fiction stories he wrote over the next dozen years, Boucher found his niche in science-fiction. He published often, and his work was well-received. As with his mysteries, Boucher wove the people he knew and the subjects that fascinated him into his works.

Many of his best works revolve around an intersection of religion and science-fiction. The possibilities of science and the moral implications of implementing science cropped up frequently in Boucher's science-fiction work. In "The Quest for St. Aquin," Boucher set the story in a futuristic society called the Technarchy, where the Roman Catholic church has been outlawed. The Pope and Thomas (of the doubting variety, of course) hear of Acquin, a holy man who converts all who listen to him. The Pope sends Thomas on a quest to find Aquin so that he might be canonized in the Church, providing additional legitimacy during a time of trouble.

Thomas is transported to Aquin's lair by a robass, a talking robotic device that uses logic and rational thought to try to persuade Thomas away from his quest. The robass questions Thomas' mission and the cleric's dedication to the church. The robass tries to tempt Thomas with a barmaid and other earthly pleasures, much like Satan had tempted Christ in his last days. The tale ends when Thomas locates Aquin and discovers the holy man's secret. The robass leaves Thomas at the lair, and the cleric is left with his thoughts, unsure of how to proceed. "The Quest for St. Aquin" is frequently listed as Boucher's best science-fiction story, if not his best short work ever.

In "Sriberdegbit," which first appeared in *Unknown Worlds*, Boucher recycles the sorcerer, Ozymandias the Great, from his mystery short story "The Compleat Werewolf." Gilbert Iles, a lawyer, is drinking at a bar. When granted a wish, Iles says "may I be eternally cursed" as an expletive. The sorcerer takes him at his word and curses him. Iles finds that he must commit a sin each day in order to survive, and the spirit Sriberdegbit is the judge of the worthiness of that sin. The tale is a fun romp, pitting the cunning of the lawyer against the spirit, talking about what constitutes sin and what may be allowed. Not surprisingly, the lawyer wants to split hairs.

Another supernatural character named Snulbug is conjured up in the story with the same name. Bill Hitchens wants to make a quick $10,000 to fund his own venture, but Snulbug explains that he is just a minor demon who can't provide cash on demand. He also can't let Hitchens change the future to make money either. This conundrum is the crux of the story, and Hitchens repeatedly tries to find ways to make next day time travel work for his profit. In the end, he is frustrated by the process. Boucher made a quick $54 from the sale of that story, unlike the twice yearly novel income.

"The Scrawny One" has a similar plot to "Snulbug." John Harker kills an old sorcerer who can summons spirits on command. When the spirit appears, Harker commands it to make him the richest man on earth. Of course, the spirit complies but plays a trick in order to thwart the man's true desire.

Boucher also tried his hand at creating a futuristic society and exploring its maturation. "Q.U.R." was part of Boucher's on-going science-fiction saga for *Astounding Science Fiction* that included stories like "Robinc" and others.

The story is set in the near future and deals with the development of usuform robots. The narrator and Dugg Quinby come up with a new line of robots designed for functionality rather than the currently proscribed humanoid form. The business venture formed by these men is dubbed Q.U.R. and puts them in direct competition with Robinc, the leading producer of humanoid robots in the Empire.

True to Boucher's nature, he added details of a civil rights movement into the story. In discussing the future, Boucher could write about policies and causes that he hoped would happen in the future. In "Q.U.R.," African-Americans have grown in political power, including the election of an African American president.

With Boucher's typical humor, the change to the laws of robot design comes about because of drinking. A nearly-impossible-to-mix drink called the Three Planets is the Martians' most popular drink. In trying to impress these visitors to earth, the lawmakers want to ply them with Three Planets. The Q.U.R. inventors develop an usuform robot that can mix the difficult drink and thus win the approval of the men who can change the laws about humanistic robots.

In the follow-up story "Robinc," the same characters return to deal with the ramifications of the new usuform robots developed in "Q.U.R." The inventors feel a backlash from Robinc for their robot development. The president of Robinc leads the public to believe that usuform robots are dangerous. The trio has to come up with a way to convince the public otherwise. In the end, the robots themselves find the solution, and Q.U.R. looks forward to a bright future.

Again Boucher used elements of civil rights in this story. The story includes some early respectful portrayals of gay men. In a time where genre fiction relegated homosexuals to victims or villains, such a move was risky; however, Boucher saw this as a part of the social justice that he championed through his writings.

Boucher also crossed genres with his short works. Just as Boucher included supernatural elements in his mysteries, he mixed mysteries into his fantasy and science-fiction tales. One of his most famous examples is "Nine-Finger Jack," a serial killer meets a planetary invasion story. John Smith, who murders his wives in the bath in the same manner as George Joseph Smith ("the Brides in the Bath" killer), is astounded to discover that his ninth wife doesn't drown. She has gills. Smith learns that she is from Venus and is part of a excursion to Earth to plot the eventual conquest of the planet. Smith's various attempts to kill his wife meet with failure, until he learns from a patient at a mental institution that Venusians can be killed by one method. After killing his wife, Smith is arrested, and the revelation of the method means the end of the Venusian attack on Earth.

Boucher uses mystery elements again in his story "Public Eye." Much like the private eye stories of the mid–1950s, Boucher developed a character four hundred years in the future who works as a private consultant to solve the odd cases in a world where murder has become almost extinct. Fers Brin is one such public eye who has to solve the murder of Professor Mase. (Fers Brin is an abbreviated version of Boucher's own character, Fergus O'Breen's name.)

The case is a relatively straightforward case of blunt trauma, but the wrong man is convicted. In this futuristic society, over twenty billion people now live on the planet. The odds of two people having the same fingerprints are less than the population; as a result, two people do have the same fingerprints.

"We Print the Truth" opens with a religious discussion of God's love for truth and the responsibility of humans to record that truth. The setting is a newspaper room, where an editor, reporter, and friends are shooting the breeze. A resident rushes in announcing his aunt's murder. The group summons the police to solve the crime. The first part of the story is sensational, but not remotely science-fiction. There's even a romantic triangle as two men fight for a girl's affections.

However, the newspapermen decide to make their own truth by announcing the end of World War II in the newspaper. Suddenly, only this little town of Grover is celebrating the defeat of the Nazis and the return of the soldiers. The manufacturing plants retool for a peacetime economy. The odd thing is that when visitors enter Grover, they too are brought into the belief of the war's end. The FBI man who comes to look into the matter forgets his mission entirely after entering the city limits.

The spell around Grover is broken when the newspaper editor calls the story a hoax, but the story doesn't explore the idea of playing God or wishes. The story ends with a mysterious stranger granting the main character a single wish, which the reader can infer for himself.

Beyond Boucher's passions for religion and mystery, two themes repeated throughout many of Boucher's science-fiction works. The first was the concept of time travel, not an uncommon plot device in the genre. In a great many of his stories, Boucher looked at a society from the point-of-view of the outsider who travels to a future world. This viewpoint allowed the author to comment on the society itself and what man can become.

Given that he wrote most of his short science-fiction works during World War II, it really shouldn't be a surprise that the other topic in many of his shorter works was totalitarian governments. In the majority of his works, Boucher included a discussion of dictatorships and the mind-numbing lack of personal freedom forced upon some people. Considering that Boucher was keenly aware of the war in Europe and Japan at that time, it's not a stretch to see the topics in his work.

The combination of these two themes began in Boucher's earliest science-fiction work. In "Barrier," he takes his character, John Brent, 500 years into the future to battle a ruthlessly totalitarian society that does not allow any dissent against its utopian policies. The government is getting ready to erect a barrier against time travel to keep the world in its perfect stasis. This perfect society has no goals or strivings since all problems have been solved. The government steps in to maintain this perfect balance. The barrier is a roadblock against all time travel crossing the year 2473. The military police of this society are called "stappers"; the name, Boucher's character points out, is a derivation of Gestapo.

In fact, Boucher makes sure that the language in this future world is something of a derivation. He writes of a world that has come up with a uniform, regular form of the English language. No more irregular verbs, and no more exceptions to the rules for English. As a linguist, Boucher has fun with the language, making it definitely unique for the era of the story without being incomprehensible.

Boucher worked on this story for months, corresponding with *Astounding's* editor, John Campbell, several times before submitting it. The time travel discussion was rather complicated.

In a three-page letter to Boucher outlining corrections, Campbell writes:

> Your time-barrier plot has one largish hole in it as suggested, which needs a bit of plugging. To wit: As is, all the assorted futuremen, particularly including the multiple-heavy vanish with the disruption of the particular path that leads to their future via the upsetter-of-the-age-of-Fantaticism-to-be. That might be O.K., but if his destruction leads to another but different future, that other chain of futures will naturally proceed to sprout time-travelers too. They will come back, hit the barrier, and be stopped. Presto!
>
> The effect of this is that any object moving (sic) through time is cutting the magnetic field.
>
> Being a line, if the time dimension is blocked at all, it's blocked at the point unavoidably, so that you can't go around it in any manner.[2]

Campbell ends the letter by adding, "One of the main angles of fun, though, is that you're practically free to design your own laws — nobody knows anything about it anyway."

Boucher worked around this by having some of the characters not understand the time travel concepts. This confusion allowed Brent a chance to explain how the final solution occurs to those characters and the readers. Based on that story, Boucher waived his next novel to Simon and Schuster so that he could work on a fantasy novel for Campbell.

Boucher allowed his social conscience to take over in "One-Way Trip." A strong opponent of capital punishment, Boucher created a society where all killing is banned, including government execution. To remove convicted criminals from society, the government opts to send prisoners into outer space to serve out their life sentences.

Boucher's interest in religion appeared in this story. The fictional society was created from the teaching of a holy man, Devarupa. Boucher used his own knowledge of spirituality and world religions to come up with a new faith that is a mixture of Christianity, Islam, Judaism, and Hinduism. As the author, he used this religion to build a Utopia that is in danger of being invaded from outside forces.

In "One-Way Trip," Gan Garrett, an agent for the World Bureau of Investigation, is on the trail of a mysterious increase in the production of lovestonite, a seemingly benign compound. (Jay Lovestone, a leading communist during the 1920s, was ousted from the American Communist Party and went on to lead the organization of trade unions across the U.S.) While looking into possible uses for the ore in Hollywood, Garrett is framed for murder and sent on his one-way trip into outer space to serve out his sentence.

Garrett's rocket is diverted to the moon, and he is soon part of a mission to save the earth from an invasion. A Hollywood set on the moon is really a planning camp for the invaders, and the extras on the set are mercenaries. Nearly too late, Garrett discovers that the lovestonite is being used to produce a deadly, new weapon that kills without bullets or blood.

Boucher included touches to remind the reader of his other series. Maureen Furness, Fergus O'Breen's sister from Boucher's mystery series, appears on the moon still in the role of Metropolis Pictures' public relations person. Inexplicably, Furness is unmarried, though carrying her married name, and is the love interest for Garrett.

In another Nazi-related story entitled "Sanctuary," Jonathan Holding is trapped in Vichy France during the war. He has been working with a scientist on matters of the other world and ghosts. The Nazis learn of this experiment and want it for their own purposes. While Holding sees the evil potential of this new science, the scientist only sees the pure science of his experiments without the application. Holding has to come up with a way to thwart the Nazis and destroy its capabilities against the Allies, while not being killed by the Nazis for his interference.

In "Conquest," a trio of space travelers crashes on to a distant planet that resembles Earth in most every respect. The only exception is the race of people who inhabit this planet. They are giants in comparison to men. However, it is man's ingenuity that wins the day, and the smaller people take over the planet and its people.

"Expedition" tells another story of interplanetary travel. A band of space travelers from Mars lands on the Earth's moon. The story unravels slowly in epistolary form as these bug-like creatures land on the moon and then earth. The back-and-forth quality of the story heightens the suspense as the Mars travelers come into contact with people we are more familiar with. In the end, the story hinges on a trick played by the humans who want to save their planet from the invaders.

Boucher's love of opera comes through in his story "Man's Reach." A robotic diva is created and sent to Venus for further voice instruction. The robot's chaperone falls madly in love with her and watches her grow from robot to human. Boucher throws in a political plot regarding a world election, but this science-fiction story is mainly about love and art.

In "The Transfer Point," Boucher uses his knowledge of allergies and asthmas to create a world where a new element in the air, agnoton, creates allergic reactions in all humans. The entire human species is reduced to three people who are trapped in a hermetically sealed chamber. Boucher's own self-referential ways appear in the story when one of the main characters in the story, Vyrko, sits down to read *Galaxy* and *Surprising*. Boucher included authors and stories by name. He quickly discovers a series of stories by author Norbert Holt that tells Vyrko's story, down to the life in the trapped rooms. Hoping to contact the author, Vyrko finds a time machine, which he uses. The machine takes him back to 1948, and Vyrko begins to write the series as Norbert Holt.

His stories find a following, and Vyrko is writing the last one when he is killed in a car accident. A friend burns the fragment of the story instead of passing the piece on to his editor. The result is the end of society, because without that final installment, the three people in the chamber can never emerge.

"Pelagic Spark" is an in-joke in the science-fiction world. L. Sprague de Camp wrote a prediction in the vein of Nostradamus, which was published in *Esquire* magazine in 1942. Boucher decided to use the vague, almost nonsensical prophecy as the kernel on which he built a story around.

De Camp's prophecy finds its way into Hitler's hands. The Führer was superstitious about such matters and tries to force the various clues into a meaningful prophecy. As the years pass, the prophecy is passed on to various hands. The interpretation and understanding of the word meanings becomes increasing off the mark. "Pelagic" eventually becomes "Pig Lace," altering the meaning of the prophecy, but making it no less real to those who believe. In the end, a descendent of de Camp reveals the prophecy as a hoax, but only after it has changed the course of history.

Translations

While Boucher had earned a graduate degree with honors in Spanish and German, he had chosen publishing over academics. However, the study of language had crept into Boucher's work in small ways. With the focus on the world precipitated by World War II, Boucher was drawn back into language through the mystery genre.

Starting in 1942, Boucher began translating the works of Georges Simenon for *Ellery Queen's Mystery Magazine*. Boucher had been laid up with a debilitating bout with his asthma that year. Phyllis and their two sons went north to Berkeley to stay with her family. Boucher went to 29 Palms with his mother. In a letter to Boucher, John W. Campbell recommended a filtered air-conditioner as a possibility for help with his on-going asthma. Boucher was disheartened by this bout of health problems. His younger son, James, was less than a year old and Boucher was missing it. He wrote, "[Jamie is] so damned little. Plumper and far more nearly human than Larry was at his age."[3]

After a month's rest, Boucher was able to go back to work again without the wracking coughs that sometimes accompanied his asthma. Still he would be months before he could resume a normal schedule.

During that time, the sheer act of creating was too strenuous for Boucher, but translating the works of others did not seem to harm his weakened condition. Boucher drew on his extensive background of linguistics to introduce American mystery readers to a world of great writers.

At first, the pairing of Georges Simenon and Anthony Boucher seems like a matter of opposites. Unlike the faithful Boucher, Simenon was a serial monogamist who once estimated he had slept with over 10,000 women in his life. Simenon wrote dark psychological novels and stories about Inspector Maigret. Simenon managed to write over 400 novels during his lifetime, completing an average book in 10 days or less.

During his recuperation, Boucher was without his library, so he could not come up with any Simenon works to translate. He was lost without his books, having only a "minute" library to fill his reading time. Dannay mailed Simenon stories to Boucher so that he could translate the works while he recovered.

Boucher was particular about which stories were translated. He read each story first in its native tongue. He looked for the hallmarks of a good mystery: plot, characterization, and the quality of writing. Boucher wanted to only translate works that would gain more attention for the foreign-language author and for *Ellery Queen's Mystery Magazine.* Then he reviewed the story again to see if story translated well into English. In one case, the dying clue rested on a word that had no English equivalent, so the translation was rendered moot. Boucher tried to keep some of the foreign flavor in the language and setting, even as he wrote for an American audience. He wrote a report on each story he read and submitted the reports to Fred Dannay who chose whether or not to commission the story.

The Simenon stories came quickly at first, due to the quantity of available material and Boucher's poor health. Boucher translated two stories in just the month of October 1942. However, by February 1946, he reported to Dannay, "I enclose the reports on the two Simenon books. We really have skimmed the cream already — I don't think there are more than 4 or 5 validly usable stories left there."[4]

Simenon had not been able to speak English prior to the war, but in 1945, he moved to Canada and later the United States. His English improved as he stayed here, in what some critics call his best period. His grasp of English allowed Simenon to read the translations, and he was not pleased with the results from his novels or short stories. Too much had been removed or added. Simenon switched publishers in the early 1950s to maintain more control over his translated works.

Despite his work for the French author's reputation in the United States, Boucher had to defend himself against Simenon's charge later that he hated the author.

> My dear God, sir!
> I have spent well over 20 years under the impression that I was one of the foremost Simenon enthusiasts & advocates in America.
> I have reviewed, at a fast rough count, 49 Simenon books. Out of such a large number, there are, I'll admit, a handful that I haven't cared much for; but my enthusiasm for the corpus of your work has been so evident that the *Times* selected me to write the long front-page feature article on The Bells of Bicêtre last spring — which your publishers quote on the jacket of The Blue Room.[5]

By 1944, Boucher was translating on a regular basis for *Ellery Queen's Mystery Magazine*. Translating required a long lead time, because the magazine had to negotiate foreign-language rights with the author, but once the contracts had been signed, a wealth of material suddenly became available to Boucher as a translator.

In February 1944, Boucher received work from the Mexican author, Antonio Helú. Dannay sent a batch of five stories to be reviewed. With their bleak worldview, Latin American mysteries tend to be inverted from their American cousins. The police and authorities are looked upon as corrupt. Thieves and killers became the anti-heroes of the stories. Unlike American mystery stories, the denouement of the Mexican story does not restore order but mocks the law instead. This was in sharp contrast to the types of mysteries that Boucher was familiar with. His own works featured policemen and detectives as the heroes.

Boucher received the stories from Dannay and read through the lot of five short stories. Boucher was troubled by the stories and wanted to call Helú directly to "talk about this whole problem of the Latin American whodunit."

Dannay replied with specific instructions on how to proceed:

> At long last I've cleared the Mexican stories — so here's the go-ahead to translate as follows:
> First, The Stickpin
> Next, The Pesos & Sidewalk, combined to make one story.
> When I've read those, I'll decide to stop or continue the series.
> Tony, take liberties in characterization, imagery, etc. Also with the style — but with this proviso: if there is anything in Helú's style that is distinctly Mexican — strange word constructions or usages — and if these do not seem amateurish or sore-thumb-y, keep them in; in other words, change liberally to improve or add distinction — but don't lose any Mexican flavor. After all, these are Mexican detective stories and therefore should not be Americanized.[6]

Boucher was able to complete the translations in less than a month. He had no difficulty with his sharp mind in trying to create a work that was both understandable to the reader and true to the original story.

> It doesn't seem to have much of the Mexican local color you mention, but I assure you that's not the result of tampering; the story just takes itself for granted as Mexican and doesn't work at it. If nothing else, though, the fabulous episode of the Procurator and the crimes passionels should prove its Latinity.
>
> I thought of creating an exotic flavor by playing on the fact that Spanish has no word for "murder." You have to say, "the crime," "the assassination," "the assassin," etc. I tried reproducing the exact word Helú used each time instead of what he would have used if writing in English. But the result was painfully awkward.[7]

Boucher was never one to rest on his laurels. He always had more ideas than time. In May 1944, Boucher suggested producing a Spanish version of *Ellery Queen's Mystery Magazine*. This idea was on the table with Mercury Publications and Lawrence Spivak, the publisher, to begin following the war. Although editorship would be in a Spanish-speaking city, Boucher suggested himself as an editorial assistant or translator. Boucher also proposed an *Ellery Queen Fantasy Magazine* to Spivak.

Dannay had to put a stop to that particular idea. Not only was Dannay worried about spreading his focus too thin from his mystery magazine, he was concerned what a full-time editorship might do to Boucher's ongoing health problems.

> About the JOB. You realize that I am planning in advance, against the day I press a button and lo!—EQMM is a monthly. In absolute confidence, I tell you that you were my first choice as Associate Editor. But the health angle, as *I* feared, makes that impossible. I wouldn't want you to take even the slightest and remotest risk.
>
> As to Spanish-language editions, that is probably out too. As I understand it, these foreign-language editions are usually handled by concerns who make a specialty of this sort of thing. In other words, if we can set EQMM up in, say, Mexico, the whole business will be handled by some other editorial office and all I'll have to do is supply copy and sorta watch what's going on.[8]

Boucher's most famous translation occurred in 1948 when he chose to translate Jorge Luis Borges' story "The Garden of Forking Paths" into English. Boucher's translation marked the first time that Borges' work had been available in English and marked a major coup for the fledgling magazine. Dannay later said, "the story is a small masterpiece."

Borges was a well-known Spanish writer, poet, and philosopher. Born in Buenos Aires in 1899, his family was bilingual in Spanish and English. He later learned French during a trip to Europe for his father's eye condition.

However, when Borges turned to writing, he felt most comfortable with Spanish and chose to work exclusively in that language.

Borges wrote "The Garden of Forking Paths" in 1941, apparently as a tribute to the 100th anniversary of Poe's short story "Murders in the Rue Morgue." In 1942 Borges and a young friend, Adolfo Bioy-Casares, published a series of spoof detective short stories, *Six Problems for Don Isidro Parodi,* under the pseudonym of "Bustos Domecq."

"The Garden of Forking Paths" itself is rather simple in plot, but has many layers, which Borges called "labyrinths." Yu Tsun is a German spy who knows the name of the town where a British artillery unit is hiding. In order to expose the troops without being captured, he murders a man named Stephen Albert, knowing that the Germans read the daily paper and will recognize the name "Albert" as that of the town where the British are hiding. The plot becomes more involved as Albert is an expert on China, who is studying Tsun's ancestors.

Ironically, the coup for the magazine led to disagreements between editor and translator. *Ellery Queen's Mystery Magazine* hosted an annual readers' contest to select the best story of the year published in the magazine. Boucher recognized the importance of the story and decided to enter "The Garden of Forking Paths" in the contest. Boucher wanted to submit the story in the contest under the original story category. Boucher called the translation an original, because the said translation had never existed before. Queen called it a reprint, as the Spanish version had been used previously in Argentinean anthologies. The story was ultimately placed in the reprints category and won second place.

Ironically, despite the accolades given to the first Borges' story, a second story by Borges was rejected outright by Dannay. "Death and the Compass" was translated by Boucher for *Ellery Queen's Mystery Magazine.* Dannay didn't care for it. Instead, the story found a home in the *New Mexico Quarterly* in 1954.

Dannay continued to want to find new and unique authors for the magazine. He proposed a United Nations Issue of *Ellery Queen's Mystery Magazine,* which would have stories from around the world. However, the idea never came to fruition. Dannay later reported, "There just weren't enough good stories to bring it off."

Even with the disappointments of the discarded international issue and the rejection of the Borges story, Boucher continued to translate for EQMM as he could. Another author whose works became available to Boucher was Thomas Narcejac, a bestselling French author who along with Pierre Boileau

Boucher and Phyllis *(left)* at the Dannays' Larchmont home. Barbara Norville in the center and Dannay and his wife to the right (courtesy Lilly Library, Indiana University, Bloomington).

is best remembered for writing *D'entre les morts,* which was later made into Alfred Hitchcock's *Vertigo*. Dannay had a few issues with the Narcejac work. "Go easy on sex! Avoid such words as damn, bastard, and bitch. Avoid all political references, especially contemporary ones — they go out of date fast."[9] Boucher completed the sanitized version of the work and recommended two more Narcejac stories for publication in June 1949.

As Boucher's other responsibilities stacked up, he had to slow his translations. By 1951, it took him almost a year to translate Boileau's "Les Fiancées."

Radio plays

In 1945, Boucher's schedule got exponentially busier. He'd been working mostly in the short story field, writing original science-fiction works or translating the stories of others. A new medium was about to be presented to him.

Boucher attended a reception for Basil Rathbone and Nigel Bruce, the wildly popular actors who played Sherlock Holmes and Dr. Watson. While he'd been a stage and film actor for a number of years in Hollywood, Rathbone had become best known for his work as Holmes. Starting in 1939 when he filmed *The Hound of the Baskervilles,* Rathbone became eternally linked with the great detective.

The radio show, *The New Adventures of Sherlock Holmes,* had gone through a number of writers in its short history. This latest version of the show had begun on October 2, 1939 with an adaptation of "The Sussex Vampire." Edith Meiser wrote the first four seasons of *The New Adventures of Sherlock Holmes.* The first few seasons were mainly adaptations of the original Conan Doyle stories, but sadly there are only 56 original stories. The show was expected to continue as a weekly radio program even after all of those were exhausted.

Meiser had long been a proponent of Holmes and Watson on the air. The show had originally debuted in 1930, the year that Sir Arthur Conan Doyle passed away. The original show had featured William Gillette. She had originally introduced the series to the National Broadcasting Company in 1930. The network had liked the series, but had felt it unlikely that a sponsor would put its name to a series based on murder and mystery when most of the radio series at the time were comedy. Meiser had personally located the sponsor, George Washington Coffee, and written the scripts. The original show went off the air in 1937, but Meiser was not satisfied.

The Hound of the Baskervilles revived interest in the radio series. After the coup of landing Rathbone and Bruce as the leads, Meiser felt the series secure. An actress in her own right, Meiser decided to leave the show to return to her roots in theater and film.

The team of Denis Green and Leslie Charteris, the successful author of the Saint series, replaced her. Green had been a fighter pilot in World War I before moving to Southern California to pursue an acting career. He had his bona fides as a devotee of Holmes; Green had appeared in the first two Holmes movies starring Basil Rathbone.

Charteris wrote for the show under the pen name of Bruce Taylor. By 1945, Charteris had other career goals in mind. At the reception, Boucher learned that Charteris, half of the current writing team for the radio show, wanted out. Charteris had aspirations of starting *The Saint Detective Magazine,* named for his character Simon Templar, and a publishing empire that would include many more mystery magazines. Charteris was tired of writing weekly radio scripts and claimed to have run out of ideas for the show.

Boucher was invited to a cocktail party for Nigel Bruce and Basil Rathbone who were visiting San Francisco to promote war bonds. He nearly missed the party as he didn't pick up his invitation until the party was underway. At the party, Boucher got to meet the actors, the writers, and the producer of the show.

Following the Rathbone reception, Boucher approached Green about putting in a good word for him with Charteris. Boucher and Green's wife, Mary, had gone to college together. Boucher hoped to edit *The Saint Detective Magazine*. He wrote the following note to Green, hoping for a possible editorial position:

> How about Anthony Boucher?
> I recently, and with the greatest regret, turned down a similar job because would mean living in New York, and my asthma couldn't take an Eastern winter; but it would seem possible, with Charteris out here, that this might be a West Coast set-up (which, incidentally, I think — and hope — is a coming trend in publishing).[10]

Despite Boucher's suggestion, nothing came of his proposal. *The Saint Mystery Magazine* would not see print for another decade, though Charteris did attempt other mystery magazines in the interim, like the *Craig Rice Crime Digest* that lasted all of two issues.

Green had other ideas for Boucher. Boucher was well known in mystery circles for his love of Doyle's canon. He'd written *The Case of the Baker Street Irregulars*, which was still a favorite among Holmes fans. Green knew all of this and suggested that Boucher apply instead for the radio writing position that Charteris had vacated.

Green pointed Boucher to Glenhall Taylor, the series' producer. Boucher met with Taylor and Edna Best, the director, in Berkeley. He was expected to submit three synopses to the pair for approval.

Boucher had reservations about being hired by Denis P.S. Conan Doyle for the position. His previous dealings with the estate had not been all pleasant. After all, Boucher had killed off a fictional version of Denis' brother, Adrian, in *Rocket to the Morgue* and had participated in *The Misadventures of Sherlock Holmes*, which the Doyle estate had vigorously resisted.

Taylor and Best saw no problem. On the strength of his three synopses, Boucher was offered the position in March 1945. Boucher accepted the offer and started writing episodes of the Sherlock Holmes show.

Originally suggested by Taylor, the collaboration was unique. Boucher continued to live in Berkeley, and Green lived in Brentwood, a suburb of Los Angeles. They rarely met, relying only the mail and an infrequent and expensive phone call to work together. When required, Boucher would take a train to Los Angeles where he would confer with Green, Taylor and Best on future scripts while taking the time to view the broadcasts.

For nearly three years, Boucher wrote a multi-page synopsis of the storyline complete with commercial breaks. He sent these to Green, who wrote the script's dialogue from the synopsis. The show typically aired about four to eight weeks after Green received Boucher's synopsis.

Boucher worked on a tight schedule for the series, but he kept to the schedule, and it worked well for both writers. Two years into their collaboration, Boucher wrote to Green, "It's a pleasure and a privilege, sir, to have you as a collaborator."[11]

The first few synopses were rather rough, and Taylor and Best complained to Boucher about his work. They chided that he needed to be "a little more" thorough in creating each scene and commercial break for Green. Even with the critiques, Boucher proclaimed that the Ellery Queen scripts he would later write were "three to five hundred % harder to write than the Holmeses...."

The show had to be exactly 24 minutes long, so the timing had to be controlled. The script was then approved by Taylor, Best and Conan Doyle who was interested in maintaining the integrity of the series based on his father's work.

The scripts and outlines were somewhat predictable. The show opened with a commercial for Petri Wine, the family that took time to bring you great wine. Following this, the narrator paid a visit to Dr. Watson's retirement home in California. The pair, along with Watson's dogs, sat before the fire, typically toasting with Petri Wine.

Of course, there were other considerations beyond the timing and the commercial breaks as well. Boucher had to rewrite a script featuring an alcoholic in it. Petri Wine Company looked askew at drunks in the scripts. Petri Wine was the show's long-running sponsor, a company that once told listeners that its sherry would taste great even in a kitchen glass.

The actors as well as the sponsor wanted special considerations. Rathbone had been a formally trained actor and enjoyed the chance to perform the Bard for the show. Boucher was also asked at times to include Shakespeare's work into his scripts.

Rathbone and Bruce only had one day per week for radio work. The films took up the rest of their week. They received the scripts in advance. The first reading would be slow to get down the details. The second reading was to ensure that the script met the length requirements. Then they would tighten up the script over the next few readings. The cast would perform once for the East Coast, and then three hours later for the West Coast. A recording was made of the East Coast performance so that it could be used if the West Coast performance was unavailable and for repeats. Many of these broadcasts are available commercially today.

Nearly all of the shows outlined by Boucher were pastiches, stories invented by Boucher using the characters and situations from the Conan Doyle stories. Boucher limited himself to two or three Doyle stories per year. Most of the original stories by Doyle had been adapted before Boucher arrived at the show. Boucher, as a fan of the Canon, used suggestions and hints from the original stories to come up with the plotlines for the new stories. There were scripts from Holmes' hiatus in Tibet as well as the cases mentioned by Watson that had never been written for publication.

Additionally, several of the scripts came from current events and holidays. The end of World War II was celebrated with the episode, *In Flanders Field*. Boucher also wrote episodes for Christmas, Thanksgiving, St. Patrick's Day, April Fool's Day, and ghost stories for Halloween.

The synopsis for his first story was dated February 14, 1943. The show was broadcast on March 26 of the same year. Boucher's first script was entitled *The Book of Tobit*. A woman is thrice widowed and the reverend who performed the last ceremony visits Holmes to ask for his help. The reference is to an Old Testament story, a standard for the religious Boucher. The Bible story is about a demon that strangles husbands on their wedding nights.

> Everyone likes Tobit — the only criticism being that both Glen and Al Scalpone knew early on what the pay-off was going to be. We feel that to help this the planting of Holmes signing the will should be held back for the end of the story.[12]

Despite the compliments about his work, Boucher was still concerned about the job in his first months there. Charteris still had some Holmes scripts in the pipeline and Boucher was concerned about the possibility of being replaced again by Charteris. However, this threat did not materialize. The late scripts from Charteris were not up to his earlier work, and Boucher was offered the long-term position.

According to Boucher's contract with Doyle and the network, all scripts from the Sherlock Holmes show belonged

> lockstockandbarrel [*sic*] to the Doyle estate and we own no part of them. I've had a lot of contacts with that estate, and know friends who have had worse ones. A recital of the infamous difficulties of Denis PS Conan Doyle would take more time than writing a script. They will prosecute to the last

drop of blood any slightest infringement. So you have to get permission from them. By they have up to now refused every offer, no matter how good, to reprint originals by Green and Boucher/Charteris. They don't want the public to realize in cold type that we've written stories that aren't Papa Doyle's.[13]

Since Boucher was writing for hire with no hopes of copyright, he worked on contracts for the script synopses. The agreement read that he was to be paid $950 per script, payable 10 days after broadcast with no additional monies for repeat episodes. His contract allowed that he would write at least eight of the 26 episodes every half year.

Writing what amounted to four short stories a month, complete with plots, characterizations, and the final surprise, some scripts were bound to work better than others in the series. The pair had 24 minutes to set the scene, introduce the characters, and solve the crime. In 1945, Green wrote about the episode named *The Paradol Chamber:*

> Oops! We're not too happy with Paradol. The main objections are these: it's a very talkie story—the action is almost nil. We feel the assumption that Holmes would accept Moriarty as a client to be illogical, and also feel that not much real sleuthing is done—Dr Paradol cracks at the end very conveniently, but rather unconvincingly for such a smart woman. Again, the scene within the chamber itself would be effective for sound effects—but nothing really happens inside of it.[14]

Boucher rewrote the script so that Holmes helped Watson explain the mystery of the Paradol Chamber and put Moriarty back in the role of antagonist. *The Paradol Chamber* became a struggle between Boucher and Taylor. The script was lighter and more humorous than most of the collaborations. Mary Watson played a major role in the episode. Boucher was concerned more with the ideas of science presented in the plot and the credibility of the story line. Taylor was more concerned with the ratings of the series and how a lighthearted adventure would be perceived by the sponsor, Petri Wine Company.

Boucher's knowledge of the Holmes' stories strengthened the show. Not only was Boucher responsible for finding mentions of cases in the Canon to write for the series Boucher was also responsible for knowing the Canon well enough to not make mistakes on Holmes' character and habits. In 1945, Boucher came up with ideas from the Canon that included the remarkable worm which was mentioned in "The Problem of Thor Bridge" and Colonel Warburton's madness from "The Engineer's Thumb."

A typical story for Holmes in this era was *Murder Beyond the Mountains,* which first appeared in January 1946. In it, Boucher used the event from "The Empty House," where Holmes explained his three-year disappearance. Holmes masqueraded as a Norwegian named Sigerson in Tibet for part of that time, and the story takes place outside the forbidden city of Lhasa. Holmes, in disguise, must solve the murder of Wah-tzun (another Boucher joke) before he can move on.

The first signs that the end of the series was at hand occurred in early 1946. Both the movie and radio contracts expired that year. MCA and its head, Jules Stein, prepared a new seven-year contract for Rathbone, but the actor reneged. The studio thought at first that Rathbone was just negotiating for more money, but it soon became obvious that he wanted out. Rathbone had done seven years of the radio show, some two hundred episodes, along with sixteen feature length films as Holmes.

Following the final episode in May 1946 before the summer break, Rathbone quit his role as Holmes. Rathbone was tired of Holmes and even wearier of being asked to sign autographs of Holmes rather than himself. Rathbone left the show in May 1946, and the show never regained its wild popularity with listeners. He would continue to be the ultimate Holmes until Jeremy Brett arrived on the scene in 1984.

With Rathbone gone, the handwriting was on the wall. Glenhall Taylor left his role as producer of the series as well, and Denis PS Conan Doyle turned over the control of the radio series to the William Morris Agency. The Petri Wine Company took control of many of the details and ran roughshod over the staff, but even they would quickly drop their sponsorship of the ailing show.

Any actor taking on this role had big shoes to fill, replacing a legend. Tom Conway replaced Rathbone. Conway had experience in taking over popular roles. Starting in 1943, Conway had taken over the Falcon role in a series of B movies from his brother, actor George Sanders. Even though he had the titular role in the Holmes series, Conway was now listed below Nigel Bruce in the credits.

The new producer, Tom McKnight, was not as easy to work with. Boucher referred to him as "Stinky." McKnight wanted more scripts further in advance, despite the terms of the Boucher-Green contracts. To get the additional scripts, he turned to other authors who had previously worked on the series and encouraged Green to write scripts without a synopsis from Boucher. Exacerbating matters, McKnight refused to pay Green any additional monies for doing more work.

> He [McKnight] is a pretentious and arrogant boor with a great deal of very real talent for production and writing — in some ways the ablest (and also

the most offensive) man I have known in radio. He is convinced that only he knows anything about Holmes. He talks (loudly, of course) about the necessity of getting back to The Good Old Days, to the Real Holmes. I was inclined to agree until I discovered that by The Good Old Days, he means not Doyle — but Meiser [McKnight's ex-wife] and Universal. He is bent on reducing Holmes to the simple formula of heavy melodrama and heavier low comedy....[15]

The contracts for the first six months of 1947 left the clause open on whether or not Boucher and Green would be the primary writers for the series. McKnight wanted Meiser back. As the first few months of the year wore on, it became apparent that Boucher would not continue as a regular contributor to the series. He and Green spent extra time on each script, trying to make it the best possible, since it might be their last.

In 1947, both Conway and Bruce left the show as well. Boucher and Green left the show on June 30, 1947. The cast changed again along with the sponsor and the network and the show limped along for another two years in various incarnations before ending.

Boucher and Green did such a good job for the Holmes show that they were asked about writing an original series for Mutual Radio. Radio shows relied on new episodes. Just as TV airs re-runs during the summer, radio shows gave their actors a summer hiatus of 13 weeks. Networks frequently ran original short-run programming during the summer.

Boucher and Green came up with *The Casebook of Gregory Hood*, a San Francisco–based antiquities expert who seemed to find current day crimes in the artifacts that he dealt with. *The Casebook of Gregory Hood* was nearly identical to *The New Adventures of Sherlock Holmes* in its opening: same sponsor, same announcement, same narrator frame for storytelling, and the same music. The narrator stopped by to visit Gregory either in his office or home, and the story was told by Hood. Hood's own Watson, Sandy Taylor, accompanied him. Taylor was Hood's lawyer and friend.

Since the show featured original characters not created by other authors, the show allowed greater leeway for Boucher's irreverent sense of humor. In one episode, a girl named Sherry was said to have been introduced to Hood by Harry Bartell, the Petri Wine spokesperson.

A typical episode for the show had Hood attempting to procure a rare antique and finding a crime that was somehow related to the antique. The show straddled the same line that many of the era's radio shows did. An unlicensed private investigator solves crime as part of his esoteric career and manages to show up the police each week. Much as Boucher's first detective

Dr. Ashwin was based on a real professor, Hood was based on a real-life importer named Richard Gump. As an inside joke, a character named Dick Gump appears in one of the radio programs.

The show had originally been planned as a summer replacement for *The New Adventures of Sherlock Holmes* in 1946, but continued for the next year when the radio network had difficulty in reaching an agreement with the Conan Doyle estate. After one year as an initial run, *The Casebook of Gregory Hood* ended, but showed up as a frequent replacement for the network over the next two years, before it moved to ABC where it played sporadically for parts of 1950 and 1951.

The show never received the same welcome as did *The New Adventures of Sherlock Holmes*. The show suffered from a constantly rotating cast. Gale Gordon, later known for his work on *The Lucille Ball Show*, starred as Hood in the first episodes and Bill Johnstone played Sandy Taylor. Gordon's time on the show was short-lived. No less than seven actors played Hood in the five year series. Boucher grew increasingly annoyed with the lack of support for the series.

> As to myself and the contest — the excellent idea you proposed of entering a Gregory Hood short story no longer appeals to me. My relations with the agency controlling the Hood program have become so unsatisfactory that I have no desire to build up their property for them, nor to associate myself too closely with it.[16]

The constant need for scripts, what Boucher later called a "steady cohabitation with a typewriter," caused him some health problems. Boucher's asthma was frequently exacerbated by stress and long hours. In 1949, he had to take a short break from the radio scripts. "Thing have got so bad, with asthma ... that I have at last had the good sense to get the hell out for a while. I'm going to spend a quiet month alone on the desert at 29 Palms and see if I can restore myself to the semblance of humanity."[17]

Boucher would have been very busy with just these two shows. However, starting in 1945 and continuing until the end of the series in 1948, Anthony Boucher became one of the silent partners writing for the radio show, *The Adventures of Ellery Queen*. Fred Dannay and Manfred Lee had decided to put Ellery on the airwaves as a way to make additional money for the writing duo. The film adventures of Queen had been a serious disappointment and the pair hoped that radio would be a better medium for their creation. The show had begun as an hour long radio drama in 1939.

The show used a unique gimmick to entice listeners. Similar to the way that the books held a Challenge to the Reader, the radio program stopped with a few minutes remaining in the show and asked listeners to solve the case. At some points during the show's run, the guests were celebrities in the studio; at other times, the guests were "normal" people in the studio. Later in the series' run, the guests would be telephoned from the studio to participate.

Despite the popularity of the Ellery Queen books, the radio show ran into problems. The producers suggested adding a secretary, and potential girlfriend for Ellery, in the character of Nikki Porter. In 1940, the show was cut to one half-hour and then was later cancelled the same year.

In late 1941, Lee and Dannay decided to resurrect the show. The writing pair had not been able to sell serialization rights for the new books and looked for another source of income. They quickly scratched a return to Hollywood and decided instead to revive the radio show.

The show began again in early 1942. The nation was at war and enjoyed the weekly adventures of Ellery Queen. However, the enjoyment of the nation came at a price for Lee and Dannay. They found it increasingly difficult to come up with an original idea every week for the mystery series. The pair started using recycled ideas, either from the earlier hour long scripts or from some of their earlier books and short stories. The formula seemed to work though; by 1943, the show boasted 15 million listeners a week.

The pressure of the deadline continued to be a burden on the writers. In 1943, Manfred Lee had remarried and was expecting a child with his new wife. He wanted several weeks off from the radio show. This caused some headaches for the show. In 1945, Dannay's wife was diagnosed with cancer, and Dannay wanted to leave the show in order to deal with her death and how to raise his young family. The show went off the air for a month in early 1945 while Lee and Dannay decided to come up with another way to handle the rigorous schedule.

Unlike the Holmes show where Rathbone and Bruce epitomized the major characters, there were no definitive actors to play the major roles in the Queen show. The show had long suffered from too many changes in cast and it returned in 1945 with a new cast.

> On the current deal, we broke with the past, fired the "actress" who'd played Nikki for almost five years [Marian Shockley] (this is a long long story) — and whose vacuity and lack of ability had caused the role to dwindle almost to the vanishing point — and hired the present actress [Barbara Terrell] who is excellent (in the opinion of both of us). Having a girl who could do anything a script demanded, we proceeded, within our severe limitations, to utilize her. That's why there's been more of Nikki-Ellery since the end of January.[18]

The new Nikki did not work out either; she was let go by July of that year for missing episodes and drinking on the job

The show decided to use unattributed authors to create the plotline for the weekly stories, and Manfred Lee would then flesh out the idea into the full half-hour script. The pair had used ghostwriters before, and they would again, giving plots to authors for some of their later novels. One of these unattributed authors was Boucher. The assignment made sense. Boucher had a good grasp of the character. He had modeled Fergus O'Breen on Queen, and Boucher's knowledge of mystery fiction made him a natural on the show.

Rather than Fred Dannay who Boucher would work with on a variety of other mystery projects, Boucher worked exclusively with Lee on the radio show; he only sent synopses to Dannay who was mourning his late wife. Lee lived in New York, even further than Denis Green's Los Angeles. The show was done almost exclusively by mail and phone.

Lee asked a lot in terms of a script from his writers. In many cases, scripts sent to him were gutted and rewritten by Lee.

> The mystery puzzle — the mathematical scramble-and-unscramble — by itself is not enough for a radio show, Tony. Mystery puzzle there must be at the bottom; but it most (sic) be clothed in *human*, dramatic terms. Also, ... delineation of situation alone is not enough; the situation must lead to something, must work itself out dramatically, must develop. Question-and-answer must be kept to a minimum; action-and-reaction to maximum.... There is no substitute for story, nor has there ever been.[19]

Lee and Boucher shared a number of common interests, so the collaboration worked fairly well. Both men were politically active and passionate about their beliefs. The Ellery who would come out of this collaboration was more socially conscious than the one who had been suggested by Dannay, who was more apolitical in his views. Ellery would fight against "bad citizenship, bigotry, and discrimination." The pair along with the actor Tom Everitt, who played Ellery, had pushed Ellery towards war work during the early 1940s, so the character had already been molded to serve a certain viewpoint.

Even with Boucher's and Lee's interests in common, the collaboration could have its rough spots. Boucher's commitment to the show was spotty at best. He was working on 2 other radio shows at the same time.

> My first temptation would be to pull out of radio completely; but the size of radio checks does cause a certain amount of second-thoughting on that. However, two weekly shows I will not undertake for 1947. And if I'm going to give up one show, I'm afraid that it will be Queen...

And doing Holmes will leave me a good deal more time for other work than doing only Queen. (And I do have a hankering to write again instead of merely plotting."[20]

In light of Boucher's health and wavering commitment to providing weekly scripts, Lee often used other writers for the series, which meant that Boucher's scripts could sit for weeks before being aired.

Several of the synopses developed by Boucher were rejected by Lee. In all fairness, the plots, at times, were outlandish. Boucher was writing three script ideas per week, something that could tax even an active mind like Boucher's. The critiques of the scripts could be scathing "There are so many things wrong with it from my standpoint that frankly, Tony, I don't know what the hell to say about it. I wouldn't dare put it on the air — I'd laugh it off myself."[21]

Boucher's synopses were much like his correspondence. He peppered each one liberally with references to mysteries and mystery writing. In one episode, he names a small country after a fictional place from the Holmes canon. In other episodes, he showed the same sort of awareness of the medium by having murders take place at the offices of *Ellery Queen's Mystery Magazine* and another murder on Ellery's own radio show.

Over the course of the collaboration, Boucher produced 77 numbered scripts for the show, which are part of the collection at Lilly Library in Bloomington. Some of the scripts are not on file. They seem to be vexed by a rule of 7, since there are two #14s, no 21, and no 28 (among others). Additionally, there were some scripts that were numbered with a letter after them, like 13a. From the tally of available scripts, Mike Nevins, in his book *The Sound of Detection: Ellery Queen's Adventures in Radio*, suggested that 81 scripts were written by Boucher; of those, eight were deemed unsuitable for the show.

Each of these scripts was profitable for Boucher. In the fifth and sixth seasons, his pay for a used plotline was approximately $500. In the seventh season, the show was put on a tighter budget; Boucher still received about $450 per show. Combined with his pay from the other two radio dramas, Boucher was at a high point in his career earnings.

Along with the tighter budget came other changes to the show. The show took another hiatus in April and May of 1947 for six weeks. The operations of the show moved west to Los Angeles along with Manfred Lee and his family. The show lost its sponsor, Anacin, and moved back to NBC from CBS. "To have gone off CBS for six weeks, to go back on the air on another network, another day, another time *for two weeks* ... and then go off again for seven weeks, returning at the beginning of AUGUST ... is all too incredible to moon over for very long. This makes radio history I'm told."[22]

Despite Boucher's schedule, the family didn't seem to equate him to weekly radio dramas.

> Most surprising aspect of it was that [Boucher's son] Larry (aged 7), who usually evinces no interest in the radio, settled down seriously and thought it was wonderful, ending up with embarrassing queries as to whether I could write a show that good. We are wondering a little as to whether or not he was disappointed when the boy turned out not to have poisoned his family.[23]

Boucher nearly missed the end of the show due to another prolonged allergic reaction. "I've been a semi-invalid almost ever since last I saw you — an amazing new allergic manifestation that left me half-deaf for weeks, following by some more familiar wheezing. I think things are straightening out now."[24] Boucher relapsed 5 weeks later. "What's been the matter with me has been mostly asthma plus an incidental virus or two. Then in addition, a combination of sterility and financial worry manages every so often to get me to the brink of a bad state of nerves."[25]

The actress playing the role of Nikki on the radio show was replaced again in early 1948, this time by Lee's wife Kaye. Not surprisingly, Lee was very pleased with the results. In May 1948, the radio show was cancelled. There was some speculation that the sponsors had grown tired of Ellery's more liberal leanings following the war. Boucher and Lee had produced an episode in early 1948 that featured an almost entirely African-American cast. The air time for *The Adventures of Ellery Queen* was sold to another show, presumably one that had not grown quite as liberal in its leanings. The schedule then held no time for the Queen radio show. "I am as thoroughly disgusted with the chicanery of mortal man as ever in my life and I could wish for a sign from heaven or anywhere else that man is not the lowest form of animation in the whole of creation."[26]

The last show written by Boucher was entitled "Misery Mike." It was quintessential Boucher; "Misery" came from the characters involvement in the opera, specifically the Miserere from Il Trovatore. With the end of the Ellery Queen radio show, Boucher was finished with writing for radio. The new legislation from the federal government, and the onset of the television age brought the era to an end and to Boucher's participation in it.

Despite those changes, Boucher didn't give up hope of finding new opportunities in radio. In 1949, he wrote to Lee Wright:

The month on the desert did a lot for my health which is now only mildly bad instead of unbearable. While I was out there all sorts of radio excitement began to pop in NY — there were no less than 3 major deals which looked 99 44/100 percent certain. I came back to Berkeley just about convinced that I'd be leaving for NY in a matter of weeks at the most. Then gradually all the deals disintegrated and radio now looks as dim as ever.[27]

Baker Street Irregulars

It should come as no surprise that the author of *The Case of the Baker Street Irregulars* and the Sherlock Holmes radio show would be an ardent fan of the Holmes canon. The Baker Street Irregulars, named after the street urchins employed by Holmes in the stories, had been founded in 1934 as a group devoted to the study of all things Sherlock Holmes. Christopher Morley, a long-time devotee of Holmes, decided to create the group following the release of Vincent Starrett's *The Private Life of Sherlock Holmes* and the release of *The Complete Sherlock Holmes* by the Doyle estate.

The group met sporadically with haphazard communications until Edgar W. Smith, a vice-president for General Motors, came to the group in 1940. He set the annual dinners for January 6 to memorialize the birthday of Holmes. Smith later founded and edited the *Baker Street Journal*, a publication regarding the writings about the Holmes stories, which Smith ran until his death in the 1960s.

Boucher was well-known to the Irregulars before his investiture in the group in 1944. Edgar Smith had written to Starrett in 1940 about *The Case of the Baker Street Irregulars* and asked what such a title could be about. Smith suspected that the book had been written by a member of BSI, assuming the unfamiliar pseudonym of Anthony Boucher to hide their identity.

> You may recall at the time the *Case of the Baker Street Irregulars* was published, my skepticism as to the identity of any such person as Anthony Boucher, and my tacit suspicion that it might be either Chris Morley or yourself.
>
> Having exchanged several letters with Boucher subsequently, however, I am at last convinced of his corporeality. The last note from him contains references which I am sure will be of interest to you, and I am taking the liberty of sending a copy of it along.
>
> You will note also that Boucher has been won over to my revised chronology.[28]

Smith took the liberty of writing to Boucher and correcting minor flaws in *The Case of the Baker Street Irregulars*. He noted that it "should be 'Sussex' and not 'Suffolk.' The bee-farm was on the 'South Downs.'"[29] Boucher had long corresponded with Holmesians across the country including Smith, Starrett, and Ned Guymon.

By the time Boucher joined the group in the mid–1940s, chapters of BSI had begun to pop-up across the country. These chapters, or scions as they were called, were each named for an allusion to a particular Holmes story. The San Francisco scion was named the Scowrers, a reference to the murderous group that Baldwin and McGinty belonged to in *The Valley of Fear*.

There doesn't seem to have been any discussion of the Irregular's chapter name. As Boucher wrote, "we are tempted to call ourselves The Scowrers; we have scoured the Bay Region for candidates."[30]

Boucher was a great fan of *The Valley of Fear*, the Holmes work that the Scowrers came from. The working class Pennsylvania coal miners appealed to the liberal side of Boucher. He wrote a positive account of their history for *Encyclopedia Britannica*. In the same vein, Boucher held the

Boucher, right, hams it up with Dean Dickensheet and Roy DeGroat at a Baker Street Irregular meeting (courtesy the White family).

Pinkertons in disdain, helping to make the final toast of the BSI meetings "Confusion to the Pinkertons."

Boucher wrote the introduction to *The Valley of Fear* in the Limited Edition Club published in 1952. He redeemed the reputation for this overlooked book. "[F]or it has become fashionable to regard it as not only the last but possibly the least of the Sherlock Holmes novels, and one of the more nearly negligible items in the Holmesian Canon.... This is a long overlooked literary landmark.... For here is, assuredly, some of the most dazzling pure detective-story-writing that even Conan Doyle ever achieved.... And disagreement with the Pinkerton version of the Molly Maguire story need not entail dislike of Doyle's admirable fictionalization of the Pinkerton account."[31]

The Scowrers were founded by Boucher and Joseph Henry Jackson, the editor at the *San Francisco Chronicle* on the night of the Trilogy Dinner, March 31, 1944. The dinner celebrated the release of not one, but three Holmes books in the same week. The books were: *Profile By Gaslight* by Edgar Smith, *The Misadventures of Sherlock Holmes* edited by Ellery Queen, and *Sherlock Holmes and Dr. Watson* edited by Christopher Morley. All across the country, the Irregulars met and toasted the event.

Jackson made sure that the event was covered in the *Chronicle*. On April 9, 1944, Jackson wrote a column about the dinner and the release of the three books. He made the comment that Holmes had crossed the line from fiction to fact with the publication of the three books, and Jackson was correct. In the Smith book and to some degree the Morley book, Holmes was treated as a flesh-and-blood person and not a character. Doyle had been relegated to a role of chronicler of Holmes tales rather than his creator.

The first meeting of the Scowrers took place at Fred Solari's restaurant on Maiden Lane just off Union Square in downtown San Francisco. The meeting only had 4 men: Boucher, Jackson, Robert Frier, and John Baxter. Boucher's "Criminal Investigations" column of February 27, 1944, in the *San Francisco Chronicle* invited all interested Holmesians to contact him via the paper. Later correspondence indicated that five men including Clint Smith had joined the organization besides Boucher and Jackson.

While there has always been a strong interest in Holmes and Watson as shown by the movies and radio shows, the Baker Street Irregulars were much stricter about membership. The group required members to have read all 56 short stories and the four novels as well as complete a written test. These stringent requirements have always kept membership to the truly devoted Holmes fans.

At the first meeting, Boucher was made "Bodymaster," so named for

McGinty of the Scowrers. Boucher had written a sonnet entitled "San Francisco to Sherlock," which he read at the meeting. As with all meetings, the festivities began with a toast to "the woman," Irene Adler. Boucher made a second toast to Hattie Doran, from "The Noble Bachelor."

Early on, the Scowrers found themselves in an awkward position. The newspaper mentions brought a number of letters from interested Holmes fans, but all of them were women. Historically, the Baker Street Irregulars had been a strictly men-only club, reflecting Holmes' own antipathy to women.

Some of the pleas to join were persuasive. Ruth Ashen of Sacramento went on for six pages on the reasons why women should be admitted. Besides these entreaties, Boucher learned that his good friend and Holmes aficionado, Lenore Glen Offord, was interested in joining the Irregulars as well.

The following month, May 1944, Boucher and the Scowrers created a women's auxiliary for The Baker Street Irregulars. The new group was called the Molly Maguires, a name equally tied to *The Valley of Fear*. Offord was given the first investiture in 1958 as "The Old Russian Woman." Later, Boucher's wife, Phyllis, would be named "Mrs. Scanlan in Perpetuity." (Boucher had been named "Scanlan" in the group, and though the Canon doesn't mention a Mrs. Scanlan, Phyllis was given that name by the group.)

Boucher, ever the promoter, wrote a letter to *Life* magazine in May 1944 to explain the change to the group. A heavily edited version of his letter appeared in the May 22nd issue that announced the addition of a women's auxiliary to the group.

The next meeting of the Scowrers and Molly Maguires was not until the first month of 1945. The January meeting of the Irregulars commemorates the birthday of Sherlock Holmes. In the second meeting of the group, Boucher presented one of three papers read that night. His work, "Holmesiana Hispanica," featured a melding of Boucher's love of Holmes and his knowledge of foreign languages. It's not surprising that Boucher would choose such a subject given his on-going translations of foreign mystery stories for *Ellery Queen's Mystery Magazine*. The paper was a hit with the Scowrers and quickly circulated through the other scions.

Boucher's most famous pamphlet on Holmes would come a few years later. Boucher took on the problem of Moriarty, trying to explain Watson's reference to a Colonel Moriarty in one story, while Professor Moriarty had been a mathematician in "The Final Problem." The piece concludes that Colonel Moriarty is just one of many identities for Colonel Sebastian Moran.

Regarding Boucher's first paper, Lenore Glen Offord gave a thumbs up to the second Scowrers meeting. "The intention was to tell you how very successful I thought the meeting was, and how much I enjoyed your oral dissertation on O2-mes; most entertaining and certainly a real contribution."[32]

In 1946, Boucher took a train to New York City to attend the BSI banquet on January 11. With that trip, he earned the honor of being the first Californian to travel across country for the annual meeting. Boucher was asked to recite the Musgrave Ritual, the eight questions from the Doyle story of the same name, to the group and gave a presentation on his work with the Holmes radio show. The group had an intense discussion over the script for "The Speckled Band" on *The New Adventures of Sherlock Holmes* and how the death of Julia Stoner was handled in the script versus the story. That episode had been aired in November of the previous year.

Boucher made his journey a fully Holmesian trip by stopping to see Vincent Starrett in Chicago as well. Boucher made this annual trek, as his finances allowed, visiting Starrett along the way to the BSI banquet. Boucher and Starrett carried on a correspondence for years about Holmes and all things mystery.

Boucher shared his experiences in New York with the Scowrers and Molly Maguires on his return to California. The group heard Boucher's account of the New York meeting and the trip to Chicago. Additionally, Boucher presented another paper to the group entitled "Prolegomena to a Holmesian Discography." Boucher used his own growing record collection as research for the article on music from the Canon.

Boucher was in demand by all parts of the organization, because of his role with the radio program. In 1947, Ben Abrahamson wrote, asking for help to "publicize the *Baker Street Journal*.... It was suggested that I write to you because of your intimate connection with the program."[33]

However, at the same time, Boucher had left the show. He replied "it's extremely doubtful that I'll be rehired, and impossible that I could present such a proposition even if I were; he loathes me personally and Irregularity in general about equally."[34]

After the 1946 meeting, a two year hiatus began for the Scowrers. In mid–1948, Boucher wrote to Jackson, expressing concern about the length of time since the last meeting. Boucher had hoped to revive the group with a discussion of putting together a collection of essays from the San Francisco scion, similar to those books published by other chapters. New officers were elected, but Jackson did not show up for the meeting. His absence might have had something to do with the disagreement the men had had over

Boucher's negative comments on reviewing and Boucher's subsequent termination from Jackson's paper.

In any event, the group's meeting did not re-invigorate the Scowrers. The group had not met again by 1951. A few members contacted Boucher personally to see if the group could be revived. "The Scowrers seem to be accursed. Frier, who was made secretary (or Harraway) to goose the Bodymaster, seems as feckless as I. I had high hopes a few months back when some young Berkeley enthusiasts, highly intelligent & knowledgeable in The Canon, decided that they would take over as resurrection men; but they have not done a damned thing."[35]

Boucher continued to handle correspondence for the group in the absence of meetings. In August of 1952, he wrote to Jackson:

> "I hate to impose on you, but it seems to me that enclosed query from Adrian Conan Doyle is one you can answer better than I could.
>
> Certainly we want the Sherlock Holmes Exhibit to hit S.F. It might even revitalize the Scowrers! (Honest, I have made several efforts to find proper Active Leaders to take over, & they always fold up too. Any ideas?)
>
> But I don't have any notions about suitable department stores. Do you or Fee [Orfelia Stull]?[36]

Nothing came of the letter, as the Doyle estate wanted about $100 per week to display the collection, a fee much too high for the department stores in the San Francisco area.

The group re-formed in the mid–1950s and began to expand with the growth of more people in the San Francisco area, providing more Sherlockians. Boucher relinquished his role as Bodymaster in 1958, but was made Toastmaster as Brother Scanlan, a role he kept until his death.

Boucher maintained strong ties to the national group as well. In 1965, he wrote, "I'll be in NY briefly on my way to London this month, & for a longer time on my way back ... [I] received tickets to "Baker Street" directed by Harold Prince in NYC. BSI not happy about the musical or its interpretation of Holmes."[37]

Mystery Writers of America

When a group of mystery writers decided to organize following the war, it was no surprise that progressive Anthony Boucher was there to help. In his roles as critic and reviewer, he was uniquely qualified to understand issues of the marketplace regarding popular fiction and mysteries in particular.

He frequently wrote about the publishing industry in his columns for the *San Francisco Chronicle*.

Boucher became one of the founding members of MWA in 1945. He proudly showed off his membership card, "Number 5." He was soon named Regional Vice President for the Northern California, San Francisco chapter, one of Mystery Writers of America's earliest chapters.

The group's early slogan "Crime Does Not Pay — Enough" was as true then as it is today. At the time, the industry had rigid price controls set at two dollars a book. Authors and agents had pushed to raise the price to $2.50, splitting the money between publishers and authors, but all of the major New York houses refused.

Boucher did note in a review column in 1947 that things had slowly begun to change with the payment of authors. "Growing prevalence of the $2.50 price for mysteries — a long needed raise, though I believe Duell and Ziff-Davis are the only firms which split the increase 50–50 with their authors."[38]

In 1948, the group approved the Basic Minimum Contract as a way to try to negotiate with New York publishers for better pay. The contract was developed by MWA's national policy committee. While the agreement was not binding to any publisher, the minimum contract idea was meant to make writers more aware of what publishers offered and what might be expected.

In talking about MWA, Boucher felt that one of the on-going (but possibly not correctable) problems with the organization was that it was not a "real" union. He felt that the screenwriters and playwrights unions gave them more bargaining power and a way to earn better pay for their efforts. However, when a chance came to become a part of the Author's Guild in 1947, the group declined the invitation.

Boucher was pleased when MWA decided to honor the Radio Writers Guild strike against the networks. MWA members were not to take on new radio work. While this would not have impacted Boucher's income from the detective shows on the air, he was for the strike and voted in favor of recognizing the guild's right to strike. After months of dickering, the strike did not take place. The guild was able to work out the details of a new contract without striking.

Boucher felt that MWA's main contributions to the mystery field were the Edgar awards, which he felt had enhanced the mystery's prestige in the field, and the yearly anthologies, which Boucher edited for a number of years. He saw the short story collections from MWA as a showcase for the talents of some of the less well-known authors.

In 1947, Boucher was invited back to New York City for a conference. "MWA is having a national convention to straighten out problems and policy, and I'll probably get to go as the SF delegate — expenses paid — the first time I've received any kind of advantageous perquisite out of my many subversive activities."[39]

Boucher was asked to be the chairman of the awards committee for 1947. Boucher would have received a second award (making four in total) as critic for his work with the *San Francisco Chronicle* in 1947, but Jud Phillips, who was serving as the president of MWA at that time, suggested Bill Weber, who wrote the Judge Lynch review column for the *Saturday Review of Literature*. Phillips hoped to receive more visibility for the Edgars if the award was given to someone outside of the organization, rather than a member. Boucher went along and Weber was named winner of the award.

Since most of the publishing world revolved around New York City, Boucher felt left out on the West Coast. Therefore, he was instrumental in starting one of the early MWA chapters, the Northern California chapter. The group still meets today. The first meeting was February 28, 1947, at Solari's restaurant. The group immediately gained attention from the local press, including the *Oakland Tribune*, which gave the group a quarter-page feature with photos.

Boucher was named Regional Vice President of the group with Lenore Glen Offord and Alfred Meyers elected Secretary and Treasurer, respectively. Along with the chapter presidents of Los Angeles and Chicago, Boucher petitioned MWA for a clarification on the by-laws to see if local members' fees could be split between the local groups and the national organization.

In hopes of expanding their membership base, the local chapter contacted the Author's Guild about sharing membership. However, the intermingling with the other group was prickly at best; Author's Guild members made disparaging comments about mystery writing during the general meetings. Discussion with the Author's Guild continued through 1947 and part of 1948 before fading out.

Beyond finding more members for the chapter, Boucher suggested an agenda of reporting on legislation that could affect writers. A committee was formed to look at the bills affecting the First Amendment introduced into the state legislature.

The group did other projects as well. Boucher helped to start a Brain Bank that provided authors with the names of MWA members who possessed specialized knowledge for use in their fiction. The group also hosted programs on how to write mystery fiction in hopes of expanding their membership.

In early 1948, the Northern California chapter of MWA took on such a collaborative novel. Each author was to write a chapter for the book. As the book was handed off to the next author, the challenge was to use the material that had already been written and add to it in a meaningful way to continue the mystery. Such books are difficult to write, especially since the plots can take wild turns at the whim of each author. The idea was modeled on the collaborative novels written by the Detection Club of England. The group wrote novels where each author had to contribute a chapter in turn, along with their suggested solution to the crimes.

The book was *The Marble Forest*, although earlier versions of the book were entitled *The Marble Maze*. Rather than list it as a collaborative work, the book was published under the pen name of Theo Durrant. The pen name was almost assuredly the creation of Boucher. William Henry Theodore Durrant assaulted and killed two members of his church and was hanged for his crimes in 1895. The name harkens back to H.H. Holmes, Boucher's other pseudonym, which also came from an executed murderer.

The Marble Forest is not a true collaborative detective novel in the manner of each author writing a successive chapter, built on the previous ones. In those works, each chapter can be rather jarringly different from the last. In *The Marble Forest*, this does not arise as Boucher provided copious written notes about the book's overall structure and plot prior to the writing. Chapters were then doled out to willing members. The novel is a seamless thriller. Boucher called the book "socialized writing."

The book was a marked departure from Boucher's normal detective novels. The action in this thriller takes precedence over detection. The book opens with a mysterious phone call announcing that Dr. Barratt's daughter Midge has been kidnapped and placed in a coffin. She has no more than five or six hours worth of air before she dies. Each chapter in the book is titled with the exact time, so the reader is constantly aware of how much time remains for Midge to live.

Barratt and his secretary, Polly, are home when a phone call comes through about Midge. One of the local girls has taken Midge to the home of an unknown person who has put Midge in a coffin and hidden her. Through a series of deductions, they determine that Midge is buried in the local cemetery. As they hunt for the young girl and hunt for the girl who took Midge, Barratt realizes that the clues and disturbed graves correspond to people who he has had difficulties with in the past.

Not everyone in town had welcomed Barratt to Red Forks when he'd moved there several years ago. He'd settled there with Alice Corbin, who had lived in the Red Forks most of her life. Barratt had become the second doctor in town, which ruffled the feathers of the older doctor. In trying to help some of the residents, family members and friends became upset with Barratt. As a result, he has more than enough enemies who might have kidnapped his daughter.

The rumors about the doctor and his behavior with Sylvia, a local woman, make the reader wonder if he is a wronged party or a callous quack. Interspersed with the chapters regarding the hunt for Midge are chapters that are told from the point-of-view of some of the cemetery's residents. Midge's dead mother tells her story, along with the granddaughter of the cemetery caretaker, and the newspaper editor's son. Their narratives tell a very different story from the rumors that pass around town.

It's not really a spoiler to write that Midge survives the ordeal. With only minutes to spare, Barratt determines who committed the crime as well as where Midge has been hidden. The girl is unharmed, and the killer pays for his crimes at the end of the book.

In 1958, *The Marble Forest* was made into the movie *Macabre* by director William Castle. Castle was best known for his works in classics such as *House on Haunted Hill, The Night Walker,* and *13 Ghosts*. Castle was known for his outrageous stunts to promote his films. For *Macabre*, he claimed that Lloyds of London had insured the audience to pay $1000 to anyone who died of fright during the movie. The movie begins with a caution to the viewers to keep an eye on their neighbors to ensure that no one goes into shock. As with several other of Castle's works, the movie has long been rumored to be in the pipeline as a possible remake starring Steve Buscemi and Rachel Leigh Cook, but nothing has come of it at this time.

The teleplay by Robb White took great liberties with the book. The number of characters were reduced, the family relationships altered, and the ending was entirely different from that of the novel. Only two of the flashbacks from the book make it into the film, and even those don't match the tone or content of the book. The final result is a film that feels suspiciously noir, rather than a work of suspense.

Boucher and Offord promoted the book tirelessly. In one instance, MWA's NorCal chapter held a contest to see if readers could guess which chapters were written by which writers in the novel. The contest was not a big success with the readers, who were more interested in the suspense than the identity of each chapter's author.

> Speaking of one-only, that's the number of answers received so far in the great Marble Forest contest. Brother, have you got a fan at Stanford. He

figured out that you had written the Prologue, Philip Whittleby and the conclusion; I am supposed to have done Nancy and your mausoleum scene! That was one guess correct, though, and unless three better ones come in Mr. Price [Boucher's father-in-law] will be the only prize-winner. Do you suppose I'll have to send his all three copies?[40]

Boucher's involvement in MWA writing projects didn't end with the collaborative novel. He was named publications chair for the group in March 1948. In this role, he began working with the members to develop anthologies that would promote the members' careers and line the coffers.

In the beginning of that position, Boucher did not have much to do. The group's previous anthology, *Murder by Experts*, had been a disappointment in sales. The publications chair did not have control over MWA's internal newsletter, *The Third Degree*. Boucher suggested a new anthology, which he dubbed *The Detective Directory*, which would later become known as *Four-and-Twenty Bloodhounds*.

Boucher's involvement in MWA culminated with his election to President of the organization in 1951. Boucher was concerned about the amount of time he would have to put into the position. He was busy with his magazine and reviewing for the Times and had little spare time for other work.

Boucher was awarded his third Edgar for mystery reviews and criticism the same year for his work in the *New York Times*, putting him in the rarefied strata of three-time winners. Many of Boucher's later photographs would show the background of his library where the three statuettes of Edgar Allan Poe sat on top of a bookcase.

Lenore Glen Offord helped Boucher in his role of president and collected the book lists for determining the Edgar awards for Best Novel that year. Boucher used his numerous contacts in the genre to help build the awards and organization.

> Haycraft and Derleth, I'm pleased to report, both accepted the committee job. Now I presume we all sit back and wait until Dorothy G. collected the publishers' lists for us. She seems to think that they'll all cooperate, and I hope to heaven she's right. Haycraft, bless him, also offers to check pseudonyms, and adds that he has heard of Marston La France is Lawrence Lariar. Good heavens, is everybody Lawrence Lariar? I can't seem to remember any books by M. la F., but possibly that's by merciful dispensation.[41]

Not only did MWA appeal to Boucher's desire for social justice, and the promotion of genre fiction, Boucher was always one to meet and talk with fellow authors about the craft of writing. MWA provided a wonderful outlet for him in this regard. Dorothea Gildar said,

> I worked for MWA as a secretary for about a year. At that time Hal Masur, who was and is a friend, wanted to entertain Tony Boucher, John Dickson Carr and Lee Wright for dinner. Being a bachelor and having no culinary skills beyond boiling eggs which he ate because they were presumably bacteria-free, he asked me to cook dinner for his guests in my tiny apartment with kitchenette which was all I could afford in those early days.
>
> I gave Lee Wright the "fixins" and she made and served the martinis (a popular drink then) while I finished the dinner comprised of grapefruits for starters, roasted leg of lamb, baked potatoes and salad, with cheese, fruit and nuts for dessert.
>
> We have a most enjoyable evening and I saw it end with regret.[42]

Even following his presidency, Boucher continued to help the group through his anthology works. Under the aegis of MWA, he collected and edited *The Quality of Murder*, his second true-crime collection. He asked many of the writers from MWA to contribute pieces on their favorite true crime works.

Boucher's organizational skills were needed for the project. He kept track of which cases had been assigned to authors. Boucher only wanted one account of any given crime. Each region had a different person helping to get the word out and to encourage authors to participate. Even so, the Nor Cal chapter of MWA contributed nearly half of the final product.

Boucher also edited the book. The pieces had been sent directly to MWA, who had in turn forwarded them on to Dutton. As Dutton possessed the only full copy of the book, Boucher struggled blindly with copyedits, using correspondence and his memory to assist.

Boucher was a hard editor for the book. "A couple of the enclosed are really very badly written — or at least they were when they came in; I've doctored them about as much as I think lies within the bounds of editorial decency."[43]

Ironically, when first asked by Dutton to edit the Best Detective Stories of the Year anthologies, Boucher turned down the request. Jeanne Lloyd, the long-time Dutton editor, had written to Boucher as he was completing *The Quality of Murder*. "It may seem funny to turn down BEST because of not enough money after doing *Quality* for free." However, Boucher relented and starting in 1963, he selected the stories in the collection and wrote an introduction.

The Quality of Murder was released in 1962, but did not sell well. This was Boucher's last anthology for the group. He later wrote about it, "I am forced to admit that readers don't buy fact crime, after the dismal failure of my MWAntho *[sic]* The Quality of Murder."[44]

Even with the poor sales, *The Quality of Murder* was a critical success. The book included some wonderful pieces of research and deduction. The book included a piece by Patrick Quentin on the Florence Maybrick case, where Quentin admitted to meeting Maybrick accidentally. James Reach wrote a piece on why Lizzie Borden was innocent using source materials rather than Pearson's account of the crimes that is still quoted today. He included a piece by Dorothy Parker on her insistence that Borden was guilty, despite any evidence to the contrary. He also managed to include the work of Edward Radin, who just happened to be one of the regional coordinators for the book.

Similar to the epilogue that Boucher had included with *The Case of the Toad-in-the-Hole*, Boucher included a reading list at the end of *The Quality of Murder*. Although it had been 25 years since he had generated the first list of fact-crime materials, Boucher included mainly material from the past 10 years in his bibliography, but managed a plug for his own *The Pocket Book of True Crime Stories*.

Boucher continued to take a stronger stand on social issues within MWA, even as his participation dwindled. He wanted the group to take a more vocal stance on issues such as payments, censorship, and other topics related to writing. In a letter to Rex Stout, Boucher commended the creator of Nero Wolfe for his work with free press issues.

> A news story on the committee to Protest Absurd Censorship (a disappointing name from the acronymic point of view), formed "to protest censorship and the conviction of Ralph Ginzburg," lists you (naturally) as one of the founders.
> I shd [sic] like to place myself at the disposal of the Committee, for whatever value my name or my personal services may have.
> I also feel strongly that MWA shd [sic] take an official position supporting the Committee's protest. I know that it is impractical & indeed virtually impossible, from an out-of-town director to exercise any influence on the Board; so let me urge you to put the issue before MWA with all the persuasiveness of which I know you are capable.[45]

Magazine of Fantasy and Science Fiction

By the 1920s, mysteries appeared more frequently in novel-length works; science-fiction flourished in the short form. While *Weird Tales*, which first appeared in 1923, is frequently listed as one of the first science-fiction outlets, its stories contained more elements of the horror and fantasy genres than what would later be called science-fiction. Boucher's first published story, "Ye Good Old Ghost Storie," appeared in that magazine when he was sixteen.

In April 1926, Hugo Gernsback, who had previously published electronics and popular science magazines, introduced *Amazing Stories*. His new magazine announced it would only publish "scientifiction" stories, an early name for what would become science-fiction (another term coined by Gernsback.) He is widely credited with being the "Father of science-fiction," and the annual fan awards from the World Science Fiction Society at the World Science Fiction Convention are named the Hugo in his honor.

As 1930 began, a new science-fiction magazine, *Astounding Stories of Super Science*, appeared. The name was quickly shortened to *Astounding Stories*. After seven years under two different editors, John W. Campbell was named to head the magazine; although unknown to anyone at that time, that appointment would later become known as the beginning of the Golden Age of Science-fiction.

Campbell insisted on "hard science" as a basis for story acceptance. Campbell was a graduate of Massachusetts Institute of Technology; his background exposed him to what science could produce in the future and how that science might affect the characters in a story. As a result, he insisted that all stories accepted under his editorship have a foundation in physics, chemistry, and biology. If a story contained a scientific premise, it had to be logical and verifiable. As a result, his works looked like a reasonable verisimilitude of the late 20th century. Many of the new stories printed in *Astounding* featured space travel 30 years before it became reality.

Campbell was also responsible for shaping new authors who would dominate science-fiction for the next generation. All of the up-and-coming authors of the day, including Isaac Asimov, wanted to work with Campbell. Mañana Literary Society authors Robert Heinlein, Theodore Sturgeon, and Scientologist L. Ron Hubbard began their careers under Campbell's helpful editorial pen.

Campbell had become the undisputed editor of the era. *Astounding Stories* became the king of the science-based stories, and *Unknown Worlds*, also edited by Campbell, held the same place in the fantasy genre. While counted as the best in the field, these two magazines were by no means the only digests on the market.

By 1941, science-fiction pulp magazines had saturated the market. Of the 20 distinct magazines published between 1938 and 1949, over 100 individual issues appeared on the newsstands in 1941 alone.

The market, always subject to precarious business cycles, could not handle so many magazines. The paper shortages that began with Pearl Harbor and the number of authors who had to go overseas to fight left these magazines with too few stories and insufficient resources to print what they had. Many of those magazines folded before the Germans did in 1945.

During the war, Boucher had helped with a large anthology, *Adventures in Space and Time*, edited by his friend, J. Francis McComas. McComas, better known as Mick, was a publisher's sales representative who traveled the country. He talked with publishers, stores and met many of the top writers of the day. He counted Craig Rice, Stuart Palmer, and other mystery authors among his friends. He and Boucher had known each other since Boucher's arrival in Los Angeles many years before.

Adventures in Space and Time was published in 1946 and contained a number of reprinted science-fiction short stories, mostly from *Astounding Stories*. The anthology's success convinced the pair that the market could bear another science-fiction magazine dedicated to their vision of fantasy and science-fiction.

Although the book appeared in 1946, the pair had been planning a possible magazine as early as 1944. Boucher had seen Fred Dannay's success with *Ellery Queen's Mystery Magazine* and wanted to emulate that in the science-fiction field. In that year, Boucher wrote to McComas that he wanted to see "Scientifiction of such a caliber..." in their magazine.

Boucher was able to approach Dannay due to his work on the Queen radio show; the two men discussed what was involved in starting a new magazine. McComas wrote in 1944, "Fantasy mag: Fred is enthused. Also, he has plans for postwar extension and expansion which might well include this mag. But paper is hellish right now (and he ain't kidding!)."[46]

As the war ended, the two would-be editors were concerned. They saw the introduction of other new mystery magazines like a proposed *Inner Sanctum Mystery Magazine* and wondered if the time for a new combined magazine of science-fiction and fantasy was passing them by. Boucher had tried and failed to secure the editor position of *The Saint Mystery Magazine* under Leslie Charteris before Boucher's radio show gig.

By 1945, *Ellery Queen's Mystery Magazine* was doing well enough that Boucher and McComas approached Fred Dannay about lending the Queen name to a magazine of fantasy. Dannay declined; his passion was mystery. He knew little of the genre that the pair wanted to enter. However, Dannay suggested that Boucher try to pitch the magazine directly to his own publisher, American Mercury, and its owner, Lawrence Spivak.

Spivak was a colorful figure who had taken over the highly praised American Mercury company, which had been originally founded by H.L. Mencken. It published a number of literate magazines and digest-sized magazines. It was responsible for *Black Mask* and some of the pulps that provided an early market for hardboiled mystery stories. In the 1950s, Spivak would be the creative force behind a new television news program entitled *Meet the Press.*

Boucher and McComas wasted no time in contacting Spivak. True to his word, Dannay had strongly recommended the pair as editors, and Spivak agreed to talk to them. Boucher and his partner traveled to New York City in January 1946.

Boucher and McComas thought the meeting went well, but the wait was insufferable. By the end of March, the pair still had not heard back from Spivak about the magazine. Even so, they set about getting the editorial parts of the magazine ready in case the telegram arrived. "I would suggest that we have editorial comment and intro written up before we meet in NYC, so that we might go over it and develop finished copy when we see LS."[47]

Their efforts were rewarded. Spivak told them to go ahead and start thinking about a line-up for the first issue of a new fantasy and horror magazine.

Boucher quickly set to work on the project. From his work in the mystery genre, he knew a number of authors who had crossed genres with some of their stories. Cross-genre short stories are frequently hard to place, and many of the authors had given up hope of selling their stories. Boucher and McComas found such works by Raymond Chandler, Dorothy B. Hughes, and Stuart Palmer.

The magazine also dealt in reprints, especially ones that had appeared in smaller, less well-known publications. Boucher and McComas put together an impressive line-up. They were able to procure works by Robert Bloch, John Dickson Carr, and H.P. Lovecraft. The magazine had come together quickly, but now the wait would feel interminable.

By August 1946, the pair had signed a letter of agreement with American Mercury that stated if the magazine had not been published by March 1947, rights would revert to Boucher and McComas. By the time 1947 rolled around, American Mercury asked to renew the letter of agreement with a new end date of January 1948. The publisher pointed to a decline in newsstand sales as the reason for the delay.

Things looked hopeful again in late 1947. American Mercury requested the list of short stories to appear in the magazine. By now, Boucher and

McComas had decided on *Fantasy and Horror* for the title of the magazine, which had been nameless until that point. They had also added to new stories to the magazine to bring the totals up to 128 pages and 50,000 words. "[Y]ou'll notice two additional opuses — both also enclosed. They are: The Lost Room by Fitz-James O'Brien — a very little known reprint. In public domain. In the Day of Our Fathers by Winona McClintic — a new story by a new author for which the standard rate of $100 should be paid."[48]

The pair tried not to get their hopes up, but in early 1946, the magazine had seemed like a sure thing. Now they were stuck in a cycle of waiting. They received another letter from Mercury, requesting to postpone the launch of the magazine again. "[T]he newsstand situation on digest-sized and pocketbooks has not improved much."[49] American Mercury pushed off a release date until the following year and discussed with the editors the possibility of increasing the price to 35¢ to defray the lowered sales.

The editors waited another year for the next letter from American Mercury. It wasn't until February 1949 before they heard from Joe Ferman, the general manager for American Mercury, about the magazine. In his latest letter, Ferman suggested adding a science-fiction story into the mix. The corporation also wanted to work to increase sales by adding "a little more sex into it." Boucher and McComas quickly agreed to add science-fiction as they were finding it difficult to delineate the differences between science-fiction and fantasy and paranormal. The editor suggested that they were open to sexual content in the stories, but they didn't want anything gratuitous in the magazine just to generate sales.

American Mercury's response was much faster this time. In May 1949, the company wrote back to suggest a name change to the magazine. The new title would be "The Magazine of Fantasy." In August, the company prepared a press release for the new magazine, announcing its October release.

A huge launch party was planned for the inaugural issue of *The Magazine of Fantasy*. The event was planned around the 100th anniversary of the death of Edgar Allan Poe, who had been a major author in the development of fantasy and horror short stories. A New York City luncheon was to be held on October 6, 1949.

The event posed problems for the two West Coast editors. McComas still worked as a sales representative for Simon and Schuster. His fall sales trip was planned for the same week as the party. Boucher had a different problem. He lived off of his earning from writing and had not been given sufficient time to save for the transcontinental flight. McComas received an advance on his expense account and paid for his co-editor's trip. Boucher agreed to re-pay McComas over time.

The editors were likely the only two people who would have trouble getting there. The rest of the invitees were among the luminaries of the mystery, horror, and fantasy genres. American Mercury invited, by telegram no less, John Dickson Carr, Fred Dannay, Basil Rathbone, Boris Karloff, and many others.

> Will you join Poe centennial fantasy and science fiction committee which we are organizing to mark the 100th anniversary of the death of Edgar Allan Poe, one of the world's greatest writers of fantasy and science fiction. An invitational luncheon will be held October 6 at the Waldorf Astoria to commemorate the date and to mark the launching of a new fantasy anthology periodical. Your acceptance carries with it no obligation of time, effort or money. By doing so you will honor Poe's contribution to an important phase of American cultural life and focus public attention on the value of fantasy and science-fiction in the world today. Please wire collect.
> Lawrence Spivak
> Anthony Boucher
> J. Francis McComas

The group chose Poe's "Masque of the Red Death" as a theme for the launch party and produced a limited edition of 150 copies of the story for the event. Basil Rathbone gave a rousing reading of "Annabelle Lee" for the crowd.

Even with the successful launch party, the magazine didn't quite live up to the expectations of the publisher or the editors. The magazine sold a respectable 57,000 net sales, but the publisher had hoped for more. As a result, the editors had to wait an agonizing month before receiving the go-ahead for a second issue of the magazine.

With that second issue, changes were instituted at the magazine. The title was changed to add the growing number of science-fiction stories in the magazine. With that issue, it became *The Magazine of Fantasy and Science Fiction* (or *F&SF* to its thousands of fans). That issue began a review column as well. Boucher was already known for his science-fiction reviews in the *Chicago Sun-Times*, but this new magazine gave him a more focused audience of science-fiction fans to talk about the latest offerings in fantasy and science-fiction. Boucher and McComas alternated duties on the review column.

The second issue sold well also, and issues three and four were requested. Boucher and McComas now had hopes that the magazine might last the year. One of the major challenges to the pair had been the notion that a national magazine could be successfully edited from the West Coast and published on the East Coast. In today's climate of cell phones and e-mail, people can interact from anywhere, but in 1950, only mail, expensive long-distance telephone calls, and even more expensive, transcontinental flights were available to communicate with Spivak in New York City.

Boucher and McComas had expected to spend the next several issues cadging stories from authors they knew, but that was not the case. In no time, the editors were deluged with new works. Boucher, Phyllis, McComas, and his wife were all put to work in managing the tidal wave of short works.

Boucher loved being a science-fiction editor and is remembered as a kind editor. Boucher went into editing with the idea that he would never send form rejection letters to the people who submitted their work to him. He recalled the help he'd received when trying to publish mystery novels and his self-proclaimed luck in working with editors like Joe Jackson and Fred Dannay. Boucher helped many new authors by suggesting changes and improvements, a far cry from the "Not for us, please try again" style of rejection that so many magazines offered. Eventually, Boucher would be forced to use form rejections, but never as frequently as most publications.

One well known example of Boucher's recognition of talent and his help to a new face in the genre was Philip K. Dick. The author, who is best known today for the film adaptations *Blade Runner* and *The Minority Report*, was at one time Boucher's student at his home in Berkeley. The efforts paid off, as Dick's first published work appeared in *The Magazine of Fantasy and Science Fiction*. Dick posthumously dedicated *Ubik* to Boucher.

In another example, Boucher helped new author Mildred Clingerman with her agent difficulties in 1954, suggesting agents and strategies. In the same letter to her, Boucher critiqued her works for *F&SF*.

Even as much as Boucher enjoyed the work, there were, of course, the occasional problems in editing a magazine. In late 1950, the publisher chided Boucher for selling his own works to other science-fiction magazines. Spivak thought that an editor should only showcase his work in his own creation. Boucher responded, concerned that his readers were apt to think he was showing favoritism toward himself and possibly Boucher couldn't sell his works elsewhere. Boucher continued to sell his work to many of the other science-fiction magazines throughout his reign at *The Magazine of Fantasy and Science Fiction*.

Over the next few years, a number of other changes came to the magazine. The magazine decided to live up to its name by adding more science-fiction to the magazine. By 1951, McComas thought that the fantasy market had been saturated. He suggested making 75 percent of the content science-fiction instead.

The Boucher-McComas partnership did not last long. McComas found that he could not keep up with the pace of full-time work as a sales rep and edit the magazine. His health suffered and in June of 1951, he wrote to Boucher, "I have reached the following conclusions about our present partnership and present to you the modification of same which are the results of my brooding. If you agree, would you sign the copy and return one of the two to me?... I have retired to a consulting position."[50] McComas reduced his income to a mere five percent of the total editorial income of *The Magazine of Fantasy and Science Fiction*.

The magazine had unexpected results. The editors were asked to start putting out a series of "Best of" anthologies from *The Magazine of Fantasy and Science Fiction*. In the third installment in the series, Boucher mentions that 16 science-fiction anthologies had been published in 1953, and the year was marked by more new magazines (and failures) than ever before.

In September 1952, the magazine became a monthly. Boucher and McComas now had steady and constant work to do for the magazine. Boucher read and edited most of the stories. McComas reviewed and approved the story list for each issue, making suggestions about order and placement, and vetoing certain stories.

More changes came to the magazine in 1954. Lawrence Spivak, who had shepherded the magazine through its formative years, sold his shares in the corporation to Joe Ferman, who had now enlisted his son Edward into the business.

Additionally, Mick McComas, Boucher's friend and co-editor, decided to retire fully from the magazine, because of health issues. "I've just finished a rather complete physical exam — more or less inspired by my ankle condition. Results: not good. High blood pressure, very bad nerves, etc, etc ad nauseam. I have been bluntly ordered to take it easy at once ... before worse things happen."[51] Boucher later attributed part of the problem to McComas' desire to write his own science-fiction works. Boucher took over sole custody as editor, which he kept until 1958.

The number of science-fiction magazines on the market continued to grow, and as it did, the market went through good times and bad. The early 1950s saw another wave of new titles, and for a while, it looked as though *The Magazine of Fantasy & Science Fiction* might not survive the onslaught. Just after retiring in 1953, McComas wrote to Boucher, "F&SF is losing money all over the place and prognosis is for worsening, rather than improvement. JWF [Joe Ferman] blames this largely — almost solely — on our editorial job. We blame it on poor distribution. Mainly, with such matters as poor promotion...."[52] By the following year, Boucher declared that the science-fiction boom seemed to be over.

One of the ways in which the magazine stood out from the others was the use of excellent cover artists. Ed Emshwiller, Chesley Bonestell and Mel Hunter accounted for many of the 1950s covers. *EQMM*'s frequent cover artist George Salter appeared in the masthead as *F&SF*'s art director until 1958.

The artwork showed innovation as well as excellence. Boucher was the first science-fiction editor to have a wraparound cover design that allowed the cover art to extend from the front cover to the spine and then the back of the magazine. While *The Magazine of Fantasy and Science Fiction* seems to be the first to try this different appearance, within a year, *Astounding* and others were trying the same.

However, the magazine was able to establish a niche in the genre. From 1949 to 1958, *The Magazine of Fantasy & Science Fiction* was the most literate of science-fiction magazines, likened on occasion to the *Atlantic Monthly* of science-fiction. Boucher's editorial influence and intelligent, sympathetic reviewing were major forces in boosting the respectability of American science-fiction

Although Boucher was a kind editor, he did not hesitate to reject stories from well-known authors who did not supply original works or whose stories did not match their reputation. Boucher rejected a story by Arthur C. Clarke that the editor couldn't make work. On another occasion in 1957, Boucher rejected a science-fiction story from John Creasey, the prolific mystery author recalling that the story had actually first appeared in 1938. Creasey did not seem to mind. He replied, "What magnificent records you keep; and what a memory!"

In a tribute to Gilbert and Sullivan, Boucher offered a glimpse into what it was like to run *The Magazine of Fantasy & Science Fiction* when he wrote "The Model of a Science Fiction Editor" (which appeared in *The Magazine of Fantasy & Science Fiction* in 1953). The first stanza of it read:

I am the very model of a modern s.f. editor.
My publisher is happy, as is each and every creditor.
I know the market trends and how to please the newsstand purchaser;
With agents and name authors my relations can be courteouser.
I've a clever knack of finding out what newsmen want to write about

And seeing that their stories spread my name in black and white about.
I've a colleague to be blamed for the unpleasant sides of bossery;
And I know the masses never get tired of flying saucery.
In short, in matters monetary, social, and promotional,
I am the very model of a pro s.f. devotional.

The position of editor had other benefits for Boucher as well. Science-fiction doesn't have quite the 150 year history dating back to Edgar Allan Poe, although in the area of fandom, science-fiction has far outpaced mystery. Boucher quickly took to the science-fiction conventions. He was also able to take family trips, often combining science-fiction conferences with trips to different parts of the United States. "We took the boys to Solacon and all had a wonderful excursion—first full-scale Family Trip we'd ever undertaken."[53]

Boucher shared his enthusiasm for the conventions with August Derleth, the author of the Solar Pons series:

> To my complete amazement (& Mick's flat disbelief) I've discovered that I love sf conventions. I even love 99% of the fans. Further amazement. My harsh remarks on critical standards in fandom, etc caused no fights but were greeted with acclaim and agreement. My staunchest and most rational supporter was EB Smith PhD! And I was not even able to start a fight by saying that what the field needed was more taste of the sort displayed by Derleth as an anthologist. Everyone agreed![54]

Boucher should have loved the science-fiction conventions. He frequently won awards for his work at *The Magazine of Fantasy & Science Fiction* at these gatherings. In 1956, Boucher was nominated for a Hugo for best professional magazine. In 1957, he won the same award. In 1958, he and Robert P. Mills, Boucher's replacement editor, were once again nominated for the same award and won.

Boucher's continuing health problems, combined with his family's health, along with problems at the magazine finally made him step down as editor in 1958. "I have been terribly overworked & in pretty bad health (my latest achievement has been coming down with erysipelas), & partly because Mother got much worse through a series of strokes & is now incapable of signing or even discussing anything."[55]

Boucher's problems with the magazine at that point were two-fold. First, he had a weekly column to write for *The New York Times Book Review*, which involved reading, critiquing, and writing about 2 to 10 books a week. Additionally, the money at *The Magazine of Fantasy & Science Fiction* had not improved much, although the magazine was now on sound financial footing. "Just too many damned quarrels with Ferman, mostly about money," Boucher wrote in 1958.

The science-fiction community was saddened, but understanding, about Boucher's decision. Isaac Asimov wrote, "Whatever is best for you, Tony,—that do. I know you have health problems and are generally overworked and I want you alive more than I want you as an editor. But how all s.f. will miss your editorial hand."[56]

Boucher was replaced at the magazine by Robert P. Mills, who had been the magazine's managing editor from its inception. Mills had worked for American Mercury for a number of years, working as managing editor for both *The Magazine of Fantasy & Science Fiction* and *Ellery Queen's Mystery Magazine*.

The reduction in Boucher's workload left more time for the family. The timing was good, as Phyllis suffered from some unexpected health problems in late 1958. Boucher reported that Phyllis had to undergo a hysterectomy shortly after his resignation as editor. "Phyllis has always been the healthiest person I know."

Even long after his resignation, Boucher was still considered the heart and soul of the magazine. In this letter from Avram Davidson, upon his becoming editor of *The Magazine of Fantasy & Science Fiction* in 1962, he reminisces about Boucher's reign at the magazine.

> Unless I deny the evidence of my sense, I must believe that I am now the editor of The Magazine of Fantasy and Science Fiction, according to what Bob Mills and Joe Ferman have told me today. And to whom should I first write and break the news, if not you?
>
> Besides it all feeling unreal, it feels unright. The Magazine of Fantasy and Science Fiction should be edited by Anthony Boucher. In a sense, in many senses, it always will be. My feelings about you and your effect on my career as a writer, I have expressed in the letter written to you at the time of your withdrawal for the Chiltern Hundreds. It still goes — in Gold and Purple. I'm somewhat of a loss to express my feelings about the Magazine itself. Adequately. Let me say, anyway, that I felt at home there from very, very early; felt that this was my kind of a magazine. And, as your kind was my kind, I hope that my kind will prove to be your kind. In trying to be a good Avram Davidson editor, rather than a poor Anthony Boucher editor — for only Anthony Boucher can be a good Anthony Boucher editor."[57]

Anthologies and introductions

One of Boucher's first forays into editing was a small book called *The Pocket Book of True Crime Stories*. This 1943 book included a variety of true crime reprints from an eclectic mix of authors.

Boucher's interest in true crime had shown itself in his own writings. He included numerous true crime cases in *Toad in the Hole* and to a lesser degree in the O'Breen cases. His pseudonym came from a notorious mass murderer. So he was conversant on the most interesting cases, and the articles about them.

Boucher sent out a mass mailing to publishers in October of 1941, asking a myriad of authors for permission to reprint articles on true crime for the anthology. The task was an arduous one. All correspondence had to be handled by mail, and Boucher had to unearth permissions from all the desired authors or locate the rights assignments made upon death from deceased writers in the collection. Boucher wrote to the Copyright office for assignments on stories by Washington Irving, Bram Stoker, and Oscar Wilde. He contacted authors, literary agents, and estates in his quest.

Even though he had an enormous workload, Boucher had a small budget for the book. Boucher was willing to pay about $25 per article for permissions. Participating authors requested anything from nothing to $75 or more. Boucher was hamstrung, because he would not receive payment until the book was completed and submitted to Pocket Books. So payment to the authors was upon publication by Pocket Books. Some authors refused to participate, unwilling to wait for the money.

Others were thrilled to participate. Hugh Wheeler and Richard Webb submitted two stories, one under the Q. Patrick name and another under the Patrick Quentin name. The pair wove a wild story of how the Lizzie Borden case might have occurred, a unique and plausible solution that did not contradict any of the known facts in the case.

Boucher wrote to Webb about it in 1942: "I am delighted with it and entranced by it and I don't believe a word of it. It's brilliant and impeccable and I wish I'd thought of it and I can't poke a possible finger through its logic, but I still think Lizzie did it."[58]

The war made it difficult to get the book completed in a timely manner. Webb wrote back to Boucher that both he and Wheeler expected to be called to duty within the next three months. Due to the paper shortage, Pocket Book telegraphed Boucher requesting either a cancellation of the book or a 40 percent reduction in the size of the planned table of contents. Boucher opted for a smaller book than he'd originally planned, and he nearly cut both the Maybrick and Borden pieces when Pocket Books decided to go to press immediately.

The result was pure Boucher. The first story in the Table of Contents was the murder of Abel by Cain from Genesis in the Bible. Other authors in the book included Bram Stoker writing about La Voisin, Oscar Wilde quipping about Thomas Griffiths Wainewright and Patrick Quentin on the Maybrick murders.

In writing to Holmes scholar Vincent Starrett, Boucher said, "Thanks greatly for the kind words on the PBook. Needless to say I don't believe Q. Patrick's Borden theory either (though I think from correspondence that QP does), but for pure novelty it was an editor's delight."[59]

The book has a preface by Lewis W. Lawes, the former warden of Sing Sing penitentiary. The prison warden said, "A friend of mine, however, insists that true murder connoisseurs are amateur criminologists. They are perennially examining the mechanisms that make assassins tick. Long hours of heated debates rise out of their inquiries and the involvements there from are occasionally scholarly, but most often, merely long-winded."[60] The book has no writings from Boucher, either in the way of an introduction to any case or a foreword. If the book had not listed his name prominently on the cover, Boucher's presence in the book would be hard to determine.

Boucher followed this up with another mystery anthology, *Great American Detective Stories*, in 1945. Boucher's story selection included a short history of the mystery story in America. "In five short stories, Edgar Allan Poe created the form and almost all of its possible variants. Bu then the English took the play away from us."[61]

Boucher chose many of the authors who represented the development of the mystery story in America, but rather than select the most recognized and anthologized story from that author, Boucher looked for less well-known works. Instead of "The Problem of Cell 13," Boucher included "The Stolen Rubens" as his Jacques Futrelle story. Likewise, he opted for lesser known works by Hammett, Chandler, Queen, Poe, Palmer, Rice, and Post along with a story by his own hand. Boucher wrote a short introduction to each work. Since the book was entitled American and not United States, Boucher chose to include a story he had translated from Mexican author, Antonia Helú.

Following the war, science-fiction anthologies came into their own as a commercially viable way of reprinting in book form the best short fiction available. This was achieved almost simultaneously with the 1946 anthologies: *The Best of Science Fiction* edited by Groff Conklin and *Adventures in Time and Space* edited by Raymond John Healy and Boucher's good friend J. Francis McComas. In 1948, Groff Conklin followed up his first effort with *A Treasury of Science Fiction*. The modern triumvirate of magazine short stories, anthologies, and novels was now in place.

Once their magazine was on fairly stable ground, Boucher and McComas edited annual anthologies of the best of *The Magazine of Fantasy and Science Fiction*. The yearly collection contained the typically erudite comments of Boucher on the state of science-fiction writing and the particular talents of each of the authors in the book. Boucher took the anthologies in new directions by including novellas, poetry and vignettes.

Following his election to President of Mystery Writers of America in 1951, Boucher opened up the same type of forum for highlighting short fiction of MWA members. He edited *Four-and-Twenty Bloodhounds* for MWA the following year.

The collection had originally been suggested by Clayton Rawson back in 1949. "Bob Arthur came up the other day with an anthology suggestion I should have thought of myself. He said, 'What about Unicorn taking it for one of their selections?' And he suggested that if they'd agree to publish, the anthology could be tailored for size. Also, of course, with a book club selection in the bag it might make a trade publisher more interested."[62] The idea was to create a mystery anthology featuring Mystery Writers of America members each year, with the organization receiving $1,000 plus any trade edition royalties. They quickly signed a contract with Simon & Schuster for an anthology dealing with Great Modern Detectives. "'Great,' of course, being defined as Created-by-MWA-members," Rawson explained wryly.

Boucher quickly organized the anthology. He sent out questionnaires to active MWA members as to the detectives created by each author and any short stories that had not been reprinted or appeared in books. Boucher was partial to works that were not overused or too familiar to the public.

As advertised, the collection contains 24 stories by MWA members of that time along with an interesting twist. Each sleuth is given a Who's Who entry. "And along with the stories you'll find the official, never-before-revealed biographies of these sleuths. You'll learn strange facts about your favorite detectives: that Miss Hildegarde Withers, for instance, is fascinated by the new self-proclaimed science of dianetics" (a jibe at fellow science-fiction writer L. Ron Hubbard).[63] Boucher credited the idea of using a "detectival Who's Who notes" to Kenneth Macgowan who had edited the mystery anthology, *Sleuths*, in 1931.

Boucher was only member from MWA's Northern California to participate. As a result, Boucher did not attend the New York book launch party, despite his role as editor. Lee Wright asked him to make a voice recording to be played for the party.

With his new career in mystery reviewing for the *New York Times*,

TRUE CRIME *Detective*

WINTER 1953   35 cents

MURDER IN THE KING'S HOUSEHOLD by F. Tennyson Jesse
see page 59

The Wanton Murder of Arnold Schuster	FRANK MULLADY
The Days of Floradora	EDMUND PEARSON
Once Aboard the Lugger	STUART PALMER
Until You Are Dead...	J. FRANCIS McCOMAS
The Murderer Was a Lady	MIRIAM ALLEN deFORD

A selection of the best TRUE CRIME CASES, new and old

The first issue of *True Crime Detective*, the second magazine edited by Boucher and McComas.

Boucher had a wide choice of opportunities to edit collections and reprints. One of his first chances was the *True Crime Detective* magazine from Casebook Publications, a division of Mercury Publications which published *The Magazine of Fantasy and Science Fiction*. Boucher edited the second periodical from the fall of 1952 until the fall of the following year. The digest-sized magazine was published quarterly, but never made it to monthly as *The Magazine of Fantasy and Science Fiction* had done.

From the start, the publishers had dual concerns about the magazine. First, Bob Mills, the managing editor of *The Magazine of Fantasy and Science Fiction* had doubts about the two men editing a second monthly publication. They knew of Boucher's poor health and didn't want the stress of two full-time jobs to harm him.

Mills and the company were also concerned about the amount of new material on true crime. The publisher didn't want to do too many "period pieces," what they defined as older crimes being retold in a new light.

Boucher used the magazine to reprint well-written stories from his friends and colleagues. Boucher contacted Joseph Jackson, who had won an Edgar for his true crime work to request a short version of the Dick Fellows story.

While the magazine contained the same high quality of work found in *The Magazine of Fantasy and Science Fiction*, the magazine did not thrive. The publishers chided Boucher and McComas after a few issues for the lack of diversity in the magazine. They wanted more variety in the types of crime presented, the length of the articles and the approaches to the crimes. Most of the articles were murders with no space given to lesser crimes.

Part of the problem with the magazine was that there were not the same number of authors dedicated to true crime as to science-fiction. Over the course of four quarterly issues, three issues had stories by Stuart Palmer, and two stories by Frank Mullady, Miriam Allen deFord and F. Tennyson Jesse each. Along with this Boucher had a story by McComas and another reprint of his own. Using such a small number of authors could have narrowed the chances for success with the magazine.

The magazine also suffered from a lack of focus in the editorial department. Ed Radin, one of the founders of MWA, was also involved in the magazine, but didn't bother to consult the two editors. He bought pieces that McComas and Boucher found sloppily written, and the pair had to then edit heavily or reject the story. The magazine was forced to pay for the pieces at higher prices than they would have liked. Boucher felt constrained in rectifying the situation because of the two men's relationship to MWA.

True Crime Detective didn't find an audience and folded after one year. Miriam Allen de Ford had this to say about the magazine:

> But true crime writers themselves, when they think of Anthony Boucher, remember chiefly his unfailing help, encouragement and applause when they did well. I know that for years I depended on him for my best reviews for my books in this category — both in the New York Times and on FM Radio KPFA. And it was largely thanks to Anthony Boucher's constant and urgent recommendations that I was able in 1965 to have my true crime magazine articles collected and published as *Murderers Sane and Mad*. I know also that I am only one of the many who had reason to be grateful to him in the past and to miss him sorely.[64]

In addition to his reviewing and his work on *The Magazine of Fantasy and Science Fiction*, Boucher was responsible for the introductions and selections for three major American lines of crime fiction: the Mercury Mysteries, the Dell Great Mystery Library, and the Collier Mystery Classics.

The Mercury Mysteries, which Boucher edited from 1952 to 1955, were deeply abridged versions of popular mystery novels. Many of the books were cut down from their original length to 60,000 words or less, in order to fit into the digest paperback form created for the books. The books went for a princely 35¢. Mercury Publications was the same organization that had created *Ellery Queen's Mystery Magazine* and *F&SF*. Lawrence Spivak and Joe Ferman were instrumental in creating the series.

Ferman wrote to Boucher, proposing the series. "From our several brief discussions, my feeling is that you could help us select for Mercury Mystery books: — Good older titles which are not too dated by the story or the style.... Good current or recent titles which may have been overlooked by the other reprint publishers. I think the suggestion of an introductory blurb is excellent."[65]

The proposed series included one title per month, produced on the first of every month. Boucher was put on a retainer of $150 a month for his services with the series. Boucher's duties not only included re-reading and selecting he books, contacting authors for reprint rights and availability, but also actual copy editing. He was picky about getting first editions only. He complained about 2nd editions and explained in detail to Ferman what was needed. He line-edited each work, making corrections to grammar and punctuation in each title.

Boucher requested a copy of the contract provided to the authors from Mercury, so he could better answer questions from authors about the rights offered. As they had with *The Magazine of Fantasy and Science Fiction*,

Ferman asked for sex appeal for the readers. Boucher replied that he looked for sex when possible, but not in every title.

Mercury Mysteries published a wide range of mystery novels from traditional mysteries like Boucher's own *The Case of the Baker Street Irregulars* (which Boucher reduced to 67,000 words) to espionage books like *The Widow-Makers* by Michael Blankfort. Boucher heartily recommended Cyril Hare's *An English Murder*: "A most violent YES!!!! I think it's perfect. Maybe even commercial."

Since Boucher selected the titles, he wrote frequently to the Fermans, suggesting titles. Boucher recommended the Lockridges, *Scarlet Imperial* by Dorothy B. Hughes, and Helen McCloy's first Dr. Basil Willing case, *Dance of Death*. Josephine Tey's *The Man in the Queue* was one of Boucher's first choices, and although he lobbied hard for *The Daughter of Time* as well, Mercury balked at the latter book.

In his introduction to *The Man in the Queue* which had been retitled *Killer in the Crowd*, Boucher says, "It's by Tey. So it's wonderful. So what are you waiting for? ... in these novels, she set a standard of sensitivity, warmth, perception, feeling for the subtlest nuances of locale and character and motivation, which has never been surpassed in the formal detective story."[66]

Each contained a miniature review column, containing bits and pieces about the subgenre and the book's place within the crime genre. Mercury felt strongly enough about Boucher's contribution that his name was prominently placed on the cover of each digest.

Boucher's position with the company did not last long. Sales figures were disappointing, and old titles tended to average out more than the recent titles. Boucher renegotiated his contract to $75 a month plus expenses associated with identifying the books and correspondence. As sales did not increase, Boucher was offered a $50 monthly retainer. By July 15, 1954, Ferman was suggesting changing Mercury Mysteries to *The Mercury Mystery Book Magazine,* and cutting each book to 120 pages. Even that suggestion did not help sales. Within a matter of months, the series was brought to a halt.

Boucher did not have to wait long for a new opportunity to select a series of classics for republication. In June 1955, Boucher was approached by Dell Modern Mystery Classic of the Month. Boucher agreed to talk to the Dell editors during a trip to New York City a few weeks hence.

Dell wanted to reprint mysteries for 35¢ that had been selected by a board of "experts" with Boucher serving on the board. One of the other board members was Louis Untermeyer, poet, biographer and mystery fan. Humphrey Bogart was the third judge for the series. The photos of the three judges were prominently displayed on the back cover of each title. From the broad category of mysteries from 1925 to 1950, Boucher was asked for his top 100 selections.

The pay for the job was handsome. Boucher made $500 in 1955 and another $500 in 1956 for his efforts. Even though his efforts mostly ceased after the initial selections, his pay was upped to $750 in 1957 for the continuing use of the Boucher name.

The group agreed on nine titles and four authors for the original publication. The authors were John Dickson Carr, Rex Stout, Agatha Christie, and Mary Roberts Rinehart. The titles were:

- *Puzzle for Fools* by Patrick Quentin
- *The Red Right Hand* by Joel Townsley Rogers
- *Trial by Fury* by Craig Rice
- *Pavilion* by Hilda Lawrence
- *The Iron Gates* by Margaret Millar
- *The Noose* by Philip MacDonald
- *Strong Poison* by Dorothy Sayers
- *The Bride Wore Black* by Cornell Woolrich
- *Laura* by Vera Caspary

In 1959, the publisher's liaison was switched to Robert Mills, who had taken over for Boucher at *F&SF*. Boucher was happy for the chance to be working with Mills again.

In 1961, Collier Books wanted to publish a series of reprints selected by Boucher and with an introduction by him. Just like the others, the choice of titles was up to Boucher. Collier agreed to pay a flat fee of $125 per title.

The deal was sweetened for Boucher by Collier's decision to reprint two of Boucher's earlier mystery titles. Collier came out with paperback versions of *The Case of the Seven of Calvary* and *The Case of the Baker Street Irregulars*, neither of which had ever been reprinted.

Likewise, Collier appealed to Boucher's knowledge of the mystery genre by asking him to write entries for their encyclopedia line. Boucher wrote a long piece for the entry for "detective story" for the encyclopedia that spanned from Poe to the 1960s. Boucher was paid $200 for his work.

In early 1962, Boucher apologized to Collier's editor for the lateness of his picks for the reprint line. "My oldest and closest friend [McComas], recuperating from a breakdown, moved in with us on his psychiatrist's request to give him a background of peace and security during a week or two of extra-intensive therapy. We finally dislodged him 4 months later, almost over the dead body of his analyst. Meanwhile my own condition got much worse."[67]

The list of possible titles started with all the books in Bruno Fischer's office. Boucher rated all of Fischer's books on an A-F scale with a few entries so bad that they only ranked a "No!" His want list included Doris Miles Disney, Lawrence Treat, Charlotte Armstrong, Michael Venning, Helen McCloy, John Dickson Carr, Elisabeth Sanxay Holding, and Ellery Queen's *The Adventures of Ellery Queen*. In late 1962 after only a few months of issuing the reprints, Colliers decided to cut down on the number of titles released each month. With a few exceptions, the titles were losing about $1000 each upon publication.

By March 1964, Collier had decided to put more Boucher selections on hold. Colliers was being bought and absorbed by Macmillan Publishing Company. Boucher was not officially told until he offered to write an introduction and short biography of Arthur W. Upfield who had passed away. Although the formal agreement had ended in November 1962, Boucher introductions continued throughout 1963.

In addition to his editorial work with all of these magazines, Boucher was frequently asked to write forewords for books by various authors. His career as a reviewer and background as an author made him a desirable name on the cover of any mystery. Over the years, Boucher wrote forewords for over fifty different titles. Each was a miniature critique of the book and its place in the genre.

Ace Books requested that Boucher write an introduction to science-fiction writer P.K. Dick's short story collection, which include the story "The Minority Report," which was later made into a movie. Boucher was paid $25 for his efforts.

With his in-depth knowledge of true crime, Boucher wrote an introduction to the collection "Crimes that Shocked America" for $100.

The Critic

> Among the extremely diverse books lumped together as "mysteries," I shall try to judge each fairly according to the best standards of the type which the author intended to produce, and not those of another type which I personally prefer.
> —*"Code for Mystery Reviewers," by Anthony Boucher*

Even if Boucher had only written his novels and begun *The Magazine of Fantasy & Science Fiction*, he would be remembered today for those efforts. However, over the course of his career, he repeatedly returned to artistic reviews and criticism as an outlet for his prolific writing and a source of ready cash.

While the titles of critic and reviewer are often used synonymously, there are distinct differences. The reviewer, not to slight his daunting task, explains the merits of a single book. Is it a good read? Does the language flow? Does the plot hold together? The emphasis is on the present, this book, and its merits.

The critic looks at the same things as the reviewer, but also puts the book into the broader perspective of the genre. The critic has to know the width and breadth of what has come before in the genre. Boucher once wrote that a reviewer wrote for the moment while the critic wrote for the ages.

Lenore Glen Offord firmly placed Boucher's work in the criticism category. "There is a difference, significant but not always recognized, between reviewing and criticism.... Anthony Boucher was a critic. He brought to his work an encyclopedic knowledge of the mystery, in both long and short forms, and could relate the subject at hand to the genre as a whole."[1]

Of course, the role of critic was made for Boucher. He was a voracious reader of not one, but two, genres. He speed-read and kept detailed notes on 3 × 5 cards about each book that he completed. The combination made Boucher the preeminent critic of his generation. It's no surprise that he won three Edgars for his criticism.

Boucher's columns were never just a disjointed series of book reviews from the past week. Each column was unified by a theme or category which was put forth to the mystery community. The reviews of several books would all tie to the theme presented.

His career as critic started early. Boucher was the theater critic for *United Progressive News* for two years. He took the job seriously, reading and viewing many more plays that he reviewed. He and his mother frequented the theater two to three times a week. In no time, he was able to compare and contrast most of the day's fare.

While he reviewed in the evening, Boucher spent his days writing his own one-act plays. A few of his efforts were produced, but most were put in a drawer. Yet his lack of commercial success did not impair his ability to review. His comments were concise and straight to the point.

Nearly ten years passed before Boucher returned to literary criticism. In the interim, he'd written seven novels and started a family. His poor health made it difficult to pursue a more robust writing career. Reading had never taxed Boucher's asthma. He couldn't handle too many trips health-wise or financially. Boucher needed a writing assignment close to home.

Reviewing was an ideal way to share Boucher's love for the genre as well as get paid to read. In addition, Boucher was able to amass a sizable collection of first edition novels that he received for review.

Of course, Boucher was by this point heavily invested in genre fiction. He'd been writing it for a decade. Reviewing seems an odd choice at first for a published author, but in the middle years of the twentieth century many mystery authors found an additional revenue source in reviews. Dorothy B. Hughes and Craig Rice also wrote reviews for newspapers and magazines, using their connections in the genre to share additional insights and gossip to make the reviews more than just a book report. Boucher's knowledge of the genre and the history of the mystery, especially his love of all things Sherlock, gave him a wealth of knowledge to draw on in making his reviews.

Reviews for the Chronicle *and* EQMM

His first experience in genre reviews came close to home, just across the bay in fact. Edward Dermot Doyle, the mystery reviewer from the *San Francisco Chronicle,* left the paper to fight in World War II, and Boucher,

Boucher at home in his office (courtesy the White family).

4F because of his asthma, was hired to temporarily fill in for the soldier. Boucher first met Doyle's editor, Joseph Henry Jackson, when Boucher suggested himself as a guest on Doyle's radio show for *The Case of the Seven of Calvary*. Before Boucher could appear on the show, Doyle went off to serve in the Army.

Boucher wasted no time in contacting Jackson. "I proceed at once to stifle my sadness and reveal the heart of a vulture. You will almost certainly have chosen his successor by now; but if you haven't or if that successor proves unsatisfactory or in his turn is drafted, please consider my hat in the ring. My prime qualification is probably that I have a wife, two children, and asthma, and should be around for some time."

After this inauspicious introduction, Boucher worked for Joseph Henry Jackson at the *Chronicle*. Jackson had joined the staff of the *Chronicle* in 1930 and remained there until his death in 1955. Jackson was the author and editor of nearly a dozen books. He made a name for himself by serving on the boards for such prestigious literary prizes as the O. Henry Memorial award and the Pulitzer Prize. In later years, Boucher would say that it was one of his good fortunes to work with such a legend so early in his career as a reviewer.

Not only did Boucher credit Jackson as being a major influence on his career, both were die-hard Sherlockians. Their friendship grew beyond the bounds of the newspaper as they became two of the co-founders of the Scowrers and Molly Maguires, the Bay area's Baker Street Irregulars chapter.

As mentioned, Boucher's columns were extraordinary for the way he dealt with not just the book at hand, but its place in the genre. The only way to do justice to his reviews is to let them speak for themselves. In this clip from one of his columns, he discusses the emergence of the spy novel in 1943. Obviously in the midst of world war, espionage came to the forefront of everyone's mind, and mystery was no exception. Not only did Boucher relate the books of 1943 to previous mysteries, but he also tied the trend to world events.

> The most interesting current phenomenon within the scope of this column is the extraordinary development of the spy novel.... To be exact, of 103 novels I've reviewed in 1943, at least 34 have had espionage or sabotage as a dominant element.... Spy novels were formerly the literary stepchildren of the mystery trade.[2]

Given the length of time that Boucher reviewed mysteries, he was able to comment on trends over the course of his career as well. In a much later

New York Times column, entitled "When Will The Spy Go Back Into The Cold?," Boucher discusses a subgenre developing from the spy novel that he christens "gothica." The notion of war had changed from World War II to Vietnam, and Boucher reflected this in his study of the genre. This new division of the spy novel was more suspenseful and feminine than its 1940s predecessors. Boucher wrote, "Mary Stewart's Edgar scroll-winning *This Rough Magic* from last year, [has] been as persistent on the bestselling list as Deighton or Fleming" and explains that "it would take a suspiciously over-male he-man to resist the charm and narrative vigor of Mary Stewart's adventure stories."[3]

Shortly after starting with the newspaper, Boucher asked about payment. In many of his reviewing jobs, Boucher took the job first and asked about the money he would be given later. While it could be an effective way to get a foot in the door, it was not the best way to negotiate the maximum fee for each piece. The payments rarely pleased Boucher, and he found himself needing more money than could be supplied by reviewing books.

> It is the question, as you might guess, of my getting some money out of this sack-profession.
>
> I gather, from things you said when we were discussing make-up changes in the threatened paper reduction, that the *Chronicle* is reasonably wealthy at present; the chief objection would doubtless be the horrifying precedent set by Paying a Reviewer.
>
> The solution could be simple: Make me a contributing editor to This World.
>
> I'm known nationally as a name reviewer — publishers quoting me in ads and jackets give the name, which only happens otherwise with Craig Rice and Dorothy Hughes outside the major NY reviewers.[4]

Boucher was able to work out an arrangement with the paper to be paid. To a man who was subsisting on royalties from books and science-fiction short stories, the extra income was a help.

Boucher was worth the price. Not only did Boucher have an encyclopedic knowledge of the genre and its history, Boucher knew most everyone in the business. In this snippet, Boucher includes details about his former editor, Marie Rodell's series of regional true crime books and the work that went into the stories.

> The Rivers of Blood of America, more formally known as the Regional Murder Series, flows gorily on ... in its second volume, *Chicago Murders*.... The Chicago volume, edited by Sewell Peaslee Wright, bristles with classics; and it's hard to tell where to start in describing its riches.[5]

His columns, besides including insightful reviews of books, had tidbits about the major authors and editors of the day. His column could read like a gossip column for the mystery world. "Today this generally profound and scholarly commentary turns into a pure society gossip column ... a cocktail party in honor of Lee Wright was proffered, or thrown, by Simon & Schuster's Western representatives."[6]

From 1942 to 1947, Boucher had a weekly column in the *San Francisco Chronicle* as the popular fiction reviewer. Boucher took over Doyle's "Department of Criminal Investigations." Following Doyle's return from war, Boucher later wrote "Murder They Say" with fellow author Lenore Glen Offord and also "Murder and Espionage" which Boucher wrote by himself early on and later with Offord.

Boucher's introduction to the world of mystery criticism was incredibly successful. He was awarded his first Edgar for literary criticism in 1946 for his work at the *San Francisco Chronicle*.

Even though Boucher had done a wonderful job for four years, it was unheard of not to let a returning veteran come back to his job. Boucher was summarily let go in 1947, when Doyle returned from war. "My five-year tenure here has been a lustrum not without luster. It's a span that has covered the rise and decline of the boomingest period in the history of the mystery novel."[7]

Boucher was given freelance work, where he wrote pieces for the paper in conjunction with his longtime friend, Lenore Glen Offord. Boucher wrote to his radio collaborator, Manny Lee: "To crown my bliss, I've now been ousted from the Chronicle by the return from the wars of their former mystery editor. Now I have neither money nor prestige."[8]

Boucher repeated the same story to Fred Dannay a few weeks later in a letter to the editor.

> I'm no longer doing mysteries for the Chronicle — Mr. Doyle came back from the wars and reclaimed his job. And I'm at the moment totally unemployed by radio — with three new original shows on the market, which sponsors seem to be treating with as much casual disdain as they bestow on Queen.
>
> All of which means that you'll probably be seeing some Nick Noble tales from me soon, if you're interested. And that I'm open to any other suggestions you might make.[9]

The truth was a little different, but Boucher did not let on to his friends. Apparently as his tenure at the *Chronicle* drew to a close, Boucher began complaining to friends at Author's Guild meetings about the rate of pay for reviewing and the working conditions at the paper. The word quickly got back to Jackson, who wasn't pleased with the bad publicity.

> What I want to tell you is that I'm afraid your contributions to The Chronicle's book section had better cease. It has come to me that on more than one occasion you have expressed yourself—once quite publicly to a group of writers—as wholly dissatisfied with the arrangement you have with the paper, and while certainly you are privileged to be dissatisfied I see no sense in continuing a connection you yourself regard as unsatisfactory.
>
> The point is not altogether whether The Chronicle's remuneration is, as you put it to a group of people, "a pittance." It's rather, I think, that The Chronicle had never paid anything to contributing reviewers until the time when you replaced, temporarily, Mr. Doyle. At that time I agreed to see if a space rate couldn't be arranged—this for the first time for anyone. Further, when Mr. Doyle returned, The Chronicle continued, at my suggestion, to pay you space for such reviews as you did in other fields—again a "first" here. Perhaps The Chronicle should do better; perhaps it shouldn't. The point is that this department did make some arrangement to pay you something, and it does not seem to me within the bounds of propriety that while it was doing so you should express yourself publicly as you have done.
>
> Further, it is reported to me that you stated flatly that "Chronicle reviewers" had to write "to policy." Entirely aside from the question of just how this might enter into the reviewing of detective stories, it is a fact that the only changes ever made in any reviews you wrote for the paper were on the grounds of (a) what seemed to me to skirt perhaps too close to libel, and (b) what seemed to me to skirt too closely to the edge of good taste. Still further, I have been able to find no other Chronicle reviewers who have this complaint to make, or, for that matter, any who feel that you are authorized to speak for "Chronicle reviewers." Again it does not seem to me proper that anyone who either feels this to be true or says publicly that it is true, should continue to do reviews for the paper.[10]

The rift with Jackson lasted for years and interfered with the two men's other mutual pastime as well. The Baker Street Irregular Scowrers did not meet during 1947–1948. There was nearly a two year gap in correspondence, before Boucher wrote some cheery letters to Jackson regarding the editor's true-crime work, *Bad Company*, which had just won the Edgar.

Jackson's enmity towards Boucher didn't extend to Boucher's co-critic. Lenore Offord took over as reviewer for the *Chronicle* in 1950.

Finally in 1951, the two men talked again. Boucher was preparing to write an introduction to the Limited Editions Club version of *The Valley of Fear*, and the two Irregulars talked about what should be included and what Boucher was writing for the introduction.

Boucher's notes to Dannay and Lee had not gone unheeded. Starting shortly after the introduction of *Ellery Queen's Mystery Magazine*, Howard Haycraft (of Haycraft-Queen Cornerstones list, *Murder For Pleasure*, and *The Art of the Mystery Story* fame) had reviewed mysteries for the digest. When Haycraft decided to step down in February 1948 to accept a position as an advisor to the Mystery Guild book club, Anthony Boucher took over the column on Haycraft's recommendation.

Boucher and Haycraft had met after the publication of *Murder for Pleasure*. Boucher had been approached about writing a book similar to *Murder For Pleasure*, but Haycraft beat him to it. Following the book's publication in 1941, Boucher wrote to the author, offering a five page detailed critique against certain points set forward by Haycraft in the book. "Page 132. Be just to Mrs. Christie. She has scarcely employed Hastings 'ad nauseum' of late. He went to the Argentine before *Ackroyd*, and I cannot recall his appearance since then save in *The ABC Murders*.... 166. Has there ever been a silent-screen Philo Vance? I doubt this statement very much."

The friends worked on a variety of projects together for MWA, and Haycraft was on the Edgar committee that nominated Boucher for his mystery criticism award in 1946.

Acting on Haycraft's suggestion, Fred Dannay approached Boucher to become the reviewer for *EQMM*. "I have had a long talk today with Howard, and it is now certain that he will not be able to continue as *EQMM*'s official reviewer. The circumstances which made Howard come to this decision are still confidential, but you will, no doubt, know about them soon. Howard was delighted when I told him that I had already written to you — in fact, Howard interrupted me to say that he was going to suggest you as his successor."[11]

Dannay started Boucher with four columns a year beginning in September 1948, which was later increased to 6 columns. Boucher and Dannay agreed to title the column "Speaking of Crime" so that the review column could be included in the magazine's Table of Contents. Boucher would title each column, which would be included as a subtitle.

In his last column at *Ellery Queen's Mystery Magazine*, Haycraft proclaimed, "Readers of EQMM are assured of that kind of criticism [announcing the emperor's new clothes] from Anthony Boucher, whose department begins in this issue."[12]

Boucher wasted no time in issuing a press release to all major publishers that he had taken over Haycraft's column in *EQMM*. Boucher found the announcements important to make. Living on the West Coast, it was impractical to have the New York publishers first send books to a New York magazine or newspaper and then to Berkeley. The time delay in getting the books from the publication to his home was prohibitive to reviewing the books in a timely fashion.

In his first column for the magazine, Boucher did a round-up of the previous year's books. The preceding year had been a cornucopia of treats in terms of the mystery genre. The fall of 1948 included *Witness for the Prosecution* by Agatha Christie, *Run to Death* by Patrick Quentin, *And Be a Villain* by Stout, and *The Fourth Postman* by Craig Rice.

Even in that first column for *EQMM*, Boucher began by dividing reviewed books into subcategories. Boucher's list featured the best book in each of the many subgenres he defined in that column. For instance, Boucher named *Wisteria Cottage* by Robert M. Coates as the best overall mystery of the year; for best pure detective story, he selected Carter Dickson's *The Skeleton in the Closet* and Edmund Crispin's *Love Lies Bleeding*. In the best hard-boiled book category he chose Williams Stuart's *Night Cry*. For best humorous mystery, Boucher selected Manning Long's *Savage Breast* and George Bagby's *In Cold Blood*. Boucher even included feminine romance-and-peril school and psychothrillers in his list.

Boucher even included more generic categories for his round-up. There were even groupings for those authors who did what they did consistently well as well as those whose current work had surpassed earlier works. Boucher also managed to include a backhanded compliment regarding the high degree of suspension of disbelief needed for a few 1948 entries, which included Craig Rice's *The Fourth Postman* and Ellery Queen's *Ten Days' Wonder*. In that first column, Boucher said about the books: "the at best tenuous relationship between the whodunit and life seemed, to me at least, totally severed."

While Boucher was not the first reviewer to categories books within the mystery genre, he was perhaps the most influential critic of a generation to do so. The designation of subgenres in the field continues to this day with the development of cozy conferences like Malice Domestic and the late lamented Eyecon for private eye fiction.

Boucher had his own favorite categories. He was mainly a fan of the traditional, puzzle mysteries; however, this didn't stop him from judging all books by their merits. Boucher was able to give equal space to all types of mysteries and extol each subcategory's virtues. In this column, Boucher discusses the emergence of the police procedural mystery, a subgenre that came into being during Boucher's tenure as a critic.

> Some attention to the actual methods by which we seek to enforce justice has, of course, been apparent in mystery fiction almost from its beginnings — though this is only one element of the detective story that can *not*

be traced back to Poe. The modern interest in the precise nature of routine and its effect upon the men engaged in it goes back at least as far as the pioneering police novels of Lawrence Treat in the early 1940s; and Sidney Kingsley's 1949 play Detective Story had its effect upon fiction, especially that of William P. McGivern.[13]

Boucher was a firm believer that good and bad books came from every possible genre. He'd had this conviction since his college days, where he couldn't see why the novels of authors like Austen and Dickens were treated as serious literature when they had been the popular entertainment of their day. He established what he called Boucher's Third Law, which stated, "the microcosm repeats the macrocosm. Within any artistic sub-genre you will find as wide a range of expression and as many levels of quality as you find within the genre itself."[14]

Together with science-fiction author Reg Bretnor, Boucher joked that the law meant 95 percent of all work was crap. However, the law says much more than that. Specifically, Boucher's law points out that ten percent of any genre fiction category will rival any book published as serious fiction. Boucher felt a desire to bring that fiction to light and to let readers know that great fiction existed in every genre.

> It is Boucher's Third Law that the microcosm repeats the macrocosm — i.e., that within any artistic sub-genre you will find as wide a range of expression and as many levels of quality as you find within the genre itself. The law is once more confirmed by observation of the still-proliferating novel of espionage and intrigue.[15]

Boucher resented the lack of respect given to genre fiction and its niche in the larger book market. In this quote, he discusses how the Michael Venning (a Craig Rice pseudonym) book, *Jethro Hammer*, was being treated as a general fiction novel, rather than a mystery, as her other books had been. "mystery novels are sure of a reasonably small sale but can never hit the jackpot; straight novels may sell nothing at all but there is no limit to their possible success. For Venning's sake I hope the trick pays off."[16]

Even as Boucher was finishing his first round-up for *Ellery Queen's Mystery Magazine*, Haycraft wrote to Boucher in the fall of 1948 to make some suggestion on improving future columns. Haycraft suggested that a column running five pages would work best in *EQMM* and recommended a monthly frequency. Doing a column less often did not mean less work, according to Haycraft. It just increased the number of books to be reviewed in each column and reduced the amount of text that could be devoted to any one title.

Taking Haycraft's suggestions, Boucher suggested making the column a monthly idea to Dannay the following March. "This time I had 40 books to cover — in about 1250 words. Some were obvious to drop as not worth mentioning; but there remains a residue..."[17] In mid 1949, Fred told Boucher that he would consider increasing the number of columns, but the inclusion of the excerpts of *Queen's Quorum*, Dannay's seminal work on short mystery fiction, had made some subscribers anxious about the amount of non-fiction in the magazine. Dannay suggested waiting until the *Queen's Quorum* was completed to discuss the matter again. In the interim, Dannay asked Boucher to cut the number of issues that the magazine printed his column to three pages every other month.

Boucher's frustration grew with each passing month. While the review job had a great deal of prestige, he was not receiving sufficient space or pay to do justice to the number of books he received on a monthly basis. Boucher vented in a note to himself. "This is to get off my chest what I do not dare write to Fred.... The Boucher content of the issues as a whole has been 1.4%, the Queen content 9.3%. In other words, practically 1 page in every 10 of EQMM is written by the editor."[18]

The situation grew tenser when Boucher was promised $150 for the 1949 year-end round-up, but received only $100. Dannay wrote and told Boucher that practically the same column had appeared in the *New York Times*. Therefore, the piece was not worth $150 to the magazine. Boucher was upset by the situation and the implications that he had cannibalized his own work between the two review columns. After a lengthy discussion, Dannay sent him the additional $50.

Even though Boucher is credited with saying that "Ellery Queen IS the American detective story," he didn't like all of the Queen books, especially some of the late 1940s titles that introduced surreal settings or circumstances. Boucher had to skate through a difficult situation when *Cat of Many Tails* came out in 1949. Boucher was expected to review Queen novels for the Queen magazine and had worked many years with both Lee and Dannay; however, he didn't like the book. Ethics won out over friendships, and Boucher wrote a tepid review that argued against the artifice of some of the Queen books. Boucher wasn't afraid to take on his editor, even though many critics labeled *Cat of Many Tails* as the best of the Queen novels with its realistic portrayal of New York City in the grips of a serial killers and the suspense in the novel.

Fred Dannay did not waste any time in responding to the negative review from Boucher.

> Tony I confess I am disappointed in your review of the *Cat* story. I had higher hopes. But, of course, I've been in this game long enough to know that no one has any right to quarrel with "the luck of the draw."
>   Nevertheless, when I compare the new Queen novel with, say, Carr's latest (*Below Suspicion*), and then compare your reviews, I have the overwhelming desire to get out of this game and try something else.
>   But what really got me was your unfair reference to "the artificiality of the Queen saga." Sure, the earlier Queen books were artificial, but even those were no more artificial than most other detective stories of the same period. But how could you even think in terms of artificiality in the face of Queen's record in the last ten years? Is *Calamity Town* artificial? Or *The Murderer is a Fox*? And even though you didn't like *Ten Days' Wonder*, is it as artificial as the great majority of detective novels?[19]

Boucher had a short, but rich reign as the reviewer for the magazine. He continued as the author of the "Speaking of Crime" column until mid–1950. After only one year as the critic for *Ellery Queen's Mystery Magazine*, he was given a second Edgar for his work.

In March 1950, Dannay had to cut "Speaking of Crime" from *EQMM*. As Dannay explained in a personal letter to Boucher later, he was forced to drop the column due to publisher Lawrence Spivak.

> His reasons were as follows: the monthly column originally had two purposes, as I myself explained them to both Spivak and Ferman. One, to render a service to EQMM readers, and two, to stimulate advertising in EQMM by mystery publishers. Mr. Spivak claimed that both purposes had failed — indeed, they had, in his opinion, both backfired badly.
>   Mr. Spivak felt that we would render a far better service to readers by devoting the two pages of review space to fiction.... I had absolutely no choice in the matter.[20]

The decision was made awkward by the fact that Spivak also published *The Magazine of Fantasy & Science Fiction*. Boucher had always enjoyed cordial relations with Spivak and making a fuss might have jeopardized that relationship and the fledgling science-fiction magazine. Dannay would like to have paid Boucher for the completed columns that had not run, but worried that the expense would have come to Spivak's attention and caused more hardship for both editors.

Boucher didn't hold a grudge on the matter. He wrote back to Dannay, "Let's pray that we can wipe all this out & resume our normal (rather high, I should say) level of friendship."[21]

In August 1950, Dannay wrote to Boucher about the review column again. Spivak had relented on his decision against the column. However, in order to cut costs, Boucher would not be the reviewer. Beginning in 1951, the column would appear monthly, but would be signed by a staff member, Robert Mills. The column would consist of reviews pulled from the major critics of the era, including Sandoe and Boucher.

Boucher's relationship with Dannay and Lee continued even after he stopped reviewing for them. Boucher wrote a nonfiction work related to his literary criticism published during in 1951. The 10-page booklet *Ellery Queen: A Double Profile* dealt with Frederic Dannay and Manfred Lee, the cousins who between them were Ellery Queen. The booklet was one of the first to detail the life of a mystery author as literary subject. The idea was radical in the era. Mystery writers, especially in the time of spy fiction and pulp novels, had very little prestige. No one expected genre fiction to have any lasting impact on the literature of the generation.

While Boucher's published biography of a mystery writer was one of the first to appear, writing about living authors is never easy. In 1951, Queen still had two decades to write. The cousins would still publish well into the late 1960s. As a result, Boucher refused all attempts to reprint the biography. The amount of work required to keep the biography up to date was not worth it to Boucher, who had moved on to writing for the *Times*.

Boucher would return to the pages of *Ellery Queen's Mystery Magazine*, when he started writing a column for them entitled "Best Mysteries of the Month," which ran from November 1957 until his death in 1968.

Boucher attempted reviews for other periodicals at this time, including *Clue: A Magazine Guide to Mysteries*. He was supposed to provide a monthly supplement to the magazine; however, the magazine collapsed after a single issue.

Science fiction reviews

Boucher wasn't limited to reviewing mysteries. In early 1949 while reviewing for *Ellery Queen's Mystery Magazine*, Mick McComas wrote to the *Los Angeles Daily News* suggesting that Boucher write a column on fantasy for the newspaper.

The editor, Scott O'Dell, was interested and wrote to Boucher. The arrangement was rather Spartan by Boucher's standards. The newspaper only offered publicity and free books. They did not pay their reviewers. Boucher negotiated a monthly column of 500 words. O'Dell wanted a column with a continuous flow of text, not individual reviews in a paragraph.

Boucher didn't respond immediately. He was in New York City for a few days and returned to Berkeley with a bad bout of asthma. Following his acceptance of the job, Boucher wrote to a number of publishers across the country and requested books. Boucher would not be the only well-known genre author to be writing for the *Los Angeles Daily News*. Other contributors included Dorothy B. Hughes, the Lockridges, and Craig Rice.

After only a few months, Boucher was able to parlay his free gig at the *Los Angeles Daily News* into a paying one. He began reviewing for the *Chicago Sun-Times* shortly after joining the California paper. Since there was no pay involved for the *Daily News*, Boucher easily switched to the other position. One of his first assignments was to first write a review of *Murder: Plain and Fanciful*, which had been edited by Boucher's fellow reviewer, James Sandoe. Sandoe had been writing reviews for the *Chicago Sun-Times* and later wrote to book reviewer editor, Emmett Dedmon, proposing a column by Boucher reviewing fantasy and science-fiction.

Dedmon contacted Boucher immediately about a position with the paper, and Boucher responded with a description of his current work situation: "I'm not sure how I should be described at present — I'm mostly busy on radio and translating."

In March 1949, Dedmon and Boucher had agreed to a bi-monthly column which covered both fantasy and science-fiction. The paper no longer had a special book section, but did carry a daily review column.

The relationship started off rather rocky. By May 10, 1949, Boucher had not received any books for the June 3 column. Again living on the West Coast had made Boucher's work more difficult as all the publishers now had to send him books directly, rather than just directing them to the newspaper.

After only six months, the *Chicago Sun-Times* showed some signs that the relationship would not be a long-term one. The newspaper cut its payment to Boucher. Boucher indicated in a return letter that the change in pay would not alter their relationship unless other more tempting offers came from editors waving contracts at him in front of his home. The reduction in the payment structure did not slow Boucher down. Instead, Boucher suggested a change to monthly from bi-monthly in early 1950.

Along with the additional space for science-fiction reviews, Boucher tried to encourage the *Sun-Times* to publish fiction. In May 1950, Boucher pushed the newspaper to reprint science-fiction and fantasy short stories. He had enclosed some of his own best work including "Expedition" with his proposal and suggested works by Robert Heinlein as well. After several weeks, he had still had not heard a response from the newspaper.

Boucher hoped to solidify his position as a science-fiction reviewer with some of the awards that were coming his way as the editor for *The Magazine of Fantasy and Science Fiction*. He quickly notified the *Sun-Times* when he was chosen Guest-of-Honor for NorWesCon, the World Science-Fiction Convention held in 1950 in Portland, Oregon.

In June 1950, Boucher learned why he hadn't heard back from Dedmon about any of the proposed changes to the reviews. The newspaper was going through some seismic shifts. *The Chicago Sun-Times* changed to a morning paper, and along with that fired 75 employees. The book review program was to be cut, but was spared at the last moment. Dedmon took on the work of four people, including book editor and drama critic.

The following month, book review columns were axed. Boucher's column and ideas were no longer used; however, Boucher was given freelance work, where he would be paid $5 to write a review based on particular books he received.

Fortunately, Boucher was not long without a science-fiction reviewing job. In the months before the *Sun-Times* cut all their reviewers, Boucher had heard through his former editor, Lee Wright, that Irita Van Doren, book editor for the *New York Herald-Tribune*, had asked Wright about hiring Boucher as a possible reviewer. Wright had indicated that Boucher was committed to the *New York Times*.

Van Doren had her own literary past. She had worked at the *Herald-Tribune* since 1926 as the book review editor. She had married into the literary Van Doren family; however, she had divorced Carl Van Doren in 1935. She later met and carried on a long-term affair with Wendell Willkie, the Republican presidential nominee of 1940.

Boucher quickly wrote back to Van Doren, explaining his current position with the *Times*. "My Times reviewing is purely piece-work; I review whatever they choose to send me, and there are no commitments either way. I do find this handling of 50% of the mystery crop rather awkward. I've always thought it better that one man should handle an entire department, so that the reader may gauge more readily just how much this man's likes and hates are apt to coincide with his own."[22]

The position that Van Doren needed to fill at the *Herald-Tribune* was Will Cuppy's mystery reviewing job. Cuppy was the somewhat reclusive humorist and reviewer who had passed away in 1949. Cuppy was best known for his work in the *New Yorker* along with his own books. Cuppy had earned his reputation as an authority on mystery by editing three mystery anthologies in the in 1940s: *World's Great Mystery Stories*; *World's Great Detective Stories*; and *Murder Without Tears*. Seemingly Cuppy was irreplaceable. The

Herald-Tribune had used anonymous reviews by staff members since Cuppy's death. Van Doren wanted to eventually appoint a replacement, but in 1950 she was only querying if Boucher would be one applicant.

A year later, she wrote again and suggested a science-fiction column, as the newspaper still had not made any decision on Cuppy's replacement. Boucher took some time to respond. He was in Los Angeles, testifying as an expert witness on the history and uses of detective fiction at the trial *Warner Brothers v Dashiell Hammett*.

Boucher had been approached on February 20, 1951, by the defense counsel for Regis Radio Corp regarding a suit filed by Warner Brothers regarding the Sam Spade radio program. WB had thought that the radio show had crept too close to *The Maltese Falcon* and contended that purchasing the rights to the novel included all future rights to the character as well. In the interim, Hammett had become involved in creating a radio show for Sam Spade, the detective from *The Maltese Falcon*.

As a result, Warner Brothers opted to sue Hammett and the radio corporation for plagiarism. Boucher was contacted as the president of Mystery Writers of America. He was asked to testify as an expert witness on the genre, on hardboiled fiction, and on the use and promotion of series characters in mystery.

Boucher was on his way to New York to pitch some ideas for the Ellery Queen television show, *The Adventures of Ellery Queen* which ran from 1950–1952. As a long-time script writer for the radio show, Boucher felt he had an in with the series, although Helene Hanff was the primary scripter for the small screen series.

Boucher pitched a story about Ellery meeting a Martian. Eugene Burr from Norman and Irving Pincus hated the idea. Of the 13 shows Boucher eventually pitched regarding the TV show, they liked only one and they asked for a treatment. The storyline involved a Gilbert and Sullivan show with Ellery and Inspector Queen as possible characters.

Boucher managed to squeeze in a trip to Hammett's attorneys while visiting New York and returned home via Los Angeles to report to the Regis Radio attorneys. Boucher's work was profitable. The corporation paid Boucher $1000 for his expert witness testimony. The judge decided that purchasing rights to a novel did not result in the sale of rights of a series character as well, and the case was decided in Regis Radio's favor.

When Boucher returned to Berkeley, he replied to Van Doren and suggested $20 (the *Times*' rate) vs. their offered $10. Van Doren countered that she could do no better. Boucher pushed the *New York Herald-Tribune* for signed reviews for mystery and also suggested a flowing text column rather than individual reviews. His work in the *New York Times* had been changed to that format recently and had strong favorable opinions from the readers.

In the year that had passed between letters from Van Doren, Boucher had assumed responsibility for all mystery reviews at the *Times*. Francis Brown, the book review editor at the *Times*, didn't want Boucher's name appearing elsewhere. Boucher suggested his H.H. Holmes pseudonym. Van Doren spoke with Brown as well, and they agreed that it was appropriate. Although most of the industry professionals knew that Boucher was Holmes, it made for two distinct public personae just as it had for Boucher's two mystery series.

Finally in September 1951 after a two-year gap, James Sandoe, who had once recommended Boucher for a science-fiction reviewer at the *Chicago Sun-Times*, became mystery editor at the *New York Herald-Tribune*. Sandoe was asked to start including notes and comments on the genre as space fillers which could be used with the column or in other places. Boucher began doing the same with his column.

Boucher was asked to lead a *Playboy* Panel entitled "1984 and Beyond" in Chicago in 1962. He participated with a number of his science fiction friends, including Heinlein, Bradbury, Clarke, Asimov and others. Boucher then edited the transcripts from the panel and along with follow-up interviews with the participants write a two-piece article on the panel that appeared in July and August 1963. The panel was considered quite prestigious because *Playboy* was one of the top-paying markets for genre fiction.

Despite such high-profile assignments, Boucher's relationship with the *Herald-Tribune* changed drastically that same year. In 1963, James Sandoe resigned and Dorothy Hughes replaced him as mystery department editor. Van Doren resigned around the same time. She went to William Morrow & Co as a part-time worker.

Shortly after her resignation, Boucher received a letter form Richard Kluger, the paper's new book editor. Kluger had plans to syndicate the *New York Herald-Tribune's* book section. He wanted Boucher to write under his own name and not the H.H. Holmes pen name. Kluger's letter had the air of dismissal in taking his case to its logical conclusion without any room for compromise. Kluger knew of the agreement 13 years before. Boucher would not be able to consent because of his work at the *Times*.

Boucher wrote back to Kluger, explaining his position and suggesting compromises, but Kluger was adamant in his demands for "Anthony Boucher" to appear on the *Herald-Tribune's* column. Kluger felt that the pen name suggested a second-class status for the *New York Herald-Tribune* as opposed to the *Times*, which got to use Boucher's "real" name.

During his tenure at the *Herald-Tribune*, Boucher also developed his own outlet for science-fiction and fantasy reviews when he and McComas started *The Magazine of Fantasy & Science Fiction*.

While Boucher and McComas were co-editors of the magazine, the review column, entitled "Recommended Reading," was listed as "by the editors" despite Boucher's obvious touches. Once McComas reduced his role at the magazine, Boucher used his own name on the column. Since Boucher was the reviewer as well as the editor of the magazine, there was no frustration over the size or frequency of the column. In this example, Boucher reviews Tolkien's latest work.

> J.R.R. Tolkien's fantasy adventure novel THE TWO TOWERS is approximately as long as three issues of this magazine, and it is only a fragment, the midsection of a trilogy with the over-all title of The Lord of the Rings of which Part I: The Fellowship of the Ring was even longer.[23]

Boucher included his own work in this November 1955 column where he became editor, critic, and subject of review. Boucher was careful to introduce, not puff up, his own work, allowing readers to make up their own minds about his collection of short stories.

> Without review, I should like (hopefully) to call your attention to my own collection, *Far and Away* (Ballantine, 35 cents).... Comments eagerly welcomed; in this case, you are the reviewer. Please let me know your verdict.[24]

Much like his introductions to the yearly best of collections for *The Magazine of Fantasy & Science Fiction*, Boucher used his interest in current events to write about the science and technology in what was being written. The ramifications of space travel had long fascinated Boucher.

> When Sputnik I was launched five months ago, a number of writers must have been at work on stories which were immediately outdated. I've been wondering what would become of such works-in-progress abruptly contradicted by history, and Charles Eric Maine's Spaceways Satellite provides the surprising answer: They get published.[25]

The big time

Boucher's longest job, that of mystery reviewer for the *New York Times Book Review*, began inauspiciously. Boucher had heard of an opening at the paper and had lobbied through his friends, Denis Green and Avram Davidson, for the position. Their efforts paid off. Just after the first of the year in 1949, Herbert Lyons, acting editor at the *New York Times Book Review (NYTBR)*, wrote to Boucher saying he had been recommended and inquiring as to whether or not Boucher had a mystery reviewing gig.

At the time, Boucher was only reviewing for *Ellery Queen's Mystery Magazine* mystery-wise, and the *Los Angeles Daily News* for fantasy and science-fiction. Boucher quickly wrote to Dannay who expressed no reservations about Boucher adding another, prestigious review organ to his list of accomplishments.

Boucher replied within days to Lyon's request for information regarding his other jobs. "Reviewing is a craft I find absorbing (I only regret that it is economically unfeasible as a fulltime profession.)"[26]

According to Lyons, the *New York Times* had not been satisfied with mystery reviews in a long time. The paper of record wanted livelier critiques of the books without revealing important plot points that would ruin the book for readers. Lyons enclosed two "practice" mysteries for Boucher to review. Boucher hurriedly reviewed the books and only in the cover letter to the first set of reviews did he mention the terms of the payment scale.

Lyons thought that Boucher was trying too hard in the first few reviews, and suggested that he loosen up a bit. Tongue-in-cheek, he suggested a move to New York City where the pace was slower. Lyons was also concerned that Boucher was too kind in his reviews. Boucher replied, "Do not get the impression that I am overly kindhearted. It was merely chance that you've picked to send me 3 of the rather few books that I've thought well of this season, which has largely been a grisly one."[27]

Boucher and Lyon spent a few weeks discussing what was expected from a reviewer in the *New York Times*. Boucher summarized their discussions as such:

> The main purposes of mystery-reviewing, it seems to me, are three, and probably in this order:
> A) to give the reader a clear idea of whether he wants to read this book.
> B) To provide a column that makes entertaining reading.
> C) To attempt, not too obtrusively, a little responsible criticism and evaluation of standards and trends.
> To which I suppose one should realistically add:
> D) to provide (if the book deserves) succinct praise which the publisher can quote in blurbs and ads.[28]

Since the paper didn't have clear guidelines for the appearance of the column, Boucher tried several approaches to handling multiple reviews each week. For one of his first columns, Boucher wrote and submitted three different versions of the column with different introductions and different styles to the column. When he didn't hear back from Lyons in weeks, Boucher grew very nervous about his job.

The pair finally came to an agreement on how the column should look. The *Times* did not want to see a bulleted list of reviews. Instead, they wanted a short introduction that tied the current trends in mystery to the books being reviewed. In requesting this format, the *Times* allowed Boucher to continue to subcategorize books. In many of the columns, Boucher selected two or three books in the same vein to discuss.

After settling on a format, Boucher was finally able to relax somewhat about his new position. In a letter to Manfred Lee, Boucher wrote: "The *NY Times* is trying me out as a mystery reviewer. After the *Chronicle* it's a delight to be paid real folding money."[29] However, the stress of the last few months with his uncertain income and the audition for the *Times* left Boucher worn out. He spent the better part of the next month at 29 Palms recuperating from a long-persisting asthma attack.

Once settled, Lyons began asking Boucher for a number of pieces beyond the columns as well. One of his first assignments for the paper was to write a longer piece on Raymond Chandler's new book, *The Little Sister*. Given Chandler's reputation, the piece was run "up front" in the *NYTBR*. Boucher didn't think the book was up to Chandler's normal standards and panned the book, disputing some of the contention that he was too nice in his reviews.

Boucher later talked about the difficulties in working for a newspaper and the occasional demands made on him to review certain books. Boucher was extremely protective of his reputation for fairness and his immunity from sales representatives from the publication.

> In short, I've been around, & I know nothing about venality in American reviewing. In additions to mysteries & s f, I've done a good deal of general reviewing; & never have I been pressured to express anything other than my own considered opinion."
>
> "On exceedingly rare occasions — possibly a half dozen times in almost 2 decades — I have been asked to review a book I had planned to skip, or to write a long review instead of a short one, presumably to keep an advertiser happy — though I don't understand just why he shd be happy to see an unfavorable opinion expressed at greater length.[30]

Shortly after the Chandler review, Lyons asked for a round-up of the current trends in the mystery story along with 12–15 good examples from

1949. Again in the trends piece, Boucher divided up the books into categories. He split out books into suspense, cold war, social consciousness, and old masters.

Although the *Times* used Boucher on a regular basis, he was not the only mystery reviewer for the newspaper at that time. The *Times* had contracted with a second reviewer at the same time to take on part of the workload. Elizabeth Bullock, who had been Boucher's fellow reviewer at the *Chicago Sun-Times* before she became a mystery editor at Farrar & Rinehart, split the duties of mystery reviewing for the *NYTBR*. Boucher knew Liz well and looked her up during his trips to New York City. Bullock did come in handy for Boucher; when *The Marble Forest* came out in 1950, Boucher was able to send the book to her to be reviewed. Boucher wasn't fond of the idea of two reviewers. He felt that the teaming would only confuse the readers of the column, since they would not know which critic had provided the reviews and whether or not, the reader agreed with the views of the critic on the book.

Harvey Breit, long-time book reviewer for the *Times*, replaced Lyons briefly in 1949 before Francis Brown was named editor in November of that year.

Unlike some of the other papers where a change in management meant the end of Boucher's work, the new editor wanted to go in a different direction than the two-reviewer column. In 1951, Boucher traveled to New York City and talked to Brown about taking over sole duties for the review column. After the meeting, Brown wrote to Boucher saying that they wanted to have him be the sole reviewer; they wanted a four month trial basis for the column before making a final decision. Boucher's pay would go up to $75 an appearance, providing a more stable income for the family. Liz Bullock only had kind comments for Boucher and his talent and gracefully bowed out.

After several years of reviewing in smaller markets and occasional pieces for the *New York Times*, Boucher was selected to be the primary mystery reviewer for the paper of record. Anthony Boucher's mystery fiction column, "Criminals at Large," made its debut in the *New York Times* on July 1, 1951. Over the next 17 years Boucher contributed 852 columns, discussing approximately six novels each week, and providing a yearly round-up of the best books. He eventually became the foremost mystery critic in America — perhaps in the world.

Besides having the ear of most of the reading world with his column in the *New York Times*, Boucher also had the backing of the two preeminent critics of the day: Howard Haycraft and Fred Dannay. Haycraft had been responsible for the history of the genre books and had written reviews for *Ellery Queen's Mystery Magazine* until 1948. Dannay, as Queen, had the attention of most of the hardcore mystery fans with his magazine. As a result, Boucher represented an entrée into field to many readers who relied on his ability to review and suggest many works to these readers. Boucher would again take over reviewing for *Ellery Queen's Mystery Magazine*, meaning that he had the role of critic for the leading vehicle for general readers and the leading magazine for mystery readers as well. It was no wonder that Boucher's quotes were coveted as blurbs for new releases.

Boucher used his pulpit wisely, not only recommending examples of his favorite puzzle stories, but also writing about all subgenres of mysteries. Boucher was the first to discover many new authors as a critic, just as he had introduced America to Borges through his translations when only a few people knew of the Argentine author before 1948. In one column he wrote, "there is a peak-in-Darien thrill about those moments when you suddenly realize that look, you are reading the first novel of a major contender."[31]

Authors as diverse as Ira Levin, H.R.F. Keating, and Ed McBain were routinely touted in Boucher's columns long before they were discovered and adopted by most of the mainstream critics. He was one of the early proclaimers of Ross Macdonald's talent. Boucher saw that the author had something special to offer the hardboiled genre. This was many years before Macdonald hit the bestsellers list following the popular, film adaptations of his novels in the 1960s.

> The entrance upon this jaded scene two years ago of Ross Macdonald was very nearly as welcome as the emergence of Hammett in *Black Mask*.... Which makes this ... the best novel in the tough tradition that I've read since *Farewell, My Lovely* ... and possibly since *The Maltese Falcon*.[32]

Boucher did not limit himself to proclaiming new talent, he helped create it. Just as Boucher had shepherded a number of careers while he was the editor of *The Magazine of Fantasy and Science Fiction*, Phyllis White credited her husband with helping a number of people in the genre. "He was a mentor. So many authors wrote to me after he had died saying that they had always written attempting to please him or feeling that he was looking over their shoulder, and not knowing how they would get along when he wasn't there."

Unlike today, where most reviewers limit contact with the authors they review, Boucher knew many of the authors he reviewed. Yet that didn't stop him from giving a poor review if he felt it was due. In this letter to Mary Collins, he pushes her to write a better book, one he knows she is capable of.

You aren't going to love me for this presumptuous letter. But since I've met, drunk with, and liked you, I feel that I owe you some explanation for the poor rating which *Sisters of Cain* gets in my column.

Hang it, you could write a damned good book, which is what makes your slipshod carelessness so exasperating. There's not one fragment of evidence in that entire opus to indicate Sophie as the murderer until she breaks down and is caught in a completely needless final attempt. And that isn't how one writes mystery novels.

You have Mrs. Rinehart's virtues. But must you swallow her vices too?

... All of which reinforces my conviction that only about three houses edit mysteries. The rest just publish them. For which reason I devoutly wish that you'd get the hell out of Scribner's as soon as your contract allows.[33]

All of his friendships and personal relationships might have caused problems for a reviewer, who is required to be scrupulous. In just a single column for the 1949 round-up, Boucher would have had to disclose his friendship with author Craig Rice along with that of about 10 other authors. He would also need to explain that his own pseudonym was H.H. Holmes, explaining his relationship to that famous murderer and why he intimately knew the case.

Boucher conscientiously disclosed his relationship to Elizabeth Bullock as a rival reviewer in his review, but he did not mention other tie-ins to his own career as a writer. Of course, in all fairness, the entire column would have consisted of disclaimers. Boucher knew most everyone.

There is no science to literary criticism and no single right answer. Reviewers disagree sharply among themselves. Ellery Queen has pointed out how small the area of agreement is in the "Best Mysteries of the Year" each year. Ten reviewers might give ten different best books. As Boucher pointed out while trying to become the sole reviewer for the *Times*, readers may find a particular reviewer with whom they agree and make choices according to that reviewer's recommendations.

Even as the premiere mystery critic of his day, Boucher met with resistance. Each reviewer walks a fine line between constant praise and continual disparagement. The critic cannot be too gentle or too rough on any one book, or his career can be tarnished as well. The reviewer's comments are dismissed as either sycophantic or snobbish, respectively.

Additionally, critics are often treated like teachers. *Those who can, do; those who can't, review.* Many reviewers are thought to be frustrated authors, feeding their sour grapes to the authors who are published. This was not the case with Boucher. He had published seven novels and myriad short stories by this point. While Boucher did not have a publishing axe to grind, many authors were concerned early on that Boucher's sole preference would be the same type of great detective, locked room puzzles that he had written.

Boucher was upfront in his likes and dislikes. Boucher wrote about his beloved locked room mysteries. "Many will agree with Sally Benson in a recent New Yorker that it is a threadbare formula; others, with me loudly at their head, will maintain that it is no more threadbare than a fugue, a sonnet or any other classically restricted form."[34]

Of course, given that he had penned several novels of puzzles and great detectives, Boucher was inclined to enjoy the old-fashioned mysteries. However, that didn't stop him from praising spy fiction, hardboiled crimes, and suspense novels. His only two pet peeves, which he openly admitted, were Mickey Spillane (whose portrayal of women as sex objects and the unrefined violence of his works disgusted Boucher) and the Had-I-But-Known school of romantic suspense, in which the female lead, whom Boucher called the idiot heroine, walked into obvious trouble alone. That is not to say that Boucher didn't have other dislikes. He had several, including ostentatiously pedantic mysteries like those of S.S. Van Dine and his imitators.

Since critics often meet with resistance from authors and fans, many publications, including the *New York Herald-Tribune* for several years during Boucher's tenure at that newspaper, print anonymous reviews to protect their reviewers from attack. Named reviewers become targets for hate mail and angry authors. There is no refuge for them with dissatisfied authors.

Because Boucher's love of the genre was apparent, many people did not feel that his reviews were harsh enough. They expected the snarky reviews that Dorothy Parker raised to an art form. Many reviewers claim that it much easier to write a scathing review than a balanced review.

Boucher was not a meek critic who did not give negative reviews. According to Phyllis White, his first responsibility was to the reader who purchased for the reviewed books, and that speaking kindly of everything served no purpose. Boucher lauded books that worked and wasn't afraid to criticize any author from Christie to Stout.

Of course, not everyone agreed with his reviews, especially authors who were not given fulsome praises. In his work "The Reviewing of Mystery Novels," Boucher wrote, "And never write an indignant letter complaining about a bad review. Such letters almost always become vulgar and scurrilous, and sound like documents from a paranoid case history. They cannot possibly change the reviewer's mind about the book in question, and no matter how much he strives for impartiality, they're bound to prejudice him somewhat against your later books."

In a correspondence with author and editor Jacques Barzun following a negative review of Barzun's anthology, *Delights of Detection*, Barzun attacks some of Boucher's ideas about the value of setting in mysteries to give historians a feel for a time and place, "how far can you really maintain that the Holmes stories are great because of their historical contents. Do you advise people to read War and Peace because it throws light on Napoleon's Russian campaign.... Hence my objections to you recommending a tale of detection on the ground that it furnishes information otherwise hard for the lay reader to come by."[35]

Boucher was not one to retreat from criticism, especially about his professional works. He responded promptly, "Naturally I do not warm to the suggestion that my reviews are dictated by personal animus. Actually the reverse is true; in the exceedingly few cases in which I do personally dislike a fellow professional, I find myself leaning over backwards to discern some merit in his work.

"I panned your antho (& rather gently, it seemed to me) for one simple reason: I thought it was a poor book. Several of my reasons I gave in the review...."[36]

Barzun was not mollified by Boucher's response and counterattacked the reviewer personally. "No one, it seems to me, gets your goat as good as I do. Before you reviewed my book you used up space to say that I became indignant whenever you praise a story for its setting. This exaggeration (to put it gently) obviously springs not from disagreement but from annoyance."[37]

Boucher tried to write back to Barzun, but his pique had begun to show with the correspondence. "You might feel less persecuted if you wd (sic) read what I write ... I objected to a story which goes so far as to reveal at the end a murderer whom the reader has never heard of, detected by a clue which he has not been told."[38]

Boucher realized that this exchange could on indefinitely and chose to end the letter with a change of subject, hoping to get the offended author off the subject of his own works and how they deserved constant praise.

One of the changes Boucher made to the policy at the *New York Times* was to start reviewing paperback originals. These books had long been looked at as cheap genre fiction and not worthy of review in the major outlets. Boucher recognized that some of the work was quite good. However, that was not good enough for Michael Avallone who wanted to see his own works reviewed in "Criminals at Large."

> Robespierre:
> The enclosed goodies are for you.
> For two years now, I have kept silent, allowing you some prime shots at me in your column plus the disgusting factor of no-review.
> NAL, Avon, and Ace for instance now are certain you don't review Avallone.
> Call it dreck, make your own excuses — but I let history judge us both. Let the school boys of tomorrow judge us.
> You scuttled The Third Degree [MWA's newsletter] and now we're lucky if we get the rag six times a year [Avallone had edited The Third Degree from 1962–1965].³⁹

Despite the reputation of being too kind in his reviews, any regular reader of "Criminals at Large" knew that Boucher wasn't afraid of telling it how it was in his opinion. His Catholic background was not in line with the growing trend in certain subgenres to portray women as whores and to use the most graphic language to describe the sleuth's dealings with these women. Some of the more graphic fiction bordered on the sadism that Boucher abhorred in Spillane.

As mentioned earlier, the Spillane books were antithetical to most things Boucher held dear. The right wing, blood-and-guts, sexist writings of Spillane went against most of Boucher's personal beliefs. The lack of plot continuity and pacing grated against what Boucher saw as a Renaissance of mystery fiction, one that he personally encouraged. In this review of a Spillane novel, Boucher leaves no doubt to his own feelings about the book.

> Fair warning: There is a new book by Mickey. It is called *The Long Wait* (Dutton).... For that reason, and for some slight ingenuity in its denouement, it may rank as the best Spillane — which is the faintest praise this department ever bestowed.⁴⁰

Shortly after Boucher was asked to review for the *New York Times*, the Mystery Writers of America elected him their President for 1951. With his new duties, Boucher was concerned that the position would take up too much of his time. However, he was assured that the position have limited duties, and he was elected to the position by MWA's membership.

He was awarded his third Edgar for mystery criticism in 1953. Boucher wrote to tell Fred Dannay of the honor. "It isn't officially released yet, but there's no harm in telling you (since you probably know anyway) that I got another Edgar for criticism. That means out of 8 annual Edgars to date, I've had it 3 times — 1945 (Chronicle), 1949 (EQMM & Times), 1952 (Times). As abominable a monopoly as you've held on the short story award."⁴¹

While Boucher was enjoying his success with the *Times*, he continued to try to make money through other efforts, including reviewing. *Manhunt* magazine approached Boucher about reviewing for their magazine. Boucher had been introduced to the editor via *Verdict*, one of *Manhunt*'s companion magazines for the St. John Publishing firm. *Verdict* was supposed to run "Coffin Corner" by H.H. Holmes, but the story was not run because the magazine was axed before the story could appear.

Boucher worked with Hal Walker at *Manhunt* in 1953. He only wrote two columns for the magazine before being cut; his third column crossed paths with the rejection letter in the mail. Hal Walker wrote that the publisher, Mr. St. John, said to kill the book review column without explanation.

Boucher frequently used his position as mystery critic to support the genre in any way he could. In 1966, he encouraged Allen Hubin in his creation of the first mystery fan magazine, *The Armchair Detective*. Hubin had begun a correspondence with Boucher, complimenting the critic's work for the *Times*.

> I have thoroughly enjoyed the Times Book Review for the past three years, and the compelling reason for my subscription has been your column of crime fiction reviews. Nowhere else have I read such knowledgeable and informative review, where the reviewer brings such a large fund of knowledge about the genre to the task, where present and past trends of crime fiction writing are considered with regard to the book at hand....[42]

In a letter to Boucher the following year, Hubin discussed the publication of a mystery journal to be published quarterly "devoted to the appreciation of mystery, detective and suspense fiction." He sent Boucher a copy of the first issue of *The Armchair Detective*; Boucher reviewed the magazine in his *New York Times* column.

It took Boucher almost four months to reply to Hubin's submission. He explained, "I've been ill a good deal this year and neglecting my correspondence shamefully." Being Boucher, he even found a few niggling errors in the first issue. Subscriptions for the magazine skyrocketed after the column appeared. Hubin would later credit Boucher for helping to get the magazine off the ground.

To complete the monumental task of reading eight to ten books a week as well as review them, Boucher made good use of speed-reading skills as well as a unique filing system of all the books he'd ever read. Using 3" × 5" index cards, Boucher kept notes on each story that he read. He used abbreviations to indicate parts of the story such as "OH" for "Our Hero" and "IH" for "Idiot Heroine," a phrase that turned up more than once in some of the romantic suspense novels. Using his note cards which numbered nearly 3000 by the time of his death, he wrote a column each week for the better part of seventeen years.

Even given his talent for reading, the pace could grate on him. Boucher complained in 1958 about, "the incredible overpublication of whodunits this fall — I've been covering from 7 to 10 a week and am that far behind still."

Since Boucher had a wealth of information on the genre at his fingertips, many mystery fans used him as a source of information on the genre. Boucher received a multitude of letters asking him obscure questions about the genre, its trends and its history. Boucher acted as a one-man library information desk. He tried, as possible, to answer each query personally although a response could sometimes take months to receive.

In one letter, Boucher addresses the issue of word counts in more recent novels for a writer. "The mystery novel has emphatically been getting shorter since the days of Van Dine & early Queen, & I at least think it's a Good Thing. The attached list of shorties certainly includes some of the worst of the year ... but also some of the best. And if John Dickson Carr & Michael Innes insist on an enormous number of words ... so do Gregory Tree & Mickey Spillane."[43]

In another instance, Boucher discussed with another reviewer the titles of books which are mentioned in mysteries, but do not exist in real life. This type of arcane information is usually just known by the hard-core fans. "In Chap 27 of *The Dutch Shoe Mystery* (page 240 of the PocketBook edition) EQ is 'writing away at a detective novel' ... & the mysterious JJMcC adds in a footnote 'The manuscript of Murder of the Marionettes, one of the detective stories Ellery wrote under his own name.' So now we know at least 1 title!"[44]

Perhaps because of his busy schedule, Boucher continued to have health problems. Boucher had to give up typing for a few days after having hand surgery. Since his livelihood came from typed copy, a speedy recovery was needed. "'Look, I can type! & and only 8 days after my operation. Have to take it moderately easy because the finger (stitches removed yesterday) start hurting after too long; but I'm far from being as helpless as I expected to be."[45]

Boucher's asthma continued to give him problems as well. He professed to finding a new doctor who kept "experimenting with new drugs and methods." He quit smoking for several months in 1958 to reduce the problems brought on by asthma and tobacco smoke. However, he returned to smoking within a few months and kept at it for the rest of his life. The result was that it took several hours in the morning for Boucher to get his breathing regulated, making speaking engagements and breakfast meetings near impossible.

With all of the health issues in his own life, Boucher was not above putting personal details in his column. His health had slowly deteriorated, and he frequently spent time in bed, reading. While his disabilities allowed him to read, his writing output was severely limited in these times. In this column, Boucher discussed the "reality" of the hardboiled novels vs. the older family manor murders. In the end, he decided that neither group necessarily better reflected the average people of the times.

> I have just spent an invalid weekend reading almost nothing but mysteries of the hard-boiled school. My impression at the moment, from which I may perhaps to some extent recover, is that an infinite weight must rest upon the consciences of Dashiell Hammett, for what he fathered, and Raymond Chandler....[46]

In the last few years of his life, Boucher found that he had to stop participating in a number of activities that he had found worthy in the past. His work in the Democratic Party was over by that time. Though he had been a member of the Democratic State Central Committee from the 18th Assembly District and 7th Congressional District, he had to stop his party activities. The work had meant trips to Fresno for political caucus and to Sacramento for state issues.

Boucher also tried taking it easy by giving up on other projects as well. "I keep making valiant resolves (which my doctor encourages) about not taking on any more commitments, but your suggestion is too tempting."[47]

Boucher's health took a turn for the worse in the middle 1960s. He'd added hypertension, which is often a side effect of certain asthma medications, to his growing list of ailments. In 1965, he wrote a fan, "Matters of health and overwork make it really impossible for me to undertake anything in the way of serious correspondence."[48]

Boucher continued his correspondence and weekly poker games with a small number of close friends. In 1963, Boucher shared with his friends the impending marriage of his son, James, to a Catholic girl. "[He] is pinned (much to his surprise) to a Catholic girl, which will shatter a 3-generation history of mixed marriages."

Even with his health problems, Boucher felt a need to continue his work with some social cause groups. He worked with Citizens against Legalized Murder, an anti-capital punishment group until 1967 when he could no longer manage the time or the trips. The student group, which met in

Berkeley, protested the fact that California was a leader in capital punishment at the time.

Boucher also did some work for the ACLU. In an ironical note, Boucher had to help the group protest the banning of Mickey Spillane books from California state parks. Given Boucher's feelings towards the author, it was a tough pill to swallow. "The authorities on Treasure Island [in the San Francisco Bay] have banned the sale of the 25¢ Signet editions of the novels of Mickey Spillane because of the protest of the chaplain's wife.... Now the Spillane novels are, frankly, abominable. I have referred to them in my *NY Times* reviews as a deliberate attempt to see how far uncensored publishing can go."[49]

Opera and Golden Voices

Boucher's love of music was apparent from the appearance of recording artists, records and divas in his short stories and radio plays. However, he couldn't express his full appreciation of the operatic voices of the 20th century through fiction so he looked for other outlets for his love of opera.

Boucher had been attending opera since his youth and had uncanny recall for most of what he'd seen and heard. Arthur Bloomfield of the *San Francisco Examiner* remembered Boucher's memory. "When I was preparing a book on the San Francisco Opera he gave me exceptionally vivid accounts of performances which took place many years ago."[50]

As a young man, Boucher had created the core of his record collection when newer orthophonic records were introduced. Old acoustic records were sold off for next to nothing, much like how CDs replaced vinyl records. Boucher acquired hundreds of these 78rpm records of the great performers of the golden age of opera. As an adult, Boucher added approximately 250 records per year to his collection. He frequented thrift shops when he was well enough and also received catalogs from specialty dealers.

By 1949, Boucher had acquired over 3,500 recordings, concentrating on the operatic recordings from the first quarter of the twentieth century. By the time of his death, he had accumulated 9,000 recordings in his personal collection. His enthusiasm had been contagious. Following her husband's death, Phyllis amassed another 4,000 records in her own library.

The University of California Santa Barbara acquired Boucher's collection after his death. The collection was so massive that the university had to send multiple temperature-controlled rigs to the house to safely transport the records. The weight of the records was so great that UCSB had to shore up the room which was to house the collection.

Nearly every singer of the Golden Age of opera was represented in Boucher's collection. In addition to American and Western European singers, his collection held recordings by performers from the Imperial Russian Court, along with Polish, Czech, Dutch and Hungarian artists seldom found outside of Europe. Many lesser known singers and unfamiliar operas and arias were included in his collection, and in many cases Boucher possessed multiple interpretations of a particular aria for comparison

In 1949, Boucher decided to share his collection with the Bay Area. He wrote and introduced himself to the producers at a new radio station in the Berkeley area, KPFA-FM. As a result, he became the host of a weekly radio program that appeared on KPFA-FM on Sundays at 8:30 P.M. The name of the show was *Golden Voices,* and it featured great voices from the twentieth century found in Boucher's extensive record collection.

Nearly every week from 1949 to his death in 1968, Boucher walked to the studio from his home, carrying a stack of records for that week's show. He taped his commentary for the program and left his records. Boucher used a stopwatch to time his commentary and recordings at the house to ensure that the program did not run over or run short.

Boucher at the mike at KPFA-FM (courtesy the White family).

The small station's future looked bleak those first few years of operation. KPFA-FM was off the air briefly in late 1950 and early 1951, due to financial difficulties. The station returned to the air in May 1951. Throughout its first 9 years, the station held numerous appeals for emergency funds to stay on the air. By 1959, these problems seemed to be resolved.

Despite making it look easy, Boucher took hours to perfect each show. He worked with Lewis Hill at KPFA. Each week, he had to submit the list of recordings to the station to be cleared for copyright before he could play those recordings. In some cases, it was easy to find who owned the material. In other cases, Boucher had to apply to the recording artist for permission to play the piece. Boucher communicated with a number of his idols and struck up a friendship with more than one operatic star.

Bloomfield remembered: "I still marvel at the absolute accuracy with which he prepared and presented his weekly half-hour program. Twenty-nine minutes and thirty second was always that — no more, no less, records always in their proper jacket and always in order, never an error and never a mispronunciation. All this — I suspect — Tony took as quote a matter of course, nothing unusual, just the way it ought to be done."[51]

Not only did Boucher handle the permissions and the planning of each week's show, he played promoter and public relations person as well. He wrote to the local papers and to friends of the opera about his show. He often let performers know that their works would be on his show. Boucher wrote to Geraldine Farrar about a show dedicated to her recordings. He began friendships with many Bay Area opera fans, who offered more suggestions for programs than weeks in a year.

Boucher also held a literary review program on KPFA-FM. He often invited local authors to appear on his show, many of whom were leftist. The Un-American Activities Committee run by the California's State Senate under the control of Senator Hugh Burns noticed Boucher's program. Boucher had the distinction of being noticed twice by the committee. He was cited in the committee's report under the name Boucher for his work at KPFA and also as William White for his political work.

Not content with just the airwaves, Boucher began writing for *Opera News* in 1950. He started with an article combining two of his passions, "Opera and Murder." Despite the magazine's enthusiasm for the article, the piece grew outdated in the years it waited for publication at *Opera News*. Boucher rewrote the article again at the beginning of 1960 when he was offered $50 for it again by *Opera News*. However, the article remained unpublished until it was later included in *Multiplying Villainies* in 1973.

Boucher included a similar column in his *Chronicle* work, discussing the murders that drive many of the most famous operas. "Last Friday the annual crime season opened at the War Memorial Opera House ... composers of opera have always found it difficult to work their characters up to the proper pitch without a murder or two."[52]

Boucher's passion for combining mystery and opera did not end there. Boucher even discussed the possibility of creating an opera from *The Maltese Falcon* after testifying in the Warner Brothers' trial regarding the rights to the famous book.

Boucher and Phyllis had been able to afford first night performances dating back to the time when Boucher was writing for three radio programs. The couple enjoyed the nights out, dressing in white tie and tails and formal gowns for the evening. Since he had become a fixture at the opera, Boucher began writing critiques of the San Francisco Opera season for *Opera News*.

Frank Merkling often had to dun Boucher for articles, which he wrote more for love than income. He chided Boucher on occasion for getting into too much "technical analysis" of specific operas rather than providing information on the songs and general storyline. Boucher often ran late and didn't have photos to accompany the piece.

Boucher also wrote a number of articles about individual artists. Near the end of his own life, Boucher wrote an obituary on Chief Caupolican, a baritone who lived in the San Francisco area. Caupolican was best known for his two seasons at the Met in the 1920s.

Boucher declared that he was the world's only, and therefore foremost, authority on Caupolican. Boucher had met Caupolican through *Golden Voices* and the two had shared many hours discussing opera. Born Emile Barrangon, Chief Caupolican was friend to both Boucher and his wife. By the time that their correspondence began in the early 1950s, Caupolican had already begun to lose his voice. In one letter to the couple, Caupolican apologized for not being in better voice to support Phyllis during a performance.

The baritone was not one to slow down with the increasing years. Caupolican married again at the age of 83 and later moved to Seattle with his new bride. He died in 1968 at the age of 93, just weeks before Boucher's own death.

Boucher did not limit himself to print and radio. He also went on television regarding opera as well. Boucher acted as host, interviewer and part-time producer for "Invitation to Opera" at KQED-TV. He also appeared on KQED's "Critics' Circle" program with opera reviews. Most of the shows dealt with the San Francisco Opera and the local opera scene.

Being Boucher, his goal was never to flaunt his own encyclopedic knowledge of opera. Instead, Boucher led his guests through questions which allowed the person being interviewed to be shown in the best light, at ease and comfortable during the program.

The end and beyond

Boucher's health began to fail in early 1968. In February and March of 1968, Boucher sent his columns via night press wire "because of illness earlier in the week." This marked the first time that his column had not been sent on time for publication. Boucher was well enough to savage Agatha Christie's *Endless Night* and another critic's remarks that had called the book "groundbreaking." Boucher felt that the book didn't play fair with the reader in the same manner that *The Murder of Roger Ackroyd* had.

Boucher produced his last column for *The New York Times* for April 21, 1968, his 852nd column for the paper of record. To the end, Boucher divided up books into subgenres. In that last column, he discussed the police procedural novel, and then went on to discuss Elizabeth Linington and Dorothy Uhnak.

For the following two weeks, Phyllis wrote to Francis Brown, editor of the *New York Times Book Review*, via collect letter, explaining why there would be no column that week. "Lung and Kidney problems. Also still under investigation, tentative estimate, 2-month illness." The following week the message was terser. "Boucher ill. No column this week."

His last ailment came on fast; Boucher suffered a fall and was rushed to the hospital with a broken rib. The X-rays revealed some problems in the lungs and he remained in the hospital. Phyllis White would later remember his last days: "He never knew about the cancer because it was very hard to diagnose him and by the time that they figured it out, he was out of it and couldn't be told anything. One of the doctors said to me, while they were all trying to figure out what was the matter with him, 'that everybody and his brother wants to get in on this.' I thought how much my husband would have enjoyed that. Like someone saying with relish, 'this will puzzle them at Scotland Yard.'" Boucher was diagnosed as having cancer, and he passed away within days.

Anthony Boucher died of lung cancer on April 29, 1968, at the Kaiser

Foundation Hospital. Despite his attacks of asthma, Boucher had been a lifetime smoker. He was frequently seen holding a pipe in family photos.

The outpouring of grief was tremendous. Boucher received praise and obituaries in *The New York Times, The Washington Post, Ellery Queen's Mystery Magazine*, and *The Magazine of Fantasy & Science Fiction*. Still, articles and obituaries did not seem to be sufficient for the man who had given so much to two genres.

The family held a service for Boucher at St. Augustine's. Boucher's body had already been cremated, so there was no casket at the service. Boucher's ashes were scattered at sea within a few days of the ceremony.

Immediately following his death, a group of authors who had been gently edited by Boucher in *The Magazine of Fantasy & Science Fiction* wanted to pay tribute to the editor. At the West Coast Science Fantasy Conference in July 1969, Len and June Moffat along with Bruce Pelz decided to sponsor a mystery conference. In the science-fiction and fantasy genres, fan conferences were quite common at that time. Yet there was nothing similar in the mystery world.

Indeed, the Moffats and Boucher had met at the 1958 World Science Fiction Convention in the Los Angeles area. Boucher took his family to many of the conferences over the years and made some fast friends among the people who wrote for *The Magazine of Fantasy & Science Fiction*. The trio along with Chuck Crayne were members of the Los Angeles Science Fiction Society (LASFS). All of them were familiar with hosting science-fiction conferences and thought that the mystery community needed one of its own.

The group decided to name the convention after Boucher, since he had only recently passed away. With Boucher's kindness to new authors and his connections, the conference was soon called Bouchercon. Phyllis White was asked for her permission to allow them to name the conference in Boucher's honor. She graciously allowed them, feeling flattered that others wanted to remember her husband. Phyllis was honored by receiving the first membership to Bouchercon and was awarded Member Number One for all following Bouchercons.

The first Bouchercon, also more formally known as the World Mystery Convention or the Anthony Boucher Memorial Mystery Convention, was held on Memorial Day weekend in 1970 in Los Angeles. This first convention did not resemble the current gathering in many respects. The timing was earlier in the year and in a constant location.

Eighty-two people attended that first effort. Robert Bloch, of *Psycho* fame, was the guest of honor at that first Bouchercon. Bloch and Boucher were old friends who had attended several conferences together. Attendees included Karen and Poul Anderson, Jon L. Breen, and Larry Niven.

The present, autumn timing of the conference began the following year. The convention date was moved to the fall as not to conflict with the Mystery Writers of America's Edgar Dinners in April. In 1971, 76 people attended the conference in Los Angeles with Bruce Pelz chairing the convention. The following year 93 people attended the conference with the Moffats and Pelz co-chairing.

For its fourth year, the conference moved to Boston and its regular October timeframe. The conference was still small and had an advanced membership of only 66. The program guide featured a mystery quiz and only two ads.

Beginning with Boston, the location of the convention changed each year. According to the convention's by-laws, Bouchercon now rotates between an Eastern location, a Midwest venue, and a Western location every three years. This allows settings as diverse as Nottingham and Anchorage to participate in the convention and to bring fans from all parts of the United States. Despite its title as the World Mystery Convention, only the U.S. and U.K. have held the convention to date.

The 1973 Bouchercon was marked by the publication of Boucher's selected criticism under the title *Multiplying Villainies*. The collection, edited by Francis M. Nevins, was the first of four books by Nevins detailing some of Boucher's best review columns. *Multiplying Villainies* begins with a tribute to Boucher by Helen McCloy, the well-known mystery novelist. She recounted stories of her first meetings with Boucher and his love of the genre.

Other anthologies were published that paid tribute to Boucher. Shortly after Boucher's death, his one-time partner in *The Magazine of Fantasy & Science Fiction*, J. Francis McComas, edited two anthologies that paid tribute to Boucher's gift. When approached about the anthologies, Phyllis thought it only fitting that McComas should serve as editor.

The first anthology was *Special Wonders,* which contained science-fiction and fantasy stories, while *Crimes and Misfortunes* had mystery short stories. Both books were published by Random House. The Nor Cal Chapter of MWA voted to take on the project, but stepped back from the project at the suggestion of the national office. Although McComas approached MWA about having its name on the cover, MWA declined saying that it could not do so without the book being an MWA anthology. As a result, they declined to be involved.

McComas purchased the use of the Boucher name for one dollar. All authors and editors worked for no compensation, and the funds went to Science-Fiction Writers of America or Mystery Writers of America, respectively. Each story was donated free of charge to the collection and contained a short piece on how the author had known Boucher and fond memories of the man. Since Phyllis had approved these two books, other suggested anthologies by Isaac Asimov and Judy Marril which were being considered by Doubleday at the same time, were scrapped.

While McComas was listed as the sole editor with Randall Garrett and Reg Bretnor assisting him, most of the correspondence was handled by Bretnor. In a curious fashion, each letter from Bretnor discusses his own wife's death from cancer the previous year as much or more as it did Boucher or the anthology.

The project had difficulties from the beginning. Boucher's long-time agent, Willis Wings, had semi-retired and was only consulting at the Collins-Knowlton-Wing, Inc agency. Phyllis grew frustrated with the project and contacted Wing. The agency wrote to Phyllis about their lack of efforts.

Wing was unhappy with the arrangement, which he still thought was with MWA. He felt that the group should have gone through his office. By bypassing his office, the anthologies had progressed without his input and guidance.

Reg Bretnor later explained to Phyllis and the agency that the anthology was not, and has never been, an MWA project, which was disingenuous at best. While the project was McComas' work, the proceeds benefited the organization and the MWA had originally been listed in the title of the anthology.

The end result was mixed. The two books have a number of great stories by well-known authors and Boucher's friends such as Poul Anderson, Asimov, Bradbury, DeFord, and William Nolan, along with wonderful anecdotes by each. However, Bretnor opted to include his own stories in the mystery anthology as well; however, Bretnor had never written for Boucher as a mystery author and could only say that he thought Boucher would like the selected story.

Even with the tributes and conventions, Boucher's most enduring legacy has been his impact on the following generation of mystery reviewers. Though no one individual critic has Boucher's influence in reviewing, the people who now review for *Ellery Queen's Mystery Magazine* and the *Times* bear a resemblance to Boucher's columns. Many of today's review columns are in a similar format to Boucher's work at *The New York Times*. Additionally, most reviewers do a yearly round-up of top books of the year as well. In today's world with the increase in the number of subgenres in mystery, Boucher's rule of treating each category with the same respect and consideration despite personal preferences is a standard that still holds true today.

Notes to Part I

The Man

1. F.M. Nevins, ed., *The Anthony Boucher Chronicles: Reviews and Commentary 1942–1947* (Shreveport, LA: Ramble House), iii.
2. Lenore Glen Offord, "A Boucher Portrait: Anthony Boucher as Seen by his Friends and Colleagues," *The Armchair Detective* January 1969: 69–76.
3. Boucher, Anthony. "Author, Author." *The Fanscient*: 4:2 (Summer 50):21–24.
4. F.M. Nevins, ed., *The Anthony Boucher Chronicles* ii.
5. F.M. Nevins, ed., *The Anthony Boucher Chronicles* iii.
6. Letter from Anthony Boucher to John Baxter, June 14, 1933. William A.P. White collection, courtesy Lilly Library, Indiana University, Bloomington, IN.
7. Letter from Anthony Boucher to Phyllis Price June 22, 1933. William A.P. White collection, courtesy Lilly Library, Indiana University, Bloomington, IN.
8. Letter from Anthony Boucher to John Baxter, June 14, 1933. William A.P. White collection, courtesy Lilly Library, Indiana University, Bloomington, IN.
9. Letter from Anthony Boucher to Phyllis Price, June 1934. William A.P. White collection, courtesy Lilly Library, Indiana University, Bloomington, IN.
10. Letter from MGM Studios to Anthony Boucher, December 10, 1934. William A.P. White collection, courtesy Lilly Library, Indiana University, Bloomington, IN.
11. Letter from Anthony Boucher to Phyllis Price, July 1934. William A.P. White collection, courtesy Lilly Library, Indiana University, Bloomington, IN.
12. Letter from Anthony Boucher to Phyllis Price, December 1935. William A.P. White collection, courtesy Lilly Library, Indiana University, Bloomington, IN.
13. Letter from Anthony Boucher to Phyllis Price, June 14, 1936. William A.P. White collection, courtesy Lilly Library, Indiana University, Bloomington, IN.
14. Letter from Anthony Boucher to Stuart Palmer, May 18, 1938. William A.P. White collection, courtesy Lilly Library, Indiana University, Bloomington, IN.
15. Letter from Anthony Boucher to Willis Kingsley Wing, January 6, 1942. William A.P. White collection, courtesy Lilly Library, Indiana University, Bloomington, IN.
16. Letter from Anthony Boucher to Stuart Palmer, June 15, 1944. William A.P. White collection, courtesy Lilly Library, Indiana University, Bloomington, IN.
17. Letter from Willis Kingsley Wing to Anthony Boucher, November 18, 1941. William A.P. White collection, courtesy Lilly Library, Indiana University, Bloomington, IN.
18. Letter from Anthony Boucher to Mick McComas, August 14, 1944. William A.P. White collection, courtesy Lilly Library, Indiana University, Bloomington, IN.
19. Letter from Mick McComas to Stuart Palmer, November 28, 1953. William A.P. White collection, courtesy Lilly Library, Indiana University, Bloomington, IN.
20. Letter from Anthony Boucher to Stuart Palmer, April 26, 1954. William A.P. White collection, courtesy Lilly Library, Indiana University, Bloomington, IN.
21. Letter from Anthony Boucher to Rex Stout, March 26, 1956. William A.P. White collection, courtesy Lilly Library, Indiana University, Bloomington, IN.
22. Lenore Glen Offord, "A Boucher Portrait" 69–76.

The Author

1. Anthony Boucher, *Exeunt Murderers*, 1st ed. (Carbondale: Southern Illinois University Press), 1983, viii.
2. *Ibid.* 187.
3. Letter from Anthony Boucher to Lee Wright, December 1936. William A.P. White collection. Courtesy Lilly Library, Indiana University, Bloomington, IN.
4. Anthony Boucher, *The Case of the Seven of Calvary* (New York: Simon and Schuster, 1937), 274–275.
5. *Ibid.*, 74.
6. *Ibid.*, 58–59.
7. Letter from Marie Rodel to Anthony Boucher, November 6, 1939. William A.P. White collection. Courtesy Lilly Library, Indiana University, Bloomington, IN.
8. Letter from Stuart Palmer to Anthony Boucher, May 17 1938. William A.P. White collection. Courtesy Lilly Library, Indiana University, Bloomington, IN.
9. Anthony Boucher, "Death on the Bay," unpublished ms. William A.P. White collection. Courtesy Lilly Library, Indiana University, Bloomington, IN.
10. *Ibid.*
11. Anthony Boucher, *The Case of the Crumpled Knave* (New York: Simon and Schuster, 1939), 40.
12. *Ibid.*, 98.
13. *Ibid.*, 44.
14. *Ibid.*, 94.
15. *Ibid.*, 114.
16. Anthony Boucher, *The Compleat Boucher* (Framingham, MA: New England Science Fiction Association, 1999), 50.
17. *Ibid.*, 81.
18. Anthony Boucher, *The Case of the Baker Street Irregulars* (New York: Simon and Schuster, 1940), 112.
19. *Ibid.*, 122.
20. Anthony Boucher, *The Case of the Solid Key* (New York: Simon and Schuster, 1941), 91.
21. *Ibid.*, 86.
22. Anthony Boucher, *The Case of the Seven Sneezes* (New York: Simon and Schuster, 1942), 7.
23. *Ibid.*, 20.
24. *Ibid.*, 55.
25. Anthony Boucher (written as H.H. Holmes), *Nine Times Nine* (New York: Duell, Sloan, and Pearce, 1940), 190.
26. *Ibid.*, 146.
27. *Ibid.*, 54–55.
28. Letter from John Dickson Carr to Anthony Boucher dated April 23, 1940. William A.P. White collection. Courtesy Lilly Library, Indiana University, Bloomington, IN.
29. Boucher, *Nine Times Nine*, 164–171.
30. Letter from Stuart Palmer to Anthony Boucher, September 3, 1940. William A.P. White collection. Courtesy Lilly Library, Indiana University, Bloomington, IN.
31. Jack Williamson, *Wonder's Child: My Life in Science Fiction* (New York, NY: St. Martin's Press, 1984), 129.
32. Anthony Boucher (written as H.H. Holmes), *Rocket to the Morgue* (New York: Duell, Sloan, and Pearce, 1942), front pages.
33. Letter from Fredric Dannay to Anthony Boucher, September 23, 1944. William A.P. White collection. Courtesy Lilly Library, Indiana University, Bloomington, IN.
34. Letter from Marie Rodell to Anthony Boucher. William A.P. White collection. Courtesy Lilly Library, Indiana University, Bloomington, IN.
35. Boucher, "Screwball Division" in *Exeunt Murderers*, 1st ed., 12.
36. Anthony Boucher, ed., *Four-and-Twenty Bloodhounds* (New York: Simon and Schuster, 1950), 217
37. Boucher, "Like Count Palmieri" in *Exeunt Murderers*, 1st ed., 102.
38. Boucher, "Crime Must Have a Stop" in *Exeunt Murderers*, 1st ed., 1983, 121.
39. Boucher, "Mystery for Christmas" in *Exeunt Murderers*, 1st ed., 1983, 200.
40. Boucher, "Ghost with a Gun" in *Exeunt Murderers*, 1st ed., 1983, 228.

The Editor

1. Letter from John W. Campbell to Anthony Boucher. William A.P. White collection. Courtesy Lilly Library, Indiana University, Bloomington, IN.
2. Lenore Glen Offord, "A Boucher Portrait," 69–76.
3. Letter from Anthony Boucher to John W. Campbell, May 20, 1942. William A.P. White collection. Courtesy Lilly Library, Indiana University, Bloomington, IN.
4. Letter from Anthony Boucher to Fred Dannay, February 1946. William A.P. White collection. Courtesy Lilly Library, Indiana University, Bloomington, IN.
5. Letter from Anthony Boucher to Georges Simenon, November 2, 1962. William A.P. White collection. Courtesy Lilly Library, Indiana University, Bloomington, IN.
6. Letter from Fred Dannay to Anthony Boucher, February 24, 1944. William A.P. White collection. Courtesy Lilly Library, Indiana University, Bloomington, IN.
7. Letter from Anthony Boucher to Fred

Dannay, March 18, 1944. William A.P. White collection. Courtesy Lilly Library, Indiana University, Bloomington, IN.

8. Letter from Fred Dannay to Anthony Boucher, September 23, 1944. William A.P. White collection. Courtesy Lilly Library, Indiana University, Bloomington, IN.

9. Letter from Fred Dannay to Anthony Boucher, November 22, 1948. William A.P. White collection. Courtesy Lilly Library, Indiana University, Bloomington, IN.

10. Letter from Anthony Boucher to Denis Green, 1945. William A.P. White collection. Courtesy Lilly Library, Indiana University, Bloomington, IN.

11. Letter from Anthony Boucher to Denis Green, March 12, 1945. William A.P. White collection. Courtesy Lilly Library, Indiana University, Bloomington, IN.

12. Letter from Denis Green to Anthony Boucher, February 9, 1943. William A.P. White collection. Courtesy Lilly Library, Indiana University, Bloomington, IN.

13. Letter from Anthony Boucher to August Derleth, September 12, 1950. William A.P. White collection. Courtesy Lilly Library, Indiana University, Bloomington, IN.

14. Letter from Denis Green to Anthony Boucher, March 22, 1945. William A.P. White collection. Courtesy Lilly Library, Indiana University, Bloomington, IN.

15. Letter from Anthony Boucher to Manfred Lee, October 14, 1946. William A.P. White collection. Courtesy Lilly Library, Indiana University, Bloomington, IN.

16. Letter from Anthony Boucher to Fred Dannay, October 16, 1946. William A.P. White collection. Courtesy Lilly Library, Indiana University, Bloomington, IN.

17. Letter from Anthony Boucher to Denis Green, March 17, 1949. William A.P. White collection. Courtesy Lilly Library, Indiana University, Bloomington, IN.

18. Letter from Manfred Lee to Anthony Boucher, April 11, 1945. William A.P. White collection. Courtesy Lilly Library, Indiana University, Bloomington, IN.

19. Letter from Manfred Lee to Anthony Boucher, May 17, 1945. William A.P. White collection. Courtesy Lilly Library, Indiana University, Bloomington, IN.

20. Letter from Anthony Boucher to Manfred Lee, April 8, 1946. William A.P. White collection. Lilly Library, Indiana University, Bloomington

21. Letter from Manfred Lee to Anthony Boucher, February 4, 1948. William A.P. White collection. Courtesy Lilly Library, Indiana University, Bloomington, IN.

22. Letter from Manfred Lee to Anthony Boucher, February 4, 1948. William A.P. White collection. Courtesy Lilly Library, Indiana University, Bloomington, IN.

23. Letter from Anthony Boucher to Manfred Lee, January 6, 1948. William A.P. White collection. Courtesy Lilly Library, Indiana University, Bloomington, IN.

24. Letter from Anthony Boucher to Manfred Lee, January 6, 1948. William A.P. White collection. Courtesy Lilly Library, Indiana University, Bloomington, IN.

25. Letter from Anthony Boucher to Manfred Lee, February 2, 1948. William A.P. White collection. Courtesy Lilly Library, Indiana University, Bloomington, IN.

26. Letter from Manfred Lee to Anthony Boucher, May 14, 1948. William A.P. White collection. Courtesy Lilly Library, Indiana University, Bloomington, IN.

27. Letter from Anthony Boucher to Lee Wright, July 9, 1949. William A.P. White collection. Courtesy Lilly Library, Indiana University, Bloomington, IN.

28. Jon Lellenberg, *Irregular Memories of the 'Thirties* (New York: Baker Street Irregulars, 1995), 242–243.

29. Jon Lellenberg, *Irregular Proceedings of the Mid 'Forties* (New York City: Baker Street Irregulars, 1995), 70.

30. *Ibid.*

31. Anthony Boucher, Introduction to Sir Author Conan Doyle, *The Valley of Fear* (New York City: Limited Editions Club, 1952), iii.

32. Letter from Lenore Glen Offord to Anthony Boucher, January 1945. William A.P. White collection. Courtesy Lilly Library, Indiana University, Bloomington, IN.

33. Lellenberg, *Irregular Proceedings of the Mid 'Forties*, 1995.

34. *Ibid.*

35. *Ibid.*, 79

36. Letter from Anthony Boucher to Joseph Jackson, August 14, 1952. William A.P. White collection. Courtesy Lilly Library, Indiana University, Bloomington, IN.

37. Letter from Anthony Boucher, April 1965. William A.P. White collection. Courtesy Lilly Library, Indiana University, Bloomington, IN.

38. Anthony Boucher, "Department of Criminal Investigations," *Ellery Queen's Mystery Magazine*, January 1947.

39. Letter from Anthony Boucher to Mick McComas, November 14, 1947. William A.P. White collection. Courtesy Lilly Library, Indiana University, Bloomington, IN.

40. Letter from Lenore Glen Offord to Anthony Boucher, March 25, 1951. William A.P. White collection. Courtesy Lilly Library, Indiana University, Bloomington, IN.

41. Letter from Lenore Glen Offord to Anthony Boucher, December 18, 1951. William A.P. White collection. Courtesy Lilly Library, Indiana University, Bloomington, IN.
42. *Remembering Anthony Boucher*; Bouchercon 25, a.k.a. Seattle, Seattle, WA (1994), 7.
43. Letter from Anthony Boucher to Jeanne Lloyd, 1961. William A.P. White collection. Courtesy Lilly Library, Indiana University, Bloomington, IN.
44. Letter from Anthony Boucher to Eric Ambler, October 22, 1964. William A.P. White collection. Courtesy Lilly Library, Indiana University, Bloomington, IN.
45. Letter from Anthony Boucher to Rex Stout, April 4, 1966. William A.P. White collection. Courtesy Lilly Library, Indiana University, Bloomington, IN.
46. Letter from Mick McComas to Anthony Boucher, July 1, 1944. William A.P. White collection. Courtesy Lilly Library, Indiana University, Bloomington, IN.
47. Letter from Mick McComas to Anthony Boucher, May 16, 1946. William A.P. White collection. Courtesy Lilly Library, Indiana University, Bloomington, IN.
48. Letter from Anthony Boucher to Joseph Ferman, October 5, 1947, in Annette McComas, *The Eureka Years* (New York: Bantam, 1982), 10.
49. Letter from Joe Ferman and American Mercury, November 10, 1947 in Annette McComas, *The Eureka Years* (New York: Bantam, 1982), 11.
50. Letter from Mick McComas to Anthony Boucher, June 7, 1951. William A.P. White collection. Courtesy Lilly Library, Indiana University, Bloomington, IN.
51. Letter from Mick McComas to Anthony Boucher, September 2, 1953. William A.P. White collection. Courtesy Lilly Library, Indiana University, Bloomington, IN.
52. Letter from Mick McComas to Anthony Boucher, October 2, 1953. William A.P. White collection. Courtesy Lilly Library, Indiana University, Bloomington, IN.
53. Letter from Anthony Boucher to Isaac Asimov, December 10, 1958. William A.P. White collection. Courtesy Lilly Library, Indiana University, Bloomington, IN.
54. Letter from Anthony Boucher to August Derleth, September 12, 1950. William A.P. White collection. Courtesy Lilly Library, Indiana University, Bloomington, IN.
55. Letter from Anthony Boucher to Lyle Cook (family attorney), April 20, 1956. William A.P. White collection. Courtesy Lilly Library, Indiana University, Bloomington, IN.
56. Letter from Isaac Asimov to Anthony Boucher, March 22, 1958. William A.P. White collection. Courtesy Lilly Library, Indiana University, Bloomington, IN.
57. Letter from Avram Davidson to Anthony Boucher, December 4, 1962. William A.P. White collection. Courtesy Lilly Library, Indiana University, Bloomington, IN.
58. Letter from Anthony Boucher to Richard Webb, May 27, 1942. William A.P. White collection. Courtesy Lilly Library, Indiana University, Bloomington, IN.
59. Letter from Anthony Boucher to Vincent Starrett, October 22, 1943. William A.P. White collection. Courtesy Lilly Library, Indiana University, Bloomington, IN.
60. Anthony Boucher, *The Pocket Book of True Crime Stories* (New York: Pocket, 1943), viii.
61. Anthony Boucher, *Great American Detective Stories* (Cleveland, OH: World, 1945), 12.
62. Letter from Clayton Rawson to Anthony Boucher, January 27, 1949. William A.P. White collection. Courtesy Lilly Library, Indiana University, Bloomington, IN.
63. Anthony Boucher, *Four and Twenty Bloodhounds* (London: Hammond, Hammond, 1950), vi.
64. Lenore Glen Offord, "A Boucher Portrait," 69–76.
65. Letter from Joe Ferman to Anthony Boucher, June 25, 1952. William A.P. White collection. Courtesy Lilly Library, Indiana University, Bloomington, IN.
66. Anthony Boucher, Introduction to Josephine Tey, *Killer in the Queue* (New York: Mercury Mysteries, 1953).
67. Letter from Anthony Boucher to the editor for *Collier's*, February 24, 1962. William A.P. White collection. Courtesy Lilly Library, Indiana University, Bloomington, IN.

The Critic

1. Lenore Glen Offord. *The Armchair Detective*, Part I, 2:2 (January 1969): 77–85
2. Anthony Boucher, "Department of Criminal Investigations," *San Francisco Chronicle*, June 6, 1943.
3. Anthony Boucher, "Criminals At Large," the *New York Times,* June 6, 1965.
4 Letter from Anthony Boucher to Joseph Jackson, March 21, 1944. William A.P. White collection. Courtesy Lilly Library, Indiana University, Bloomington, IN.
5. Anthony Boucher, "Department of Criminal Investigations," *San Francisco Chronicle*, June 24, 1945
6. Anthony Boucher, "Department of Criminal Investigations," *San Francisco Chronicle*, July 29, 1945.

7. Anthony Boucher, "Department of Criminal Investigations," *San Francisco Chronicle*, August 31, 1947.
8. Letter from Anthony Boucher to Manfred Lee, August 12, 1947. William A.P. White collection. Courtesy Lilly Library, Indiana University, Bloomington, IN.
9. Letter from Anthony Boucher to Fred Dannay, September 17, 1947. William A.P. White collection. Courtesy Lilly Library, Indiana University, Bloomington, IN.
10. Letter from Joseph Henry Jackson to Anthony Boucher, October 22, 1947. William A.P. White collection. Courtesy Lilly Library, Indiana University, Bloomington, IN.
11. Letter from Fred Dannay to Anthony Boucher. William A.P. White collection. Courtesy Lilly Library, Indiana University, Bloomington, IN.
12. Howard Haycraft, *Ellery Queen's Mystery Magazine*, August 16, 1948.
13. Anthony Boucher, "Criminals At Large," the *New York Times*, December 2, 1956.
14. Phyllis White and Lawrence White, "A Family Portrait," *Berkeley Historical Society* 1985: 20.
15. Anthony Boucher, "Criminals At Large," the *New York Times*, December 5, 1965.
16. Anthony Boucher, "Department of Criminal Investigations," *San Francisco Chronicle*, August 27, 1944.
17. Letter from Anthony Boucher to Fred Dannay, March 1949. William A.P. White collection. Courtesy Lilly Library, Indiana University, Bloomington, IN.
18. Note from Anthony Boucher to self, July 15, 1949. William A.P. White collection. Courtesy Lilly Library, Indiana University, Bloomington, IN.
19. Letter from Fred Dannay to Anthony Boucher, September 17, 1949. William A.P. White collection. Courtesy Lilly Library, Indiana University, Bloomington, IN.
20. Letter from Fred Dannay to Anthony Boucher, April, 1950. William A.P. White collection. Courtesy Lilly Library, Indiana University, Bloomington, IN.
21. Letter from Anthony Boucher to Fred Dannay, 1950. William A.P. White collection. Courtesy Lilly Library, Indiana University, Bloomington, IN.
22. Letter from Anthony Boucher to Irita Van Doren, March 31, 1950. William A.P. White collection. Courtesy Lilly Library, Indiana University, Bloomington, IN.
23. Anthony Boucher, "Recommended Reading," the *Magazine of Fantasy & Science Fiction*, August 1955.
24. Anthony Boucher, "Recommended Reading," the *Magazine of Fantasy & Science Fiction*, November 1955
25. Anthony Boucher, "Recommended Reading," the *Magazine of Fantasy & Science Fiction*, April 1958.
26. Letter from Anthony Boucher to Herbert Lyons, January 24, 1949. William A.P. White collection. Courtesy Lilly Library, Indiana University, Bloomington, IN.
27. Letter from Anthony Boucher to Herbert Lyons, February 7, 1949. William A.P. White collection. Courtesy Lilly Library, Indiana University, Bloomington, IN.
28. Letter from Anthony Boucher to Herbert Lyons, February 11, 1949. William A.P. White collection. Courtesy Lilly Library, Indiana University, Bloomington, IN.
29. Letter from Anthony Boucher to Manfred Lee, March 3, 1949. William A.P. White collection. Courtesy Lilly Library, Indiana University, Bloomington, IN.
30. Letter from Anthony Boucher to Charles McCabe, June 6, 1961. William A.P. White collection. Courtesy Lilly Library, Indiana University, Bloomington, IN.
31. Anthony Boucher, "Department of Criminal Investigations," *San Francisco Chronicle*, August 31, 1947.
32. Anthony Boucher, "Criminals At Large," the *New York Times*, August 5, 1951
33. Letter from Anthony Boucher to Mary Collins, October 14, 1943. William A.P. White collection. Courtesy Lilly Library, Indiana University, Bloomington, IN.
34. Anthony Boucher, "Department of Criminal Investigations." *San Francisco Chronicle*, February 27, 1944.
35. Letter from Jacques Barzun to Anthony Boucher, December 5, 1958. William A.P. White collection. Courtesy Lilly Library, Indiana University, Bloomington, IN.
36. Letter from Anthony Boucher to Jacques Barzun, June 16, 1961. William A.P. White collection. Courtesy Lilly Library, Indiana University, Bloomington, IN.
37. Letter from Jacques Barzun to Anthony Boucher, June 20, 1961. William A.P. White collection. Courtesy Lilly Library, Indiana University, Bloomington, IN.
38. Letter from Anthony Boucher to Jacques Barzun, June 22, 1961. William A.P. White collection. Courtesy Lilly Library, Indiana University, Bloomington, IN.
39. Letter from Michael Avallone to Anthony Boucher, August 20, 1967. William A.P. White collection. Courtesy Lilly Library, Indiana University, Bloomington, IN.
40. Anthony Boucher, "Criminals At Large," the *New York Times*, November 11, 1951.
41. Letter from Anthony Boucher to Fred

Dannay, April 15, 1953. William A.P. White collection. Courtesy Lilly Library, Indiana University, Bloomington, IN.

42. Letter from Allen J. Hubin to Anthony Boucher, November 28, 1966. William A.P. White collection. Courtesy Lilly Library, Indiana University, Bloomington, IN.

43. Letter from Anthony Boucher to Lenore Glen Offord, December 16, 1951. William A.P. White collection. Courtesy Lilly Library, Indiana University, Bloomington, IN.

44. Letter from Anthony Boucher to Lenore Glen Offord, William A.P. White collection. Courtesy Lilly Library, Indiana University, Bloomington, IN.

45. Letter from Anthony Boucher. March 19, 1956. William A.P. White collection. Courtesy Lilly Library, Indiana University, Bloomington, IN.

46. Anthony Boucher, "Department of Criminal Investigations." *San Francisco Chronicle*, November 25, 1945.

47. Letter from Anthony Boucher to Theodore Cogswell, August 1958. William A.P. White collection. Courtesy Lilly Library, Indiana University, Bloomington, IN.

48. Letter from Anthony Boucher to Mr. Aucott, February 16, 1965. William A.P. White collection. Courtesy Lilly Library, Indiana University, Bloomington, IN.

49. Letter from Anthony Boucher to Ernest Besig (ACLU). William A.P. White collection. Courtesy Lilly Library, Indiana University, Bloomington, IN.

50. Lenore Glen Offord, "A Boucher Portrait," 69–76.

51. *Ibid*.

52. Anthony Boucher, "Department of Criminal Investigations," *San Francisco Chronicle*, October 1, 1944.

Part II

Novels by William A.P. White as Anthony Boucher

He also used the pen name H.H. Holmes, as noted.

The Case of the Seven of Cavalry (Simon & Schuster, 1937). Reprints: Macmillan, (Murder Revisited Series, No. 8, 1954); Collier #AS97, 1961; Collier #01759, 1967; in *Four Novels*, Zomba, 1984. Protagonist: Dr. Ashwin.

The Case of the Toad-in-the-Hole (unpublished) Protagonist: Dr. Ashwin.

The Case of the Crumpled Knave (Simon & Schuster, 1939). Reprints: Popular Library Book #154, 1954; Pyramid #R-1585, 1967; in *Four Novels*, Zomba Books, 1984. Protagonist: Fergus O'Breen.

The Case of the Baker Street Irregulars (Simon & Schuster, 1940) Reprints: Tower, 1947; as *Blood on Baker Street* (condensed), Mercury, 1953; Collier #AS147, 1962; Collier #07151, 1967; Gregg, 1980; Carroll and Graf, with Otto Penzler introduction, 1986; Carroll (UK), 1996.

Nine Times Nine, as H.H. Holmes (Duell, Sloan, & Pearce, 1940). Reprints: Penguin #553; (as Anthony Boucher): Collier #AS334, 1962; in *Four Novels*, Zomba, 1984; International Polygonics, 1986. Protagonist: Sister Ursula.

The Case of the Solid Key (Simon & Schuster, 1941). Reprints: Pyramid #X-1733, 1968. Protagonist: Fergus O'Breen.

The Case of the Seven Sneezes (Simon & Schuster, 1942). Reprints: Dell Book #334, 1942; Pyramid #R-1542, 1966. Fergus O'Breen.

Rocket to the Morgue, as H.H. Holmes (Duell, Sloan & Pearce, 1942). Reprints: Phantom, 1943; Two Complete Detective Books, 1944; (as Anthony Boucher) Dell #591, 1952; Pyramid #X1681, 1967; in *Four Novels*, Zomba, 1984; International Polygonics, 1988. Protagonist: Sister Ursula.

The Marble Forest by Theo Durrant, a Northern California Mystery Writers of America collaborative novel with Boucher contributing episodes and editing (Knopf, 1951). Reprint: as *The Big Fear*, Popular Library, 1953. Film: *Macabre* (director: William Castle).

Articles

"The Best Tricks of the Mystery Trade." *The Mystery Writer's Handbook*, 1956.
"The Biggest Stumbling Block." *The Mystery Writer's Handbook*, 1956.
"The Borderlands of Sanity — From Charm to Murder: The Case of Neville Heath." *True Crime Detective*, Fall (October), 1952.
The "Dear Wish" to Baffle Time. *The Sunday New York Times*, November 12, 1961.
"Department of Abject Apology," with Mick McComas. *The Magazine of Fantasy & Science Fiction*, October 1953.
"Do You Believe —." *Mercury Mystery Book Magazine*, March 1956.
"Ellery Queen: A Double Profile," 12-page pamphlet, 1951.
"The Ethics of the Mystery Novel." *Tricolor*, October 1944; *The Art of the Mystery Story*, 1946.
"A Fiction Writer Admires Dewey."
"G. & S. Notes from England." *Niekas* #11, June 1965.
Gardner, Erle Stanley. *Encyclopedia Britannica*.
"The Glass of the Future," [as Herman Mudgett] *The Magazine of Fantasy & Science Fiction*, January 1955; *The Best of Fantasy & Science Fiction*: Fifth Series, 1956.
Hammett, (Samuel) Dashiell. *Encyclopedia Britannica*.
"Have You Looked in Your Attic Lately? The cases of Theodore Edward Coneys and Otto Sanhuber." Pocket Books, 1961.
"The Hess Murder Case." *San Francisco Chronicle*, November 1, 1942
"Holmes on the Range," as Able Baker. *The Third Degree*, December 1963.
"It's Murder, Amigos: The Mystery Story Takes Root in Latin America." *Publisher's Weekly*, April 19, 1947.
"The Model of a Science Fiction Editor." *The Magazine of Fantasy & Science Fiction*, October 1953.
Molly Maguires. *The Encyclopedia Britannica*, 1956.
"Murder Up to Date." *The Writer*, July 1954; as "What Kind of Mystery Story Appeals to Today's Public," *The Mystery Writer's Handbook*, 1956.
"My Favorite Murder: The Tragedy of Samuel Savile Kent." *True Crime Detective*, Spring (March), 1953.
"Mystery & Science Fiction." *The American Peoples Encyclopedia*. 1953–1956.

"The Naming of Names," as Herman Mudgett. *The Magazine of Fantasy & Science Fiction*, October 1953.

"Of Fortune and Faro," *Opera News*, January 15, 1966.

"On a Day Unknown: The Case of August Sangret." *Ed McBain's Mystery Book*, September 1960.

"On the Difficulties of Getting Mr. Anderson's First Name Correctly Spelled." *Vorpel Glass*, February 1963.

"Opera and Murder." *Multiplying Villainies*, 1973.

"Out of Patience…" *Ellery Queen's Mystery Magazine*, December 1953.

"Out on a Limb." *Unknown Worlds*, October 1941.

"Playboy Panel," paper from the panel discussion on science fiction in Chicago in 1962. Final text was published in two parts in *Playboy* in July and August 1963.

"Pseudonyms are Murder." *The Third Degree*, December 1958.

"The Publishing of Science Fiction. Modern Science Fiction: Its Meaning and Its Future," 1953.

"Ray Bradbury, Beginner." *Ray Bradbury Review*, 1952.

Report on the Sexual Behavior of the Extra-Sensory Perceptor, as Herman Mudgett. *The Magazine of Fantasy & Science Fiction*, August 1954; *The Best of Fantasy & Science Fiction*: Fifth Series, 1956.

"The Reviewing of Mystery Novels"

"The Roles of Reviewer and Editor in Science Fiction." *Dinky Bird* #11, July 1964.

"The Science Fiction Books of 1963: A Survey." *Neikas* #9, September 1964.

"Silent, upon two peaks…, as Herman Mudgett. *The Magazine of Fantasy & Science Fiction*, July 1955; *The Best of Fantasy & Science Fiction: Fifth Series*, 1956.

"Sonnet of the Unsleeping Dead" (verse). *Weird Tales*, 1935; *Dark of the Moon*, 1945.

"Note on 'A Tale of the Ragged Mountain'" *The Magazine of Fantasy & Science Fiction*, March 1958; *Ellery Queen's Mystery Magazine*, February 1965.

"The Tongue of Men and of Angels" (tongue recipes). *American Cookery*, January 1943

"The Trojan Horse Opera." *The Art of the Mystery Story*, 1946.

"There Was a Young Man of Cape Horn" (limerick) as Herman Mudgett. *The Magazine of Fantasy & Science Fiction*, August 1951.

"The 12 Days of Christmas." *The Zed* #782, Winter 1955.

"Wanted: A Fanzine," *Mystery Writers Annual*, 1964.

"Wizards of a Small Planet." *Playboy*, 1958; *Space Digest*, February 1959; as "Science Fiction Still Leads Science Fact," *The New York Times Sunday Magazine*, December 1, 1957; SF '58: *The Year's Greatest Science Fiction and Fantasy*, 1958.

"You and the Reviews and the Reviewers." *The Mystery Writer's Handbook*, 1956.

Collected Short Stories

The Compleat Anthony Boucher

"The Ambassadors" (*Startling Stories*, June 1952; *Future Tense*, 1953; *Galaxy of Ghouls*, 1955; *Fifty Short Science Fiction Tales*, 1963; *The Shape of Things*, 1965).

"The Anomaly of the Empty Man" (*The Magazine of Fantasy & Science Fiction*, April 1952; [reprints altered and corrected a plot error] *Crooks' Tour* [MWA Anthology], 1954; *Shock*, May 1960; *The Science-Fictional Sherlock Holmes*, 1960 [and new edition in 1968]; *Cream of the Crime* [MWA Anthology] 1962, *The Misadventures of Sherlock Holmes*, Sebastian Wolfe, ed., 1989).

"Balaam" (*Nine Tales of Space and Time*, Raymond J. Healy, 1954; *Best SF Four: Science Fiction Stories*, 1961).

"Barrier" (*Astounding Science Fiction*, September 1942; *Astounding Science Fiction* [British], 1942; *Six Great Short Novels of Science Fiction*, 1954; *Spectrum IV*, 1965).

"The Chronokinesis of Jonathan Hull" (*Astounding Science Fiction*, June 1946; *Astounding Science Fiction* [British], 1948; *Great Stories of Science Fiction*, 1951).

"The Complete Werewolf" (*Unknown Worlds*, April 1942).

"Conquest" (*Star Science Fiction Stories #2*, Frederik Pohl, ed., 1953).

"Elsewhen" (*Astounding Science Fiction*, January 1943; *Murder, Plain and Fanciful*, 1948).

"Expedition" (*Thrilling Wonder Stories*, August 1943; *Best of Science Fiction*, 1946; Invasion from Mars, 1949).

"The First" (*The Magazine of Fantasy and Science Fiction*, October 1952).

"Gandolphus" (*Other Worlds Science Fiction*, June 1952; *The Magazine of Fantasy & Science Fiction*, December 1956; *A Decade of Fantasy & Science Fiction*, 1960).

"The Ghost of Me" (*Unknown Worlds*, June 1942).

"The Greatest Tertian" (*Illustrious Client's Third Case Book*, 1953; *Invaders of Earth*, Geoff Conklin, ed., 1952; *The Science Fiction Sherlock Holmes*, 1960).

"Khartoum: a prose limerick" (*Stefantasy*, August 1955; *Inside Science Fiction*, September 1958).

"A Kind of Madness" (*Ellery Queen's Mystery Magazine*, August 1972).

"Man's Reach" (*The Magazine of Fantasy & Science Fiction*, November 1972).

"Mary Celestial" with Miriam Allen DeFord (*The Magazine of Fantasy & Science Fiction*, May 1955).

"The Model of a Science Fiction Editor" (*The Magazine of Fantasy & Science Fiction*, October 1953).

"Mr. Lupescu" (*Weird Tales*, September 1945; *The Sleeping and the Dead*, 1947; *Avon Detective Mysteries #3*, 1947; *Shot in the Dark*, 1950).

"Nellthu" (*The Magazine of Fantasy & Science Fiction*, August 1955; *The Best of Fantasy & Science Fiction: Fifth Series*, 1956; *Playboy*, July 1956; *Deals With the Devil*, 1958; *The Dark Side*, 1965).

"Nine-Finger Jack" (*Esquire*, May 1951; *The Magazine of Fantasy & Science Fiction*, August 1952; *The Best Science-Fiction Stories: 1952*, 1952; *20 Great Tales of* Murder [MWA Anthology], 1961; *Ellery Queen's Mystery Magazine*, September 1964; *The Saint Detective Magazine*, January 1958; *The Saint Magazine Reader*, 1966; as "The Saga of Nine-Finger Jack," *Everybody's Magazine*, February 1962; dramatic adaptation by George Lowther for *NBC Matinee Theatre*, October 30, 1957).

"One-way Trip" (*Astounding Science Fiction*, August 1943).

"The Other Inauguration" (*The Magazine of Fantasy & Science Fiction*, March 1953; *Science Fiction Terror Tales*, 1955).

"Pelagic Spark" (*Astounding Science Fiction*, June 1943).

"The Pink Caterpillar" (*Adventure*, February 1945).

"The Public Eye" (*Thrilling Wonder Stories*, April 1953; *The Best Detective Stories of the Year—1953*, 1953; *Spaces, Time, and Crime*, 1964).

"The Quest for Saint Aquin" (*New Tales of Space and Time*, Raymond J. Healy, ed., 1951; *Fantasy & Science Fiction*, January 1959; *Best SF Five: Science Fiction Stories*, 1963; *The Worlds of Science Fiction*, 1963; *One Hundred Years of Science Fiction*, 1968).

"Q.U.R.," as H.H. Holmes (*Astounding Science Fiction*, March 1943).

"Rappacini's Other Daughter"

"Recipe for Curry De Luxe" (*Cooking Out of This World*, Anne McCaffrey, ed., Ballantine, 1957).

"Review Copy," as H. H. Holmes (*The Magazine of Fantasy & Science Fiction*, Fall, 1949).

"Robinc," as H. H. Holmes (*Astounding Science Fiction*, September 1943).

"Sanctuary," as H.H. Holmes (*Astounding Science Fiction*, June 1943).

"The Scrawny One" (*Weird Tales*, May 1949, *Cavalier*, June 1961).

"Secret of the House," as HH Holmes (*Galaxy Science Fiction*, March 1953).

"A Shape of Time" (*The Future is Now*, William F. Nolan, ed., 1970).

"Snulbug" (*Unknown Worlds*, December 1941).

"Sriberdegibit" (*Unknown Worlds*, June 1943; *Unknown Worlds* [British], 1943; *The Magazine of Fantasy & Science Fiction*, March 1954).

"Star Bride" (*Thrilling Wonder Stories*, December 1951; *Stories for Tomorrow*, 1954; *Wonder Stories*, 1963).

"The Star Dummy" (*Fantastic*, Fall, 1952; *The Omnibus of Science Fiction*, 1952).

"Summer's Cloud" (*The Acolyte*, Summer 1944).

"The Tenderizers" (*The Magazine of Fantasy & Science Fiction*, January 1972).

"They Bite" (*Unknown Worlds*, August 1943).

"Transfer Point" (*Galaxy Science Fiction*, November 1950; *Adventures in Tomorrow*, 1951; *A Shadow of Tomorrow*, 1953).

"The Way I Heard It" (*The Acolyte*, Fall, 1944).
"We Print the Truth" (*Astounding Science Fiction*, December 1943).

The Compleat Werewolf

"The Complete Werewolf" (*Unknown Worlds*, April 1942; *Unknown Worlds* [British], 1945; *From Unknown Worlds*, 1949; *Beyond Human Ken*, 1952).
"Expedition" (*Thrilling Wonder Stories*, August 1943).
"The Ghost of Me" (*Unknown Worlds*, June 1942; *Astounding Science Fiction* [British], 1942; *Beyond the Barriers of Space and Time*, 1954).
"Mr. Lupescu" (*Weird Tales*, September 1945; *The Sleeping and the Dead: Thirty Uncanny Tales*, 1947; Avon Detective Mysteries #3, 1947; *Shot in the Dark*, 1950; adaptation by Doris Gilbert, CBS-TV, May 1, 1951).
"The Pink Caterpillar" (*Adventure*, February 1945; *Avon Fantasy Reader No. 17*, November 1951; *Fantasy & Science Fiction*, December 1958; *Tales for a Rainy Night* [MWA Anthology], 1961)
"Q.U.R.," as H.H. Holmes (*Astounding Science Fiction*, March 1943; *Adventures in Time and Space*, 1946).
"Robinc" (*Astounding Science Fiction*, September 1943; *The Robot and the Man*, 1953).
"Snulbug" (*Unknown Worlds*, December 1941; *Unknown Worlds* [British], 1948; *The Magazine of Fantasy & Science Fiction*, May 1953; *The Best from Fantasy & Science Fiction: Third Series*, 1954; *The Unknown*, 1963).
"They Bite" (*Unknown Worlds*, August 1943; *Unknown Worlds* [British], 1943; *The Magazine of Fantasy & Science Fiction*, December 1952; *Alfred Hitchcock Presents My Favorites in Suspense*, 1954; *Zacherly's Vulture Stew*, 1960).
"We Print the Truth" (*Astounding Science Fiction*, December 1943).

Exeunt Murderers

"Black Murder," (*Ellery Queen's Mystery Magazine*, September 1943; *Great American Detective Stories*, 1945).
"The Catalyst" (*Black Mask*, July 1945; as "The Numbers Man," *Ellery Queen's Mystery Magazine*, June 1953; *A Pride of Felons: Twenty Stories by Members of the Mystery Writers of America*, 1963; *Ellery Queen's Anthology, 1963 Mid-Year Edition*, 1963).
"Code Zed" (*World's Great Spy Stories*, Vincent Starrett, ed., 1944).
"Coffin Corner," as H.H. Holmes (*The Female of the Species*, Ellery Queen, ed., 1943; *The Great Women Detectives and Criminals*, 1946).
"Crime Must Have a Stop" (*Ellery Queen's Mystery Magazine*, February 1951; *Eat, Drink and Be Buried* [MWA Anthology], 1956; *For Tomorrow We Die*, 1958; *Ellery Queen's Anthology, 1964 Midyear Edition*, 1964).
"Death of a Patriarch" (*Exeunt Murderers*, Francis M. Nevins, ed., 1983).
"Design for Dying" (*Detective Short Stories*, September 1941).
"The Ghost with a Gun" (*Master Detective*, Vol. 32, No. 4, June 1945).
"The Girl Who Married a Monster" (*Ellery Queen's Mystery Magazine*, February 1954; *Butcher, Baker, Murder-Maker* [MWA Anthology], 1954).

"Like Count Palmieri" (*Ellery Queen's Mystery Magazine*, February 1946; *Planned Departures: A Crime Writers Association Anthology*, 1958; *Ellery Queen's 1965 Anthology*, 1965).

"A Matter of Scholarship" (*Ellery Queen's Mystery Magazine*, April 1955; *Ellery Queen's 1963 Anthology*, 1963).

"Mystery for Christmas" (*Ellery Queen's Mystery Magazine*, January 1943; *The Saint's Choice of Hollywood Crime*, 1946; *Crime for Two* [MWA Anthology], 1955; *Ellery Queen's 1962 Anthology*, 1962).

"The Punt and the Pass" (*Short Stories*, November 26, 1945).

"QL 696.C9" (*Ellery Queen's Mystery Magazine*, May 1943; *Famous Stories of Code and Cipher*, 1947; *Verdict*, 1953).

"The Retired Hangman" (*Shadow Mystery Magazine*, February and March 1947; *Best Detective Stories of the Year—1948*, 1948; as "Murder Was Their Business," *Ellery Queen's Mystery Magazine*, November 1955).

"Rumor, Inc.: A Nick Noble Story" (*Ellery Queen's Mystery Magazine*, January 1945).

"Screwball Division" (*Ellery Queen's Mystery Magazine*, September 1942; *Four and Twenty Bloodhounds*, 1950).

"The Smoke-filled Locked Room" (*The Locked Room Reader*, Hans Stefan Santesson, ed., 1968).

"The Statement of Jerry Malloy" (*Dangerous Dames*, by Brett Halliday, 1955; *Ellery Queen's Mystery Magazine*, November 1958).

"The Stripper," as H.H. Holmes (*Ellery Queen's Mystery Magazine*, May 1945; [as Anthony Boucher] *Twentieth Century Detective Stories*, 1948; *The Harlot Killer*, 1953; *Verdict*, July 1953; *Bodies and Spirits*, 1964).

"Threnody" (*Maiden Murders* [MWA Anthology], John Dickson Carr, ed., 1952; as "Death Can Be Beautiful," *Ellery Queen's Mystery Magazine*, April 1962).

"The Ultimate Clue" (*Ellery Queen's Mystery Magazine*, October 1960; *Ellery Queen's Sixteenth Mystery Annual*, 1961; *Mystery: A Treasury for Younger Readers*, 1963).

Far and Away

"The Anomaly of the Empty Man" (*The Magazine of Fantasy & Science Fiction*, April 1952).

"Balaam" (*Nine Tales of Space and Time*, Raymond J. Healy, ed., 1954).

"Elsewhen" (*Astounding Science Fiction*, January 1943).

"The First" (*The Magazine of Fantasy & Science Fiction*, October 1952).

"The Other Inauguration" (*The Magazine of Fantasy & Science Fiction*, March 1953).

"Review Copy" (*The Magazine of Fantasy & Science Fiction*, Fall, 1949).

"Secret of the House" (*Galaxy Science Fiction*, March 1953).

"Snulbug" (*Unknown Worlds*, December 1941).

"Sriberdegibit" (*Unknown Worlds*, June 1943).

"Star Bride" (*Thrilling Wonder Stories*, December 1951).

"They Bite" (*Unknown Worlds*, August 1943).

Uncollected and Unpublished Short Stories

Unless noted as published, these stories are unpublished and exist only at the Lilly Library at Indiana University, Bloomington.

"The Accuracy of Norbert Holt"
"The Adventure of the Bogle-Wolf" (*The Illustrious Client's Second Casebook*, J.N. Williamson, ed., 1944; *The Game is Afoot*, Marvin Kaye, ed., 1984)
"The Adventure of the Illustrious Impostor" (*The Misadventures of Sherlock Holmes*, Ellery Queen, ed., 1944)
"The Adventure of the Murdered Muse"
"The Adventure of the Undying Detective"
"Arsene Lupin vs. Colonel Linnaus" (*Ellery Queen's Mystery Magazine*, November 1944)
"Aunt Louisa," 1944
"Before the Fact"
"Breakfast Scene"
"The Captain," 1943
"The Case of the Villain's Identity" (*Radio Writer*, April 1948)
"Caste"
"Christmas Story"
"The Clue of the Knave of Diamonds" (*Ellery Queen's Mystery Magazine*, May 1963)
    [novella form of *The Case of the Crumpled Knave* that preceded the 1939 novel]
"The Coat"
"The Corpse of Cagliostro"
"Crime and Quillans," 1938
"Death of the Undead," 1936
"Death on the Bay: A Dr. Ashwin Story"
"Double Cross of Lorraine," 1943
"Footnote to Dunne" (*Arkham Sampler*, Autumn 1949)
"Gadget for Murder"
"Galligrew," written by Anthony Boucher for pictures by Frances Baxter (children's story)

"The Green Men of San Pedro"
"Integrity"
"It Will Have Blood"
"John and the Radio"
"The Last"
"The Last Hand" (*Ellery Queen's Mystery Magazine*, September 1958; as "A Little Honest Stud," *Masters of Mayhem* [MWA Anthology], 1965)
"Lousy Fencer"
"A Major in Philosophy," as A.P. White
"The Maskeleyne Cipher: A Dr. Ashwin Short Story"
"Mr. Pettie Protests"
"Murder by Jove" (*Look*, September 6, 1944)
"Murder in Miniature"
"The Butler Did It"
"The Woman Who Fed Cats"
"The Woman Who Married Her Widower"
"Murder of a Martian: A Colonel Rand Story"
"Murder on V-Day" (*Look*, January 1945)
"My Dear Ellerby"
"November Fifth" (*Trailer Dust*, October 1946)
"One Way Trip" (*Astounding Science Fiction*, August 1943)
"Operator A"
"Ouroboros Unbound"
"Palace: A Story for Children," as A.P. White
"Prelude"
"Quest," written in 1931 for English class at USC
"The Request of Dajos Kunyadi"
"Requiescant," written as A.P. Sweeney, rejected by *Esquire*
"Reunion En Route"
"The Riddle of Khorzuk," early science fiction, 1936, rejected by *Weird Tales*
"Salem"
San Francisco Murders, Joseph Henry Jackson, ed., story "The Legends" by Boucher), Duell, Sloan, and Pearce, 1947.
"The Seat of the Matter," published posthumously in 1970
"Tarvish"
"Terror at Sunset," early science fiction, 1936, rejected by *Weird Tales*
"Toy Cassowary" (*The Acolyte*, Winter 1945)
"Transcontinental Alibi" (*Mystery Book Magazine*, Spring 1950)
"Vacancy with Corpse," as H.H. Holmes (*Mystery Book Magazine*, February 1946)
"Wilber" (picture book)
"Wildfire at Midnight," early work, rejected by *Popular Publications*
"Ye Good Old Ghost Storie," as William A.P. White (*Weird Tales*, January 1927, his first published story)

Sherlockiana

"On the Nomenclature of the Brothers Moriarty" (San Francisco: Beaune, 1966). This was originally printed by Edwin B. Hill in 1941 in an edition of 25 copies with a short postscript by Vincent Starrett. The entire text is a letter from Boucher to Christopher Morley about the problem of the three Moriarty brothers.

"The Case of the Sixty-First Adventure" (*The San Francisco Chronicle*, This World, November 29, 1942).

"Jack El Destripador," *The Misadventures of Sherlock Holmes*, 1944. Synopsized translation of an anonymous novel.

"Sonnet: San Francisco to Sherlock." *A Baker Street Four-Wheeler*, 1944. Presented at the first meeting of the Scowrers.

"Was the Later Holmes an Impostor?" *Profile by Gaslight*, 1944.

"Holmesiana Hispanica: A Tentative Bibliography." The Scowrers, 1945. reprinted in *The Baker Street Journal*, 1947.

"Ballads of the Later Holmes." *The Baker Street Journal*, 1946.

"Prolegomena to a Holmesian Discography." *The Baker Street Journal*, 1946.

"The Records of Baker Street." *The Baker Street Journal*, 1949.

"An Aborted Avatar." *The Baker Street Journal*, July 1959.

"A Short Biography of Sherlock Holmes." *The Baker Street Irregulars*, 1959.

"Sherlock Holmes and Science Fiction," Introduction to *The Science-Fictional Sherlock Holmes*, 1960; *The Baker Street Journal*, 1960; *New Frontiers*, August 1960.

"A Note on Scowrers." *The Vemissa Herald*, Spring 1962; *West by One and by One*, 1965

"The Best and Wisest Man," two-part, two-hour radio program with Boucher introducing and discussing audio-Sherlock. Originally recorded at the KPFA-FM studios in Berkeley, California. The show was aired on WBAI-FM, New York, on September 21 and 28, 1963.

"Baker Street Immortal." *The New York Times Book Review*, January 21, 1968.

"Footnote to a Footnote." *The Baker Street Journal*, 1968.

Plays and Screenplays

These plays and screenplays are unpublished and exist only at the Lilly Library at Indiana University, Bloomington, or with the White family in their personal archives.

Charlie McCarthy, Detective
Confessional
Death of a Hero. The Story of a Dictator's Double
Don Juan
Episodio Historico
The Immortal
Jack the Giant-Killer
Jasmine
The Knight
Kuniqunde
Little Princess
Los De Rojas
Milk
The Moon is Gibbous: A Guignol Monologue
The Open Window (a play in one act)
Panacea
Panache: A Heroic Melodrama
The Petard of Death
The Plume (a one-act play)
Rave Notice or Critics Have Fun, Too.
Roy Rogers Screen Treatment
Second Semester
The Shade
Sheep's Clothing
Sigh No More, Ladies!
Something That Happens
Theomore
The Werewolf of the Moors

Reviews

Chicago Sun-Times, 1948–1950
Clue, a Guide to Mysteries, 1948
The Magazine of Fantasy & Science Fiction, fall 1949 to January 1959
Ellery Queen's Mystery Magazine: "Speaking of Crime," 1948–1950; "Best Mysteries of the Month," November 1957–February 1968
Los Angeles Daily News, 1948–1949
Manhunt: "The Murder Market," H. H. Holmes, November–December 1953; "Verdict of Two" (with J. Francis McComas), February and May 1964
New York Herald Tribune, 1950–1963
New York Times, "Criminals at Large," 1949–1968
Opera News, 1949–1968
San Francisco Chronicle, "Department of Criminal Investigations," 1942–1946; "Murder and Espionage," 1942–1946; "Murder, They Say," 1946–1947; and miscellaneous reviews.
Pacifica Radio, "Escape," 1961–1968

Radio Plays

The Adventures of Ellery Queen

All episodes were written in conjunction with Manfred B. Lee.
Network affiliation: CBS, June 18, 1939–1940; NBC, 1942–1944; CBS, 1945–1947; NBC, 1947; ABC, 1947–1948.
Sponsors: Gulf Oil, Bromo-Selzer, Anacin

Season 5

"The Corpse of Mr. Entwhistle," June 13, 1945
"The Absent Automatic," June 20, 1945
"Mr. 1 and Mr. 2," June 27, 1945
"Nikki's Rich Uncle," July 4, 1945
"The Gentleman Burglar," July 18, 1945
"The Torture Victim," July 25, 1945
"Nick the Knife," August 1, 1945
"The Clue in C Major," August 8, 1945
"The Time of Death," August 15, 1945

Season 6

"The Man Who was Afraid," September 5, 1945
"The Lost Soul," September 19, 1945
"The Green House," September 26, 1945
"Ellery Queen, Cupid," October 3, 1945
"The Kid Glove Killer," October 10, 1945
"The Other Man," October 17, 1945
"The Repentant Thief," October 24, 1945
"The Hallowe'en Murder," October 31, 1945
"The Message in Red," November 7, 1945
"The Happy Marriage," November 14, 1945
"The Ape's Boss," November 21, 1945
"The Doodle of Mr. O'Drew," November 28, 1945

"The Peddler of Death," December 5, 1945
"The Man With Two Faces," December 12, 1945
"The Man Who Loved Murders," December 26, 1945
"The Lost Hoard," on January 2, 1946
"The Various Deaths of Mr. Frayne," on January 9, 1946
"The Green Eye," January 16, 1946
"Ellery Queen's Tragedy," January 30, 1946
"The Living Dead," February 13, 1946
"The Three Fencers," February 20, 1946
"The Ninth Mrs. Pook," February 27, 1946
"The Phantom Shadow," March 6, 1946
"The Clue of the Elephant," March 13, 1946
"The Armchair Detective," March 27, 1946
"The Death Wish," April 3, 1946
"The Girl Who Couldn't Get Married," April 10, 1946
"Nikki Porter, Murder Victim," April 17, 1946
"The Man Who Bought One Grape," April 24, 1946
"The Rhubarb Solution," May 1, 1946
"The Hollywood Murder Case," on May 22, 1946
"The Laughing Woman," May 29, 1946
"Mr. Warren's Profession," June 5, 1946
"Cokey and the Pizza," June 19, 1946
"The Double Die," June 26, 1946
"The Ultra-Modern Murder," July 17, 1946
"The Man Who Got Away with Murder," July 31, 1946
"Bis to Cal," August 14, 1946

Season 7

"Ellery Queen, Criminal," October 9, 1946
"The Woman Who Died Several Times," October 23, 1946
"Ellery Queen's Rival," October 30, 1946
"The Crime of Inspector Queen," November 6, 1946
"Ellery Queen, Gigolo," December 4, 1946
"The Unhappy New Year," January 1, 1947
"The Man Who Could Vanish," January 8, 1947
"The Crooked Man," March 12, 1947
"The Specialist in Cops," March 19, 1947
"The Man Who Murdered a City," April 2, 1947

Season 8

"Murder for Americans," August 17, 1947
"The Man Who Squared the Circle," September 21, 1947
"The Saga of Ruffy Rux," November 27, 1947
"Nikki Porter, Bride," December 11, 1947
"The Melancholy Bride," December 18, 1947
"The Private Eye," January 22, 1948

"A Question of Color," February 12, 1948
"The Old Sinner," February 19, 1948
"The Lynching of Mr. Cue," March 11, 1948
"The Farmer's Daughter," March 25, 1948
"The K.I. Case," April 8, 1948
"The Slicer," April 15, 1948
"The Three Frogs," April 29, 1948
"One Diamond," May 6, 1948
"Nikki Porter, Starlet," May 13, 1948
"Misery Mike," May 20, 1948

UNUSED SYNOPSES

#12 "The Beethoven Manuscript"
#15 "The Quisling Quarterback"
#61" May Tenth"
#62 "The Modern Fagin"
#63 "The Giant at Large"
#71 "The King of the Jungle"
#73 "The Hostages to Fortune"
#77 "The Green-Eyed Murder"

Gregory Hood

Network affiliation: Mutual Broadcasting System
Sponsor: Petri Wine

"The Three Silver Pesos," June 3, 1946
"The Black Museum," June 10, 1946
"The Murder of Gregory Hood," June 17, 1946
"The Adventure of the Beeswax Candle," June 24, 1946
"Murder in Celluloid," July 1, 1946
"The Derringer Society," July 8, 1946
"South of the Border," July 15, 1946
"The Red Capsule," July 22, 1946
"The Forgetful Murder," July 29, 1946
"The Double Diamond," August 5, 1946
"The Venerable Thugs," August 12, 1946
"The Mad Danger," August 19, 1946
"The Ghost Town Mortuary," August 26, 1946
"Gregory Hood's First Case," September 2, 1946
"The Elusive Violin," September 9, 1946
"The Missing Memoirs," September 16, 1946
"The Frightened Librarian," September 23, 1946
"Gregory Hood, Suspect," September 30, 1946
"The Adventure of the Sad Clown," October 7, 1946
"The Killer Who Gave a Damn," October 14, 1946

Untitled, November 11, 1946
"The Four Hundred Mile Murder," November 18, 1946
"The White Masters," November 25, 1946

The New Adventures of Sherlock Holmes

All episodes were written in conjunction with Denis Green.
Network Affiliation: NBC Blue Network, Mutual Broadcasting System
Sponsors: Bromo Quinine, Parker Pen, Petri Wine, Kreml Hair Tonic for Men
Many of these broadcasts have survived and are available on cassette and CD.

1945

"The Book of Tobit," March 28, 1945
"The Amateur Mendicant Society," April 2, 1945
"The Curious Affair of the Viennese Strangler," April 9, 1945
"The Remarkable Worm," April 16, 1945
"The Case of the Notorious Canary Trainer," April 23, 1945
"The Affair of the Unfortunate Tobacconists," April 30, 1945
"The Case of the Purloined Ruby," May 7, 1945
"In Flanders Field," May 14, 1945
"The Singular Affair of the Paradol Chamber," May 21, 1945
"The Dance of Death," May 28, 1945
"The Limping Ghost," September 3, 1945
"The Story of Colonel Warburton's Madness," September 10, 1945
"The Case of the Out-of-Date Murder," September 17, 1945
"The Eyes of Mr. Leyton," September 24, 1945
"The Problem of Thor Bridge," October 1, 1945
"The Case of the Vanishing Elephant," October 8, 1945
"The Manor House Case," October 15, 1945
"The Great Gandolfo," October 22, 1945
"Murder By Moonlight," October 29, 1945
"The Gunpowder Plot" (alternate Title: "The Fifth of November"), November 5, 1945
"The Adventure of the Speckled Band," November 12, 1945
"The Adventure of the Double Zero," November 19, 1945
"The Accidental Murderess," November 26, 1945
"Murder in the Casbah," December 3, 1945
"A Scandal in Bohemia," December 10, 1945
"The Case of the Second Generation," December 17, 1945
"The Night before Christmas," December 24, 1945
"The Case of the Iron Box," December 31, 1945

1946

"The Strange Case of the Murder in Wax (Alternate title: "The Hampton Heath Murder Case"), January 7, 1946

"Murder Beyond the Mountains (Alternate title: "Murder in the Himalayas or Murder in Tibet"), January 14, 1946
"The Adventure of the Tell-Tale Pigeon Feathers," January 21, 1946
"The Strange Case of the Demon Barber (Alternate title: "Sweeney Todd, the Demon Barber"), January 28, 1946
"The Indiscretion of Mr. Edwards (Alternate title: "Cross of Damascus"), February 4, 1946
"The Case of the Guileless Gypsies," February 11, 1946
"The Camberwell Poisoning Case," February 18, 1946
"The Adventure of the Terrifying Cats (Alternate title: "Murder at the Opera"), February 25, 1946 (an ill Nigel Bruce was replaced by Eric Snowden)
"The Adventure of the Submarine Caves," March 4, 1946
"The Adventure of the Living Doll," March 11, 1946
"The Blarney Stone Murder," March 18, 1946
"The Strange Case of the Girl with the Gazelle," March 25, 1946
"The April Fool's Day Adventure," April 1, 1946
"The Singular Affair of the Disappearing Scientists," April 8, 1946
"The Adventure of the Headless Monk," April 15, 1946
"The Tankerville Club Scandal," April 22, 1946
"The Waltz of Death," April 29, 1946
"The Man With the Twisted Lip," May 6, 1946
"The Singular Affair of the Uneasy Easy Chair," May 13, 1946
"The Haunting of Sherlock Holmes," May 20, 1946 (an ill Nigel Bruce replaced by Joseph Kearns)
"The Singular Affair of the Baconian Cipher," May 27, 1946 (Basil Rathbone's last show as Holmes. He would be replaced by Tom Conway.)
"The Stuttering Ghost," October 12, 1946 (Show moved to Saturdays at 9:30 P.M.)
"The Case of the Hungry Cat," October 26, 1946
"The Adventure of the Original Hamlet," November 2, 1946
"The Singular Affair of the Dying Schoolboys," November 9, 1946
"The Adventure of the Genuine Guarnerius (Alternate title: "The Mystery of the Murdered Violinist"), November 16, 1946
"The Adventure of *The Sally Martin*," November 23, 1946
"The Strange Death of Mrs. Abernetty," November 30, 1946
"The Singular Affair of the Coptic Compass," December 7, 1946
"The Adventure of the Elusive Emerald," December 14, 1946
"The Adventure of the Grand Old Man," December 21, 1946
"The White Cockerel," December 28, 1946

1947

"The Darlington Substitution Case," January 4, 1947
"The Singular Affair of the Babbling Butler," January 27, 1947
"The Strange Case of the Persecuted Millionaire," February 10, 1947
"Cue for Murder," March 3, 1947
"The Adventure of the Scarlet Worm," March 24, 1947
"The Adventure of the Maltree Abbey," March 31, 1947

"The Adventure of the Tolling Bell," April 4, 1947
"The Island of Death," April 28, 1947
"The Harley Street Murders," May 19, 1947
"The Murder in the Locked Room," June 9, 1947
"The Adventure of the Innocent Murderess," June 30, 1947

Opera Programs

Golden Age Records, KFPA, May 1949–August 1950
Golden Voices, KFPA, May 1951–April 1968
Critics at Large; Canadian Broadcasting Corporation, 1960–1962

Anthologies

Edited by Boucher

Best Detective Stories of the Year, Volumes 18–23, edited and introduced by Boucher, plus a special volume in 1969.

Best of Fantasy and Science Fiction, edited and introduced by Boucher. Little Brown, 1952. Second Series, Little Brown, 1953. Third Series, Little Brown, 1954. Fourth Series, Little Brown, 1955. Fifth Series, Little Brown, 1956. Sixth Series, Little Brown, 1957. Seventh Series, Little Brown, 1958. Eighth Series, Little Brown, 1959.

Crimes That Shocked America. Brant House and Boucher, eds.. New York: Ace, 1961.

Fatal Caress, Richard Hindry Barker, ed. introduction by Boucher. Duell, Sloan and Pearce, 1947.

Four and Twenty Bloodhounds, selected by and introduced by Boucher, Simon & Schuster, 1950.

Great American Detective Stories, introduction by Boucher, World Publishing, 1945.

The Pocket Book of True Crime Stories Pocket Books, 1943.

The Quality of Murder, Dutton, 1962.

The Quintessence of Queen, Avon, 1962.

A Treasure of Great Science Fiction, Doubleday, 1959.

Posthumous Collections

Special Wonder, The Anthony Boucher Memorial Anthology of Fantasy and Science Fiction, complied by J. Francis McComas. Random House, 1970.

Crime and Misfortunes, The Anthony Boucher Memorial Anthology of Mysteries, complied by J. Francis McComas. Random House, 1970.

Boucher's Choicest, compiled by Jeanne F. Bernkopf. Dutton, 1969.

Multiplying Villainies: Selected Mystery Criticism 1942–1968, compiled by Francis M. Nevins. Bouchercon, 1973.

Exeunt Murderers, compiled by Francis M. Nevins. Southern Illinois University Press, 1983.

The Anthony Boucher Chronicles, Volume I, compiled by Francis M. Nevins. Ramble House, 2001.
The Anthony Boucher Chronicles, Volume II, compiled by Francis M. Nevins. Ramble House, 2002.
The Anthony Boucher Chronicles, Volume III, compiled by Francis M. Nevins. Ramble House, 2002.

Forewords, Introductions, and Prefaces

Bacon, Peggy. *Lady Marked for Murder*. New York: Mercury, 1953.
Barker, Richard Hindry. *Fatal Caress*. New York: Dell.
Black, Thomas. *The Pinball Murders*. New York: Mercury.
Blackstock, Charity Lee *The Foggy, Foggy Dew*. London: House and Maxwell, 1959.
Blankfort, Michael. *The Widow-Makers*. New York: Mercury.
Blochman, Lawrence G. *See You at the Morgue*. New York: Collier, 1962.
Brackett, Leigh. *No Good From a Corpse*. New York: Collier, 1962.
Brand, Christianna. *Green For Danger*. New York: Bantam, 1965.
Burke, Thomas. "The Hands of Mr. Ottermole." In *Murder by Experts* (MWA Anthology). New York: Ziff, 1947.
Carey, Bernice. *The Frightened Widow*. New York: Mercury, 1954.
_____. *The Missing Heiress*. New York: Mercury.
Carr, John Dickson. *The Blind Barber*. New York: Collier, 1962.
_____. *Hag's Nook*. New York: Collier, 1962.
Cheney, Peter. *Dark Foreword*. New York: Dodd, Mead, 1952.
Chesterton, Gilbert Keith. *The Adventures of Father Brown*. New York: Dell, 1962.
Cogswell, Theodore R. *The Wall Around the World*. New York: Pyramid, 1967.
Conan Doyle, Sir Arthur. *The Valley of Fear*. New York: Limited Editions Club, 1952.
Cunningham, A.B. *Blood Runs Cold*. New York: Mercury, 1954.
Davis, Dorothy Salisbury. *The Clay Hand*. New York: Collier, 1962.
Davis, Mildred. *They Buried a Man*. New York: Mercury.
Derleth, August. *The Reminiscences of Solar Pons*. Sauk City, WI: Mycroft and Moran, 1961.
Dick, Philip K. *The Variable Man and Other Stories*. New York: Ace, 1957.
Eshleman, John. *The Deadly Chase*. New York: Mercury, 1955.
Fish, Robert L. *The Incredible Schlock Homes*. New York: Simon and Schuster, 1965.
Fitt, Mary. *Pity for Pamela*. New York: Collier, 1962.
Freeman, R. Austin. *Mr. Pottermack's Oversight*. New York: Collier, 1962.
Gault, William Campbell. *Vein of Violence*. New York: Award, 1964.
Gilbert, Anthony. *The Wrong Body*. New York: Mercury.

Gruber, Frank. *Kiss The Boss Goodbye.* New York: Mercury, 1954.
Gross, Jerry. *Crimes that Shocked America.* Brant House and Anthony Boucher, eds. New York: Ace Books, 1961.
Hare, Cyril. *Best Detective Stories.* New York: Mercury, 1962.
Healy, Raymond J. *New Tales of Time and Space.* New York: Pocket, 1951.
Heyer, Georgette. *A Blunt Instrument.* New York: Bantam, 1966.
Hunt, Peter. *Oscar Slater: The Great Suspect.* New York: Colliers, 1962.
Innes, Michael. *Hamlet, Revenge!* New York: Collier, 1962.
Jay, Charlotte. *Arms for Adonis.* New York: Collier, 1962.
Jess, F. Tennyson. *Comments on Cain.* New York: Collier, 1962.
Johns, Veronica Parker. *Murder by the Day.* New York: Mercury.
Knight, Damon Francis. *Far Out.* New York: Simon and Schuster, 1960.
Knowland, Helen. *Baltimore Madame.* New York: Mercury, 1954.
Kutak, Rosemary. *I am the Cat.* New York: Collier, 1962.
Kuttner, Henry. *Henry Kuttner: A Memorial Symposium.* Berkeley, California: Sevagram, 1958.
Latimer, Jonathan. *The Dead Don't Care.* New York: Mercury.
Lustgarten, Edgar. *The Murder and the Trial.* New York: Collier, 1957
McBain, Ed. *The 87th Precinct.* New York: Simon and Schuster, 1959.
McCloy, Helen. *Cue for Murder.* New York: Collier, 1965.
MacDonald, Philip. *Murder Gone Mad.* New York: Mercury.
Marsh, Ngaio. *The Bride of Death.* New York: Mercury, 1955.
Moyes, Patricia. *Murder By 3s.* New York: Holt, Rinehart, and Winston, 1965.
Offord, Lenore Glen. *Clues to Burn.* New York: Mercury Publication.
Perutz, Leo. *The Master of the Day of Judgment.* New York: Collier, 1962.
Post, Melville Davisson. *Uncle Abner.* New York: Collier, 1962.
Queen, Ellery. *Cat of Many Tails.* New York: Bantam, 1965.
_____. *The Quintessence of Queen.* New York: Random House, 1962.
Rawson, Clayton. *The Footprints on the Ceiling.* New York: Collier, 1962.
Reeves, Robert. *Come Out Killing.* New York: Mercury, 1955.
Shattuck, Richard. *The Wedding Guest Sat on a Stone.* New York: Mercury, 1962.
_____. *With Blood and Kiss.* New York: Mercury, 1953.
Sherwood, John. *Murder of a Mistress.* New York: Mercury, 1954.
Simenon, Georges, *The Short Cases of Inspector Maigret.* New York: Doubleday, 1959.
Stoker, Bram. *Dracula,* 1965.
Talbot, Hake. *Rim of the Pit.* New York: Bantam, 1965.
Teilhet, Darwin and Hildegarde Teilhet. *The Screaming Bride.* New York: Mercury, 1954.
Tey, Josephine. *Killer in the Crowd.* New York: Mercury, 1954.
Tyre, Nedra. *Death is a Lover.* New York: Mercury, 1950.
Verne, Jules. *The Mysterious Island.*
Verne, Jules. *Around the World in 80 Days.*
Woolrich, Cornell. *The Bride Wore Black.* New York: Collier, 1962.

As Editor

The Magazine of Fantasy & Science Fiction, Fall 1949–August 1958; edited in collaboration with J. Francis McComas, Fall 1949–August 1954.
True Crime Detective, Fall 1952–Fall 1953.
Mercury Mysteries, 1952–1955.
Dell Great Mystery Library, January 1957–July 1960.
Collier Mystery Classics, 1962.
The World's Great Novels of Detection, 1965.

Translations

Unless noted as published, these translations are unpublished and exist only at the Lilly Library at Indiana University, Bloomington, or with the White family in their personal archives.

Anonimo
    "The Ballad of Blanca-Nina"
    "The Ballad of Julianesa"
    "To Christ Crucified"
Arangesola
    "I wish in the first place to confess to you"
Azorin
    "Spanish Readings"
Becquer
    "From the Rimas"
Bhartrihari
    "You and I and I am You"
Boileau, Pierre
    "The Brides"
    "Counterplan"
    "Triangle" (*Ellery Queen's Mystery Magazine*, December 1948)
    "Monsieur Lucien, Burglar"
Borges, Jorge Luis
    "Death and the Compass" (*New Mexico Quarterly*, 1954)
    "The Garden of Forking Paths" (*Ellery Queen's Mystery Magazine*, August 1948)
Branco, Francisco A.
    "The Dwarfs' Club"
    "Breton de los Herrevos, Manuel"
    Marcela or Which of the Three? (a play)
Camoens, Luis De
    "Letrilla"
Dario, Ruben
    "Cyrano in Spain"
    "Metepsychosis"

Duchateau, Andre-Paul
 "Boomerang"
Goethe, Johann Wolfgang con
 "Egmont"
 "The Erlking"
 "The Godlike"
 "Gretchen at the Spinning Wheel"
 "The Harper's Song"
Gongora
 "Romance"
Heine
 "The Asra"
 "The Home-coming"
 "I'll Not Believe in Heaven"
 "I'll Not Complain"
 "There Was an Aged Monarch"
 "To My Mother, B. Heine"
Helu, Antonio
 "Professional Debut"
 "The Stickpin" (*Ellery Queen's Mystery Magazine*, November 1944)
 El Fistol de Corbata"
 "El Hombre de la Otra Acera"
 "Las Tres Bolas de Billar"
 "Piropos a Media Noche"
 "Veinte Mil Pesos En El Bolsillo"
Jimenez"
 "An Autumn Air"
Klopstock"
 "The Band of Roses"
Machado, Antonio
 "Philip IV"
 "Sage Counsels"
Marquina
 "En Flandes se ha puesto el sol"
Marti
 "Paraphrases"
Messac, Regis
 "The Detective Novel and the Influence of Scientific Thought. A treatise on 19th century detective works including Conan Doyle and others."
Mistral, Gabriela
 "Ballade"
 "Nocturne"
 "Morike"
 "Think On't, O Spirit!"
Narcejac, Thomas
 "The Police are on the Stairs" (*Ellery Queen's Mystery Magazine*, February 1951)
 "The Vampire"

Perutz, Leo
   "Specimen A"
Pushkin
   "Elegy"
   "I Loved You"
Schnitzler, Arthur
   "Comedy of Seduction"
Silva, Jose Asuncion
   "Egalite"
   "Future"
   "Lazarus" (translated from Jose Ascuncion Silva, *Dark of the Moon*, 1947)
   "Mal Du siecle"
   "Nocturne"
   "A Poem"
   "Zoosperms"
Simenon, George
   "Affaire Zilioouk" (*Ellery Queen's Mystery Magazine*, May 1944)
   "The Case of Arnold Schuttringer"
   "The Case of the Three Bicyclists" (*Ellery Queen's Mystery Magazine*, August 1948)
   "The Château of Missing Men"
   "The Château de l'Aresenic"
   "File No. 16"
   "The Little House at Croix-Rousse"
   "MMR Maigret's Admirer"
   "Nouchi"
   "The Old Lady of Bayeux" (*Ellery Queen's Mystery Magazine*, August 1952)
   "The Polish Officer"
   "The Safe of the S.S.S."
   "The Secret of Fort Bayard" (*Ellery Queen's Mystery Magazine*, November 1943)
   "Stan the Killer"
   "The Stronger Vessel" (*Ellery Queen's Mystery Magazine*, January 1951)
   "The Thirteen Culprits"
   "The Three Rembrandts" (*Ellery Queen's Mystery Magazine*, September 1943)
   "The Timmermans"
   "The Tracy Enigma" (*Ellery Queen's Mystery Magazine*, May 1947)
   "The Vanished Corpse or the Man Who Killed No One"
Storm
   "El lago de abejas"
Trinam, Hieronyme
   "Your Mouth Has Found"
Unamuno, Migeul de
   "The Secret Life"
Verdi
   "Rigoletto"

Villaespesa
    "Animae Rerum"
    "The Hesperides"
Zorrilla, Hose
    Don Juan Tenorio (a play)

Articles About Boucher

Boucher, Anthony. "Author, Author" department of *The Fanscient* 4:2 (Summer 50): 21–24.

Christopher, Joseph. "Anthony Boucher Reviews C. S. Lewis: From Anthony Boucher's *San Francisco Chronicle* Reviews of 1942–1948." *The Lamp-Post of the Southern California C.S. Lewis Society* 26:3–4 (Fall-Winter 2002): 41–49.

_____. "In the C.S. Lewis Tradition: Two Short Stories by Anthony Boucher." *Mythlore* 2:3/7 (Winter 1971): 25.

_____. "The Order of Martha of Bethany." *Extrapolation* 45:4 (Winter 2004): 348–367.

_____. "The Pride of Sister Ursula." *Performance for a Lifetime: A Festschrift Honoring Dorothy Harrell Brown: Essays on Women, Religion, and the Renaissance.* Barbara C. Ewell and Mary A. McCay, eds. New Orleans: Loyola University New Orleans, 1997, 140–158.

_____. "The Theological Comedies of Anthony Boucher." *Journal of Myth, Fantasy, and Romanticism* 1:2 (Spring 1992): 46–57. (Australian journal from the University of Queensland; the essay was editorially shortened.)

_____. "Usuform Robotics: Anthony Boucher's Future History." *Niekas Science Fiction and Fantasy No. 42* ([December] 1990): 22–33, 64–66.

_____, Dickensheet, D.W. and Briney, R.E. "A. Boucher Bibliography." *The Armchair Detective* Part I, 2:2 (January 1969): 77–85; Part II, 2:3 (April 1969): 143–155; Part III, 2:4 (July 1969): 263–273. (Also separately published with Lenore Glen Offord's "Anthony Boucher as Seen by his Friends and Colleagues" for the Northern California Chapter of the Mystery Writers of America.)

_____. "A Consummation Devoutly to Be Wished: Four More Collections of Anthony Boucher's Mysteries." *The Mystery Fancier* 9:2 (March/April 1987): 9–19. Fan writing.

Duncan, Karen. *Remembering Anthony Boucher: Bouchercon 25.* Accord Communication, 1994.

Hahn, Robert, ed. *Sincerely, Tony/Faithfully, Vincent. The Correspondence of Anthony Boucher and Vincent Starrett.* Chicago, IL: Catullus, 1975.

Jeffers, H. Paul. *The 2005 Christmas Annual: Once a Week in Baker Street: The Boucher-Green Years.* Baker Street Journal, Winter 2005.

Marks, Jeffrey. "Anthony Boucher's Sister Ursula," *Mystery Reader's Journal*. Religious Mysteries, Part 1 Volume 20, No. 1, Spring 2004.

Nevins, Francis M. "Anthony Boucher." *Mystery* 3:2 (September 81): 18–19.

———. *Exeunt Murderers*. "Introduction: The World of Anthony Boucher." Southern Illinois University Press, 1983.

———. *Exeunt Murderers*. "A Checklist of the Fiction of Anthony Boucher." Southern Illinois University Press, 1983.

Offord, Lenore Glen compiler. "A Boucher Portrait: Anthony Boucher as Seen by His Friends and Colleagues." White Bear Lake, MN: Allen J. Hubin, 1969. Offprint from *The Armchair Detective* Part I, 2:2 (January 1969): 77–85.

Penzler, Otto. "Introduction." *The Case of the Baker Street Irregulars* (Simon & Schuster, 1940), by Anthony Boucher. Gregg Press Mystery Fiction Series.

Spencer, David G. "The Case of the Man Who Could Do Everything." *Rhodomagnetic Digest* 2:2 (September 50): 7–10.

White, Lawrence, and P. White. *Boucher: A Family Portrait*. Berkeley Historical Society: 1985.

Appendix: Boucher Choices for Best Books, 1951–1967

From his column in the New York Times.

1951

The Devil in Velvet by John Dickson Carr
They Came to Baghdad by Agatha Christie
A Gentle Murderer by Dorothy Salisbury Davis
An English Murder by Cyril Hare
A Rough Shot & Time to Kill by Geoffrey Household
The Paper Thunderbolt by Michael Innes
Mr. Byculla by Eric Linklater
The Way Some People Die by Ross Macdonald
Shield for Murder by William P. McGivern
Night at the Vulcan by Ngaio Marsh
Murder on the Left Bank by Elliott Paul
The Origin of Evil by Ellery Queen
Mr. Blessington's Imperialist Plot by John Sherwood
Black Sheep, Run & The Golden Door by Bart Spicer
The 31st of February by Julian Symons
Big Shot by Lawrence Treat

1952

Epitaph for a Spy by Eric Ambler
Barbary Hoard by John Appleby
The Inward Eye by Peggy Bacon
Catch a Tiger by Owen Cameron
Mrs. McGinty's Dead by Agatha Christie
The Key to Nicholas Street by Stanley Ellin
Deadlock by Ruth Fenisong
The Bloody Bokhara by William Campbell Gault
Death has Deep Roots by Michael Gilbert
They Died Laughing by Alan Green

The Ivory Grin by Ross Macdonald
Vanish in an Instant by Margaret Millar
Black Widow by Patrick Quentin
The Long Green by Bart Spicer
The Daughter of Time by Josephine Tey

1953

Fear to Tread by Michael Gilbert
Post Mortem by Guy Cullingford
Meet Me at the Morgue by Ross Macdonald
The Canvas Coffin by William Campbell Gault
Speak Justly of the Dead by E.C.R. Lorac
Their Nearest and Dearest by Bernice Carey
The Singing Sands by Josephine Tey
A Kiss Before Dying by Ira Levin
Beat Not the Bones by Charlotte Jay
The Case of the Hesitant Hostess by Erle Stanley Gardner
Reputation for a Song by Edward Grierson

1954

The Whisper in the Gloom by Nicholas Blake
The Time of the Fire by Marc Brandel
The Third Bullet and Other Stories by John Dickson Carr
The Long Goodbye by Raymond Chandler
A Pocket Full of Rye by Agatha Christie
Dead Man's Shoes by Michael Innes
The Fugitive Eye by Charlotte Jay
Find a Victim by John Ross Macdonald
Rogue Cop by William P. McGivern
Murder in Pastiche by Marion Mainwaring
Lucinda by Howard Rigby
A Shilling for Candles by Josephine Tey

1955

Tour De Force by Christianna Brand
The Tall Dark Man by Anne Chamberlain
The Mean Streets by Thomas B. Dewey
Room For Murder by Dorothy Miles Disney
The Rare Adventure by Bernard Ferguson
F.O.B. Murder by Bert and Delores Hitchens
The Yellow Turban by Charlotte Jay
The Best That Ever Did It by Ed Lacy
Scales of Justice by Ngaio Marsh
All Through the Night by Whit Masterson
Beast in View by Margaret Millar
Somewhere in This City by Maurice Procter
The Evil of the Day by Thomas Sterling

1956

A Dram of Poison by Charlotte Armstrong
The Man Who Didn't Fly by Margot Bennett
A Tangled Web by Nicholas Blake
The Lenient Beast by Frederic Brown
A Capitol Offense by Jocelyn Davis
The Second Man by Edward Grierson
Compulsion by Meyer Levin
Cop Hater and The Mugger by Ed McBain
The Barbarous Coast by Ross Macdonald
Harm Intended by Richard Parker
Inspector Queen's Own Case by Ellery Queen
Murder in Haiti by John Vandercrook

1957

The Tiger Among Us by Leigh Brackett
The Night of the Good Children by Marjorie Carleton
Fire, Burn! by John Dickson Carr
Death of an Old Sinner by Dorothy Salisbury Davis
Be Shot for Sixpence by Michael Gilbert
The Con Man by Ed McBain
Stopover: Tokyo by John P. Marquand
Gideon's Night by J.J. Marric
An Air That Kills by Margaret Millar
Bunny Lake is Missing by Evelyn Piper
What Rough Beast by John Trench
The Bushman Who Came Back by Arthur Upfield

1958

The Woman in the Woods by Lee Blackstock
The Devil's Agent by Hans Habe
Untimely Death by Cyril Hare
Blind Date by Leigh Howard
Killer's Choice by Ed McBain
The Doomsters by Ross Macdonald
A Stir of Echoes by Richard Matheson
The Midnight Plumber by Maurice Procter
The Finishing Stroke by Ellery Queen
The April Robin Murders by Craig Rice and Ed McBain
The Stopped Clock by Joel Townley
Heat Wave by Caesar Smith
The Color of Murder by Julian Symons

1959

Devil by the Sea by Nina Bawden
The End of Violence & Seven Steps East by Ben Benson
Lament for Four Brides by Evelyn Berckman

Psycho by Robert Bloch
No Grave for a Lady by John and Emery Bonett
The Foggy, Foggy Dew by Charity Blackstock
Scandal at High Chimneys by John Dickson Carr
The Hours Before Dawn by Celia Fremlin
Blood and Judgment by Michael Gilbert
The Chinese Bell Murders by Robert van Gulik
King's Ransom & 'Till Death & Killer's Wedge by Ed McBain
The Listening Walls by Margaret Millar
The Twisted Ones by Vin Parker
A Dream of Falling by Mary O. Rank
The Sands of Windee & Journey to the Hangman by Arthur Upfield

1960

Passage of Arms by Eric Ambler
The Traces of Brillhart by Herbert Brean
Cat Among the Pigeons by Agatha Christie
The Devil's Own by Peter Curtis
Uncle Paul by Celia Fremlin
Strike for a Kingdom by Menna Gallie
Watcher in the Shadows by Geoffrey Household
Give the Boys a Great Big Hand by Ed McBain
The End of the Night by John D. MacDonald
The Ferguson Affair by Ross Macdonald
Send Another Hearse by Harold Q. Masur
Dead Men Don't Ski by Patricia Moyes
Versus Inspector Maigret by Georges Simenon
My Brother Michael by Mary Stewart
The Progress of a Crime by Julian Symons

1961

Counsel for the Defense by Jeffrey Ashford
Wait for the Wedding by Celia Fremlin
The Case of the Curious Spinster by Erle Stanley Gardner
The House of Soldiers by Andrew Garve
The Cipher by Alex Gordon
The Red Pavilion by Robert van Gulik
The Wrong Side of the Sky by Gavin Lyall
The Wycherly Woman by Ross Macdonald
Gideon's Fire by J.J. Marric
The Eye of the Needle by Thomas Walsh
That Night it Rained by Evelyn Waugh
Killing Time by Donald E. Westlake
The Smartest Grave by R.J. White

1962

The D.L. by Jeffrey Ashford
The Demoniacs by John Dickson Carr

The Pale Horse by Agatha Christie
When I Grow Rich by Joan Fleming
The Chinese Nail Murder by Robert van Gulik
Murder by Proxy by Brett Halliday
The Spoilt Kill by Mary Kelly
The Zebra-Striped Hearse by Ross Macdonald
Commorant's Isle by Allan MacKinnon
How Like An Angel by Margaret Millar
The Plain Man by Julian Symons
361 by Donald E. Westlake
Perfect Pigeon by Richard Wormser

1963

The Light of Day by Eric Ambler
A Little Less Than Kind by Charlotte Armstrong
It's Different Abroad by Henry Calvin
The Mirror Crack'd by Agatha Christie
Black Sister by Dagmar Edqvist
The Trouble Makers by Celia Fremlin
The Massingham Affair by Edward Grierson
The Expendable Man by Dorothy B. Hughes
Dead of Summer by Mary Kelly
The Assassination Bureau, LTD by Jack London
Gideon's Ride by J.J. Marric
Murder a la Mode by Patricia Moyes
The Player on the Other Side by Ellery Queen

1964

A Kind of Anger by Eric Ambler
The Clocks by Agatha Christie
Question of Loyalty by Nicolas Freeling
The Incident at the Merry Hippo by Elspeth Huxley
The Night of the Generals by Hans Helmut Kirst
The Spy Who Came in from the Cold by John Le Carre
Greenmask! by Elizabeth Linnington
The Chill by Ross Macdonald
Gideon's Vote by J.J. Marric
Burning is a Substitute for Love by Jennie Melville
The Fiend by Margaret Millar
The Road to Hell... by Hubert Monteilhet
Five Times Maigret by Georges Simenon
The Rough Magic by Mary Stewart

1965

Funeral in Berlin by Len Deighton
For Kicks by Dick Francis
The Jealous One by Celia Fremlin
Double Barrel by Nicolas Freeling

The Quiller Memorandum by Adam Hall
The Day the Call Came by Thomas Hinde
Cunning as a Fox by Kyle Hunt
The Perfect Murder by H.R.F. Keating
Midnight Plus One by Gavin Lyall
The Far Side of the Dollar by Ross Macdonald
Petrovka 38 by Julian Semyonov
Maigret Cinq by Georges Simenon
Airs Above the Ground by Mary Stewart

1966

The Hands of Innocence by Jeffrey Ashford
At Bertram's Hotel by Agatha Christie
Odds Against by Dick Francis
The King of the Rainy County by Nicolas Freeling
The Crack in the Teacup by Michael Gilbert
Blind Spot by Joseph Harrington
Saturday the Rabbi Went Hungry by Harry Kemelman
The Pedestal by George Lanning
Black Money by Ross Macdonald
The Crimson Madness of Little Doom by Mark McShane
Killer Dolphin by Ngaio Marsh
The Night is a Time for Listening by Elliot West
The Spy in the Ointment by Donald E. Westlake

1967

A Most Contagious Game by Catherine Aird
Lemon in the Basket by Charlotte Armstrong
A Parade of Cockeyed Creatures or Did Someone Murder Our Wandering Boy? by George Baxt
The Hochmann Miniatures by Robert L. Fish
Flying Finish by Dick Francis
The Walking Stick by Winston Graham
The Tower by P.M. Hubbard
Sly as a Serpent by Kyle Hunt
Murder Against the Grain by Emma Lathen
Something Wrong by Elizabeth Linnington
The Last One Left by John D. MacDonald
Murder Fantastical by Patricia Moyes
God Save the Mark by Donald E. Westlake

Bibliography

The majority of my research was done at Indiana University in Bloomington. The bulk of the Anthony Boucher papers are housed in the Lilly Library as the William A.P. White collection. The entire collection takes up 62 boxes and totals some 30,000 individual pieces of paper. I had the good fortune to spend the following dates on campus, doing research: June 7 and August 16–20, 2004; October 17, 2005; October 12 and December 22, 2006; and March 6 and 16, 2007.

The collection is divided into three sections. Memorabilia included old date books, drawings, and medical records. The writings consisted of most of Boucher's known output, including a large number of unpublished works. The correspondence section included letters to and from luminaries such as Fred Dannay, Stuart Palmer, Craig Rice, Isaac Asimov, Charlotte Armstrong, James Sandoe, John W. Campbell, Poul Anderson, and of course all letters with his mother and wife. Additionally, all correspondence and records for Boucher's work for Mystery Writers of America, *The Magazine of Fantasy & Science Fiction*, *True Crime Detective*, and others is included there.

I was also fortunate enough to spend time with the White family and receive access to documents not contained in the Lilly Library. I received copies of family documents and genealogy, such as the "Price Family History" and "Jataka," a family-written account of the family. Along with that, many personal documents belonging to Phyllis White were available for me to peruse.

Adey, Robert. *Locked Room Murders*. Minneapolis, MN: Crossover, 1991.
Albert, Walter. *Detective and Mystery Fiction: An International Bibliography of Secondary Sources*. Madison, IN: Brownstone, 1985.
Bernkopf, Jeanne F, ed. *Boucher's Choicest*. New York: Dutton, 1969.
Blankfort, Michael. *The Widow-Makers*. New York: Mercury, 1946.

Blau, Peter. E-mail interview, April 25, 2007.
Borges, Jorge Luis. "Death and the Compass." *New Mexico Quarterly*, 1954.
Borges, Jorge Luis. "The Garden of Forking Paths." *Ellery Queen's Mystery Magazine*, August 1948.
Boucher, Anthony. "Author, Author" department of *The Fanscient* 4:2 (Summer 50): 21–24.
_____. *The Case of the Baker Street Irregulars*. New York: Simon & Schuster, 1940.
_____. *The Case of the Crumpled Knave*. New York: Simon & Schuster, 1939.
_____. *The Case of the Seven of Cavalry*. New York: Simon & Schuster, 1937.
_____. *The Case of the Seven Sneezes*. New York: Simon & Schuster, 1942.
_____. *The Case of the Solid Key*. New York: Simon & Schuster, 1941.
_____. *The Case of the Toad-in-the-Hole*. Unpublished ms. circa 1938 at Indiana University.
_____. *The Compleat Boucher: The Complete Science Fiction and Fantasy of Anthony Boucher*. Framingham, MA: Nesfa, 1999.
_____. *The Compleat Werewolf*. New York: Simon & Schuster, 1969.
_____. "Death on the Bay: A Dr. Ashwin Story." Unpublished ms. at Indiana University.
_____. *Ellery Queen: A Double Profile*. Boston: Little, Brown, 1951.
_____. *Far and Away*. New York: Ballantine, 1954.
_____. "It Will Have Blood." Unpublished ms. at Indiana University.
_____. "Murder of a Martian: A Colonel Rand Story." Unpublished ms. at Indiana University.
_____. *Panache: A Heroic Melodrama*. Unpublished play from the White estate.
_____. *The Petard of Death*. Unpublished play from the White estate.
_____. *The Plume*. Unpublished play from the White estate.
_____. *Rave Notice or Critics Have Fun, Too*. Unpublished play from the White estate.
_____. "A Short Biography of Sherlock Holmes." *The Baker Street Irregulars*, 1959.
_____. "Sonnet: San Francisco to Sherlock." *A Baker Street Four-Wheeler*, 1944.
_____. "Toy Cassowary." *The Acolyte*, Winter 1945.
_____, ed. *Four and Twenty Bloodhounds*. New York: Simon & Schuster, 1950.
_____, ed. *Great American Detective Stories*. New York: World, 1945.
_____, ed. *The Pocket Book of True Crime Stories*. New York: Pocket, 1943.
_____, ed. *The Quality of Murder*. New York: Dutton, 1962.
_____, ed. *A Treasure of Great Science Fiction*. New York: Doubleday, 1959.
Boucher, Anthony, host. *Golden Voices*. Berkeley, CA: KFPA radio programs February 29, 1968, and May 15, 1964.
Boucher, Anthony, and Denis Green. "The Amateur Mendicant Society," episode of *The New Adventures of Sherlock Holmes*. New York: Mutual Broadcasting System, April 2, 1945.
_____. "The Book of Tobit," episode of *The New Adventures of Sherlock Holmes*. New York: Mutual Broadcasting System, March 28, 1945.
_____. "The Camberwell Poisoning Case," episode of *The New Adventures of Sherlock Holmes*. New York: Mutual Broadcasting System, February 18, 1946.
_____. "The Case of the Notorious Canary Trainer,." episode of *The New Adventures of Sherlock Holmes*. New York: Mutual Broadcasting System, April 23, 1945.

_____. "The Great Gandolfo," episode of *The New Adventures of Sherlock Holmes*. New York: Mutual Broadcasting System, October 22, 1945.

_____. "The Indiscretion of Mr. Edwards," episode of *The New Adventures of Sherlock Holmes*. New York: Mutual Broadcasting System, February 4, 1946.

_____. "Murder Beyond the Mountains," episode of *The New Adventures of Sherlock Holmes*. New York: Mutual Broadcasting System, 14 Jan 1946.

_____. "The Murder of Gregory Hood," episode of *The Adventures of Gregory Hood*. New York: Mutual Broadcasting System, June 17, 1946.

_____. "The Mystery of the Headless Monk," episode of *The New Adventures of Sherlock Holmes*. New York: Mutual Broadcasting System, April 15, 1946.

_____. "The Paradol Chamber," episode of *The New Adventures of Sherlock Holmes*. New York: Mutual Broadcasting System, May 21, 1945.

_____. "South of the Border," episode of *The Adventures of Gregory Hood*. New York: Mutual Broadcasting System, July 15, 1946.

_____. "The Strange Adventure of the Uneasy Easy Chair," episode of *The New Adventures of Sherlock Holmes*. New York: Mutual Broadcasting System, May 13, 1946.

_____. "The Strange Case of the Demon Barber," episode of *The New Adventures of Sherlock Holmes*. New York: Mutual Broadcasting System, January 28, 1946.

_____. "The Strange Case of the Murder in Wax," episode of *The New Adventures of Sherlock Holmes*. New York: Mutual Broadcasting System, January 7, 1946.

Boucher, Anthony, and J. Francis McComas, eds. *True Crime Detective*. Spring 1953.

_____. *True Crime Detective*. Summer 1953.

_____. *True Crime Detective*. Fall 1953.

_____. *True Crime Detective*. Winter 1953.

Christopher, Joseph, D.W. Dickensheet and R.E. Briney. "A. Boucher Bibliography," *The Armchair Detective* Part I, 2:2 (January 1969): 77–85; Part II, 2:3 (April 1969): 143–155; Part III, 2:4 (July 1969): 263–273. (Also separately published in Lenore Glen Offord's "Anthony Boucher as Seen by his Friends and Colleagues" for the Northern California Chapter of the Mystery Writers of America.)

Crayne, Dian. E-mail interview, August 2, 2005.

Duncan, Karen. *Remembering Anthony Boucher: Bouchercon 25*. Accord Communication, 1994.

Durrant, Theo. *The Marble Forest*. New York: Knopf, 1951.

Greene, Douglas. E-mail interview, November 16, 2002.

Grost, Michael. "Visitors from Science Fiction: Isaac Asimov, Jorge Luis Borges, Anthony Boucher, J.G. Ballard and Others." *A Guide to Classic Mystery and Detection*. http://home.aol.com/mg4273/classics.htm, accessed May 19, 2007.

Hahn, Robert, ed. *Sincerely, Tony/Faithfully, Vincent. The Correspondence of Anthony Boucher and Vincent Starrett*. Chicago, IL: Catullus, 1975.

Holmes, H.H. *Nine Times Nine*. New York: Duell, Sloan, & Pearce, 1940.

_____. *Rocket to the Morgue*. New York: Duell, Sloan & Pearce, 1942.

_____. "Vacancy with Corpse." *Mystery Book Magazine*, February 1946.

Jackson, Joseph Henry, ed. *San Francisco Murders*. New York: Duell, Sloan, and Pearce, 1947.

Jeffers, H. Paul. *The 2005 Christmas Annual: Once a Week in Baker Street: The Boucher-Green Years*. Baker Street Journal, Winter 2005.

Klinger, Leslie. Phone interview. October 18, 2005.
Lellenberg, Jon L. *Irregular Crises of the Late Forties: Archival History of the Baker Street Irregulars*. New York: Baker Street Productions, 1995.
_____. *Irregular Proceeding of the Mid-Forties: Archival History of the Baker Street Irregulars*. New York: Baker Street Productions, 1995.
Marks, Jeffrey. "Anthony Boucher's Sister Ursula." *Mystery Reader's Journal*. Religious Mysteries, Part 1 Volume 20, No. 1, Spring 2004.
McComas, J. Francis, ed. *Crime and Misfortunes: The Anthony Boucher Memorial Anthology of Mysteries*. New York: Random House, 1970.
_____. *Special Wonder:, The Anthony Boucher Memorial Anthology of Fantasy and Science Fiction*. New York: Random House, 1970.
Narcejac, Thomas. "The Police are on the Stairs." *Ellery Queen's Mystery Magazine*, February 1951.
Nevins, Francis M. "Anthony Boucher." *Mystery* 3:2 (September 81): 18–19.
_____. Personal interview, April 18, 2005.
_____, ed. *The Anthony Boucher Chronicles, Volume I*. Shreveport, LA: Ramble House, 2001.
_____, ed. *The Anthony Boucher Chronicles, Volume II*. Shreveport, LA: Ramble House, 2002.
_____, ed. *The Anthony Boucher Chronicles, Volume III*. Shreveport, LA: Ramble House, 2002.
_____, ed. *Exeunt Murderers*. Carbondale: Southern Illinois University Press, 1983.
_____, ed. *Multiplying Villainies: Selected Mystery Criticism 1942–1968*. Bouchercon Book, 1973.
_____, ed. *The Sound of Detection: Ellery Queen's Adventures in Radio*. Arlington, VA: Kirby, 2002.
Offord, Lenore Glen, compiler. "A Boucher Portrait: Anthony Boucher as Seen by His Friends and Colleagues. White Bear Lake, MN: Allen J. Hubin, 1969. Offprint from *The Armchair Detective* Part I, 2:2 (January 1969): 77–85.
Penzler, Otto. "Introduction." *The Case of the Baker Street Irregulars*. Boston: Gregg, 1980.
Queen, Ellery. *The Quintessence of Queen*. New York: Avon, 1962.
_____, ed. *The Misadventures of Sherlock Holmes*. Boston: Little, Brown, 1944.
Resnick, Michael. E-mail interview, May 31, 2004.
Silverberg, Robert. E-mail interview, July 12, 2003.
Spencer, David G. "The Case of the Man Who Could Do Everything." *Rhodomagnetic Digest* 2:2 (September 50): 7–10.
Van Gelder, Gordon. Various e-mail interviews, 2005 through 2007.
Vande Water, William. Various e-mail interviews, 2004 through 2007.
White, James. E-mail interview. 3 June 2004, 20 Aug 2006, 22 December 2006.
White, Lawrence. Personal interview, June 11–14, 2004, and various e-mail interviews, November 2004 to March 2007.
_____, and P. White. *Boucher: A Family Portrait*. Berkeley Historical Society, 1985.

Index

"An Aborted Avatar" 178
Abrahamson, Ben 95
ACLU 152
The Acolyte 63
Adey, Robert 53
"The Adventure of the Bogle-Wolf" 176
"The Adventure of the Illustrious Impostor" 176
Adventures in Space and Time 105, 115
The Adventures of Ellery Queen (radio show) 24, 81, 86, 87, 88, 89, 90, 181–183
The Adventures of Ellery Queen (television show) 138
The Adventures of Sherlock Holmes 41, 42
Amazing Stories 104
"The Ambassadors" 172
Anderson, Poul 28, 158, 159
"The Anomaly of the Empty Man" 172, 175
The Anthony Boucher Chronicles, Volumes I, II, and III 189
The Armchair Detective 149
Armstrong, Charlotte 122
"Arsene Lupin vs. Colonel Linnaus" 176
Asimov, Isaac 104, 113, 139, 159
Astounding Stories 56, 66, 68, 70, 104, 105
Atlantic Monthly 111
Avallone, Michael 147, 148

"Baker Street Immortal" 178
Baker Street Irregulars (organization) 42, 65, 91, 92, 93, 94, 95, 96; The Scowrers and Molly McGuires 92, 93, 94, 95, 96, 126, 129
Baker Street Journal 91, 95
"Balaam" 172, 175
"Ballads of the Later Holmes" 178
"The Barrier" 70, 172
Barzun, Jacques 147

Best, Edna 80, 81
"The Best and Wisest Man" 178
Best Detective Stories of the Year 188
Best of Fantasy and Science Fiction 188
The Best of Science Fiction 115
"The Best Tricks of the Mystery Trade" 170
The Big Bow Mystery 51
"The Biggest Stumbling Block" 170
Bimbos of the Death Sun 57
Black Mask 106
"Black Murder" 60, 174
Bloch, Robert 106, 157, 158
Bogart, Humphrey 121
Bonestell, Chesley 111
"The Borderlands of Sanity—From Charm to Murder: The Case of Neville Heath" 170
Borges, Jorge Luis 76, 77, 144, 193
Boucher, Anthony: asthma 10, 11, 17, 20, 21, 23, 26, 72–74, 76, 86, 90, 91, 112, 124, 126, 136, 142, 150, 151, 157; Berkeley 22, 24; birth 7; Catholicism 10, 27, 28, 33, 47, 48, 66, 67, 69, 114, 148, 151; *Chicago Sun-Times* 108, 136, 137, 139, 180; and civil rights and social justice 61, 68, 88, 90, 101, 103; death 156, 157; as editor 108–113; impossible crimes 44, 45, 49, 51–53, 57; intertextuality 32, 40, 43, 49, 55, 57, 67, 72, 73; Los Angeles 16, 17, 22, 24, 34; *Los Angeles Daily News* 135, 136, 141, 180; *The New York Herald Tribune* 25, 49, 137, 138, 139, 146, 180; opera 27, 60, 90, 152, 153–156; Pasadena High School 12, 13; Pasadena Junior College 13; politics 23, 60, 64, 70, 71, 92, 151, 154; reading habits 11, 12, 16, 25, 29; Ross Sanitarium 11, 12; *San Francisco Chronicle* 22, 24, 25, 92, 96, 97, 98, 124, 126, 128, 129, 148, 180; source of pen name 9, 10, 25, 48, 49, 99, 139, 140, 145, 171; Stanford genius

study 11; *United Progressive News* 16, 18, 20, 30, 34, 124; University of California, Berkeley 13, 14, 15, 19, 22, 23, 29, 30, 31, 40, 73; University of Southern California 13; wedding 20; as White, William Parker 7, 10; writing process 37, 41, 58, 61, 62, 78
Bouchercon 3, 4, 157, 158
Bradbury, Ray 55, 139, 159
Breen, Jon 51, 158
Breit, Harvey 143
Bretnor, Reg 132, 159
Brown, Francis 139, 143, 156
Bruce, Nigel 23, 24, 79, 80, 81, 84, 87
"The Bruce-Partington Plans" 60
Bullock, Elizabeth 143

Campbell, John W. 55, 56, 57, 66, 70, 71, 73, 104
The "Canary" Murder Mystery 51
Carr, John Dickson 33, 51, 56, 59, 102, 106, 108, 121, 122, 131, 134, 150
Cartmill, Cleve 17, 20, 30, 66
The Case of the Baker Street Irregulars 41–43, 45, 49, 51, 52, 80, 91, 92, 120, 121, 169
The Case of the Crumpled Knave 37–39, 47, 169
"The Case of the Illustrious Impostor" 59
The Case of the Seven of Calvary 19, 30–34, 36, 43, 50, 59, 121, 126, 169
The Case of the Seven Sneezes 36, 45–47, 57, 169
"The Case of the Sixty-First Adventure" 178
The Case of the Solid Key 36, 40, 43–45, 49, 169
The Case of the Toad-in-the-Hole 34, 35, 103, 114, 169
"The Case of the Villain's Identity" 176
The Casebook of Gregory Hood 24, 85, 86, 183, 184
Castle, William 100
"The Catalyst" 63, 174
Caupolican, Chief 155
Chandler, Raymond 106, 115, 142
Charteris, Leslie 24, 79, 80, 82
Chesterton, G.K. 10, 38, 44
The Chinese Orange Mystery 51
Christie, Agatha 38, 46, 62, 121, 130, 131, 156
"The Chronokinesis of Jonathan Hull" 40, 172
Citizens Against Legalized Murder 151, 152
Clarke, Arthur C. 111, 139
Clingerman, Mildred 109
Clue: A Magazine Guide to Mysteries 135, 180
The Clue of the Crumpled Knave 36, 176
"Code Zed" 63, 174
"Coffin Corner" 58, 174
Collins, Mary 145
The Compleat Anthony Boucher 172
"The Compleat Werewolf" 40, 67, 172, 174
Conan Doyle, Adrian 55, 56, 96

Conan Doyle, Sir Arthur 32, 33, 82, 85
Conan Doyle, Denis PS 80, 81, 82, 84, 86
Conklin, Groff 115
"Conquest" 72, 172
Conway, Tom 84
Craig Rice Crime Digest 80
Crayne, Chuck 157
Creasey, John 111
Crime and Misfortune 158, 159, 188
"Crime Must Have a Stop" 61, 174
Critics at Large 187
Cuppy, Will 137, 138

Dannay, Fred 11, 24, 29, 56, 59, 60, 62, 63, 74–78, 86, 87, 88, 105, 106, 108, 109, 128, 129, 130, 133, 134, 141, 144, 148
Davidson, Avram 113, 140
"The "Dear Wish" to Baffle Time" . 170
"Death of a Patriarch" 60, 174
"Death on the Bay" 36
De Camp, L. Sprague 55, 73
Dedmon, Emmett 136, 137
DeFord, Miriam Allen 118, 119, 159
"Department of Abject Apology" 170
Derleth, August 112
"Design for Dying" 62, 174
Devil in the White City 49
Dick, Philip K. 109, 122
Dickson, Carter *see* Carr, John Dickson
"Do You Believe—" 170
Doyle, Edward Dermot 124, 128
Durrant, Theo 99

Ellery Queen: A Double Profile 135, 170
Ellery Queen Fantasy Magazine 76, 105
Ellery Queen's Mystery Magazine 24, 59–62, 73–77, 89, 94, 105, 111, 119, 124, 130–134, 135, 141, 144, 148, 157, 159, 180
"Elsewhen" 40, 172, 175
Emshwiller, Ed 111
Encyclopedia Britannica 92
"The Ethics of the Mystery Novel" 170
Everitt, Tom 88
Exeunt Murderers 58, 174, 188
"Expedition" 72, 172, 174
The Exploits of Sherlock Holmes 56

Far and Away 140, 175
Ferman, Edward 110
Ferman, Joe 107, 110, 111, 113, 119
"A Fiction Writer Admires Dewey" 170
"The First" 172, 175
Fischer, Bruno 122
"Footnote to a Footnote" 178
Four-and-Twenty Bloodhounds 101, 116, 188
Futrelle, Jacques 115

"Gandolphus" 41, 172
Gardner, Erle Stanley 33
Gernsback, Hugo 104

Index

"The Ghost of Me" 172, 174
"The Ghost with the Gun" 63, 174
"The Girl Who Married a Monster" 61, 174
Golden Age Records 187
Golden Voices 27, 153, 154, 187
Gordon, Gale 86
Great American Detective Stories 115, 188
"The Greatest Tertian" 172
Green, Denis 24, 25, 79, 80, 81, 83, 84, 85, 88, 140, 184
The Greene Murder Case 41
Guymon, Ned 92

Halter, Paul 51
Hamilton, Ed 20
Hammett, Dashiell 138, 144
Haycraft, Howard 130, 132, 144
Haycraft-Queen Cornerstone 57, 130
Healy, Raymond John 115
Heinlein, Robert 20, 55, 66, 104, 136, 139
Helú, Antonio 75, 76, 115, 194
Hine, Annie Boucher 9
Hitchcock, Alfred 78
Hoch, Ed 51
Holmes, H.H. 49, 55, 99
Holmes, Sherlock 36, 41, 43, 55, 60, 65, 79, 80, 82–84
"Holmesiana Hispanica" 94, 178
The Hound of the Baskervilles 79
Hubbard, L. Ron 66, 104, 116
Hubin, Al 149
Hughes, Dorothy B. 106, 120, 124, 127, 136, 139
Hunter, Mel 111

Indiana University 4, 34, 89
Inner Sanctum Mystery Magazine 105
Irving, Washington 114
"It Will Have Blood" 36

"Jack El Destripador" 178
Jackson, Joseph Henry 93, 95, 96, 109, 118, 126, 129
Jesse, F. Tennyson 118

Karloff, Boris 108
Keating, H.R.F 144
The Kennel Murder Mystery 51
"A Kind of Madness" 172
Kluger, Richard 139
Knox, Father Ronald 39

Landru, Henri 34, 49
"The Last Hand" 177
Lawes, Lewis W. 115
Lee, Gypsy Rose 31
Lee, Manfred 24, 86, 87, 88, 89, 90, 128, 129, 135, 142, 181
Levin, Ira 144
Life 94

"Like Count Palmieri" 60, 175
Locked Room Murders 53
Lovecraft, H.P. 106
Lovestone, Jay 71
Lyons, Herbert 141, 142

Macabre 100, 169
Macdonald, Ross 144
The Magazine of Fantasy and Science Fiction 4, 25, 26, 65, 108–113, 116, 118, 119, 123, 134, 140, 144, 157, 158, 192
The Maltese Falcon 138, 144, 155
Mañana Literary Society 20, 21, 55, 66
Manhunt 149, 180
"Man's Reach" 72, 172
The Marble Forest 99, 100, 101, 169
Marple, Jane 48
"A Matter of Scholarship" 64, 175
McBain, Ed 144
McCloy, Helen 122, 158
McComas, J. Francis "Mick" 17, 23, 25, 26, 28, 55, 105, 107, 108, 109, 110, 111, 115, 116, 118, 121, 122, 135, 140, 158
McCrumb, Sharyn 57
McKnight, Tom 84, 85
Meet the Press 106
Meiser, Edith 24, 79, 85
Mencken, H.L. 106
Mercury Mysteries 119, 120, 192
Mercury Publications 76, 106, 107, 108
Merkling, Frank 155
Millar, Margaret 3, 29
Mills, Robert P. 112, 113, 118, 121, 135
The Misadventures of Sherlock Holmes 56, 80, 93
"Mr. Lupescu" 172, 174
"The Model of a Science Fiction Editor" 111, 112, 170, 173
Moffat, Len and June 157
Morley, Christopher 91, 93
Mullady, Frank 118
Multiplying Villainies 155, 158, 188
Murder by Experts 101
"Murder by Jove" 177
"Murder of a Martian" 39
"Murder on V-Day" 177
"The Murders in the Rue Morgue" 51, 77
"The Musgrave Ritual" 42, 95
"My Favorite Murder: The Tragedy of Samuel Savile Kent" 170
"Mystery for Christmas" 61, 175
The Mystery of Edwin Drood 32
Mystery Writers of America 22, 65, 96, 97, 98, 99, 101–103, 116, 118, 148, 158, 159; Edgars 22, 97, 98, 101, 128, 134, 148, 158

Narcejac, Thomas 77, 78, 194
"Nellthu" 173
Nevins, Mike 4, 58, 89, 189
The New Adventures of Sherlock Holmes 23,

24, 65, 79, 80–86, 89, 91, 95, 184–186; *The Book of Tobit* 82, 184; *Murder Beyond the Mountains* 83, 84, 185; *The Paradol Chamber* 83
New Mexico Quarterly 77
New York Times 3, 4, 25, 26, 101, 112, 116, 127, 133, 137, 140–145, 147–149, 156, 157, 159, 180
"Nine-Finger Jack" 68, 173
Nine Times Nine 47–52, 54, 59, 169
Noble, Nick 59
"A Note on Scowrers" 178
"November Fifth" 177

O'Breen, Fergus 34, 37–47, 57, 69, 71, 88
O'Breen, Maureen 41–43, 45, 46, 71
O'Dell, Scott 135
"Of Fortune and Faro " 170
Offord, Lenore 22, 94, 95, 98, 100, 101, 123, 128, 129
"On a Day Unknown: The Case of August Sangret" 171
"On the Difficulties of Getting Mr. Anderson's First Name Correctly Spelled" 171
"On the Nomenclature of the Brothers Moriarty" 178
101 Years of Entertainment 56
"One-Way Trip" 71, 173, 175
"Opera and Murder" 171
Opera News 27, 154, 180
"The Other Inauguration" 173, 175
"Out of Patience..." 171
"Out on a Limb" 171

Pacifica Radio 180
Palmer, Stuart 20, 33, 35, 54, 105, 106, 115, 118
Parker, Dorothy 103, 146
Parker, William Owen 8
"The Pelagic Spark" 73, 173
Phillips, Jud 98
"The Pink Caterpillar" 40, 173, 174
Playboy 139, 171
The Pocket Book of True Crime 103, 113, 188
Poe, Edgar Allan 107, 108, 112, 115
Porter, Nikki 87, 88
Price, Dr. Lawrence 14, 15, 18, 20, 40
Price, Mary "Minnie" (nee Bell) 14, 15
The Private Life of Sherlock Holmes 91
"Prolegomena to a Holmesian Discography" 95, 178
"Pseudonyms are Murder" 171
"Public Eye" 69, 173
"The Punt and the Pass" 60, 175

"QL.696.C9" 60, 175
The Quality of Murder 102, 103, 188
Queen, Ellery 11, 29, 32, 33, 37, 38, 46, 51, 65, 87, 88. 115, 122, 131, 133, 145, 150
Quentin, Patrick 31, 103, 114, 115, 121, 131

"The Quest for St. Aquin" 67, 173
The Quintessence of Queen 188
"Q.U.R." 67, 68, 173, 174

Radin, Ed 118
Rathbone, Basil 23, 24, 79, 80, 81, 84, 87, 108
Rawson, Clayton 51, 116
"The Records of Baker Street" 178
"The Retired Hangman" 64, 175
"Review Copy" 173, 175
"The Reviewing of Mystery Novels 171
Rice, Craig 31, 105, 115, 121, 122, 124, 127, 131, 132, 136, 145
Rinehart, Mary Roberts 121, 145
"Robinc" 68, 173, 174
Rocket to the Morgue 21, 49, 54–57, 64, 80, 169
Rodell, Marie 21, 35, 49, 50, 57, 127
"The Roles of Reviewer and Editor in Science Fiction" 171
"Rumor, Inc." 60, 175
Ryder, Dr. 32

The Saint Mystery Magazine 79, 80, 105
Salter, George 111
San Francisco Opera 27
"Sanctuary" 71, 72, 173
Sandoe, James 136, 139
Sayers, Dorothy L. 10, 39, 121
"The Science Fiction Books of 1963: A Survey" 171
"The Scrawny One" 67, 173
"The Screwball Division" 59, 175
"The Seat of the Matter" 177
"Secret of the House" 173, 175
"A Shape of Time" 173
"Sherlock Holmes and Science Fiction" 178
"A Short Biography of Sherlock Holmes" 178
The Sign of the Four 42
Simenon, Georges 73–75, 194
Sister Ursula 25, 44, 47, 48, 54, 58
Smith, Edgar W. 91, 92, 93
"The Smoke-Filled Locked Room" 64, 175
"Snulbug" 67, 173–175
"Sonnet: San Francisco to Sherlock" 178
Special Wonders 158, 159, 188
"The Speckled Band" 41, 51, 95
Spillane, Mickey 146, 148, 150, 152
Spivak, Lawrence 76, 105, 106, 109, 110, 119, 134
"Sriberdegbit" 67, 173, 175
"Star Bride" 172, 175
"The Star Dummy" 173
Starrett, Vincent 91, 92, 95
"The Statement of Jerry Malloy" 64, 175
Stewart, Mary 127
Stoker, Bram 114, 115
Stout, Rex 26, 103, 121, 131
"The Stripper" 58, 175

Index   213

Sturgeon, Theodore 104
"Summer's Cloud" 173

Taylor, Glenhall 80, 81, 82, 83, 84
"The Tenderizers" 173
Tey, Josephine 120
"They Bite" 173–175
The Three Coffins 52–54
"*Threnody*" 30, 175
Tolkien, J.R.R. 140
"Toy Cassowary" 177
"Transcontinental Alibi" 62, 63, 177
"Transfer Point" 72
A Treasure of Great Science Fiction 188
"The Trojan Horse Opera" 171
True Crime Detective 26, 118, 192
"The 12 Days of Christmas" 171

"The Ultimate Clue" 64, 175
"Unknown Worlds" 67
Unknown Worlds (fantasy magazine) 104
Untermeyer, Louis 121
Upfield, Arthur 122

"Vacancy with Corpse" 58, 177
The Valley of Fear 92, 93, 129
Vance, Philo 32
Van Dine, S.S. 39, 51, 146, 150
Van Doren, Carl 137
Van Doren, Irita 137, 138, 139
Verdict 149

Walker, Hal 149
"Wanted: A Fanzine" 171
"Was the Later Holmes an Impostor?" 178
"The Way I Heard It" 63, 174
"We Print the Truth" 69, 174
Weber, Bill 98
Weird Tales 12, 17, 21, 29, 103
White, James (son) 11, 21, 28, 73, 151
White, James Taylor (father) 7–9
White, Lawrence (son) 20, 21, 28, 90
White, Mary Ellen (nee Parker) 8, 9, 13, 16, 20, 21, 26
White, Phyllis (wife) 4, 9, 14–18, 20, 21, 30, 55, 73, 94, 109, 113, 144, 146, 156, 157, 158, 159
Wilde, Oscar 114, 115
Williamson, Jack 55
Willkie, Wendell 137
Wimsey, Lord Peter 10
Wing, Willis Kingsley 33–36, 45, 159
"Wizards of a Small Planet" 171
Woolrich, Cornell 121
Wright, Lee 19, 21, 30, 31, 35, 45, 49, 64, 90, 91, 102, 116, 128, 137

"Ye Good Old Ghost Storie" 177
"You and the Reviews and the Reviewers" 171